WILD ABOUT GROUP TIME

Between the Lions®

PBS KIDS℠

Wild About Group Time

Simple Literacy Plans for Preschool

by the *Between the Lions*® Staff

Based on the Award-Winning PBS KIDS® Literacy Series

Gryphon House

BETWEEN THE LIONS is produced by WGBH Boston, Sirius Thinking, Ltd., and Mississippi Public Broadcasting.

BETWEEN THE LIONS is funded in part by The Corporation for Public Broadcasting, a cooperative agreement from the U.S. Department of Education's Ready To Learn grant, and by the Barksdale Reading Institute. National corporate funding is provided by Chick-fil-A, Inc.

Corporation for Public Broadcasting

A private corporation funded by the American people

BARKSDALE READING INSTITUTE

Visit us on the Web at: pbskids.org/lions

Printed in China through Asia Pacific Offset, April 2010. This product conforms to CPSIA 2008.
Published by Gryphon House, Inc.
10770 Columbia Pike, Suite 201
Silver Spring, MD 20901
301.595.9500
301.595.0051 (fax)
800.638.0928 (toll-free)

Visit us on the web at www.gryphonhouse.com.

Library of Congress Cataloging-in-Publication Data

Wild about group time / by the Between the Lions Staff.
p. cm.
ISBN 978-0-87659-305-9
1. Literacy. 2. Language awareness in children. 3. Education, Elementary.
LC149.W43 2010
372.6--dc22

2010000175

Table of Contents

Introduction

Between the Lions is an award-winning children's television series named for a family of lions—Theo, Cleo, Lionel, and Leona—who run a library like no other. The doors "between the lions" swing open to reveal a place in which characters pop off the pages of books, letters sing, and words come alive.

This book, *Wild About Group Time,* is a unique educational tool by the same people who created *Between the Lions*. You can use this book during group time, circle time, floor time, or anytime, to teach key literacy skills to young children. *Wild About Group Time* is designed to help young children develop a strong foundation in early literacy. The lessons follow a program scope and sequence (see pages 12–13), which is aligned with state preschool standards as well as national Head Start frameworks.

This introduction provides an overview of *Wild About Group Time*, the literacy scope and sequence used in the book, a checklist to help you set up your classroom, as well as a glossary that explains the meaning of important literacy terms.

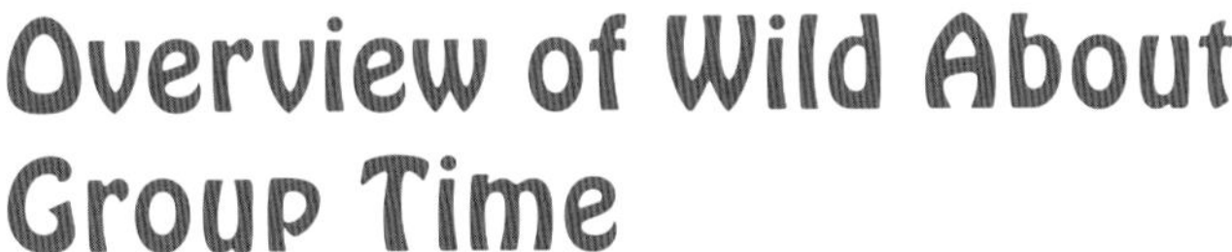

Overview of Wild About Group Time

Each of the ten chapters of *Wild About Group Time* focuses on one topic, which reflect things that are interesting to young children and themes that teachers usually cover each year. The following are the topics in *Wild About Group Time*:

- Families
- Feelings
- Friends
- Houses and Homes
- Colors
- Silly Animal Stories
- Helping
- Things That Grow
- Food
- Silly Stories

Each group-time activity has the following components:

- Title
- Age (3+, 4+)
- Literacy Skill Focus (from the scope and sequence)
- Related Themes
- Vocabulary
- What Children Will Learn
- Materials
- Preparation (if necessary)
- What to Do
- Simplify It
- Add a Challenge
- Book Suggestions

The Literacy Scope and Sequence—The Building Blocks of Literacy

It is essential that all children develop these building blocks of literacy. Each component is described below and then presented in chart form.

Oral Language: Listening and Speaking

Research tells us that before children become readers, they need to listen and talk a lot. Keep your classroom alive with the sounds of children talking, singing, and playing with the sounds in words.

Begin group time with a conversation about the topic—introducing new words and concepts and inviting children to talk about their lives. Throughout the day, create opportunities for children to listen to environmental sounds, music, songs, poems, chants, and stories. Focused talk around listening activities builds children's listening and speaking vocabulary.

Book Appreciation and Knowledge

Love of books and the joys of reading are at the heart of a successful literacy program. Children enjoy many different kinds of books, including favorite folktales, rhyming books, alphabet books, and concept books. Include a variety of books in your classroom to spark children's interest in books.

Story Comprehension

A strong foundation in story comprehension in preschool will help children become good readers in elementary school. Build opportunities for children to make connections between stories and their lives; predict what will happen next in a story; and understand that stories have a beginning, middle, and end. Fun after-reading activities, such as storyboard retellings and character interviews, help children deepen their understanding of a story.

Phonological and Phonemic Awareness

Words and their sounds are what children "play with" to build a solid foundation in phonological awareness. Use the word-play activities in *Wild About Group Time* to help children learn listening, rhyming, alliteration, and blending sound skills.

Concepts of Print

The activities in *Wild About Group Time* help children learn that print conveys meaning and that there are many great reasons to read and to write. As they watch you read books during group time, children notice that reading is done from top to bottom and from left to right. Song and poem charts, environmental print, and writing activities also help children learn about letters and words, the spaces between words, and the direction in which words are read on a page.

Alphabet Knowledge and Letter Recognition

Name games, word walls, word cards, and alphabet, song, and poem charts help children recognize letters in familiar words and associate the names of letters with their shapes and sounds. Tactile letter shaping, letter sorting, writing, art, and movement activities offer multiple ways for children to learn how to form letters.

Beginning Writing

Children are motivated to learn to write when they discover that what they think and say can be written down and read by others. They learn to write by observing others write. Observing what you write on class charts shows children that charts can describe their experiences. Children can also respond to stories by drawing, scribbling, or dictating their stories, thoughts, and ideas. The activities in *Wild About Group Time* provide guidelines,

information, ideas, and activities to teach children skills that will prepare them to become good readers and writers. When introducing a new skill, whether it is singing a new song, identifying a rhyming pattern, or distinguishing letters with straight lines from those with curved lines, use the following instructional sequence to scaffold or support children's learning.

- **Model the skill** by demonstrating how to do it step by step. Think aloud so children can understand your thought process.
- **Invite children to practice** the skill along with you.
- **Encourage children to perform** the skill on their own, providing guidance when needed.

Reading Aloud

Reading books aloud is the foundation of early literacy. Researchers have concluded that reading aloud may be the most important thing we can do to prepare toddlers and preschoolers for learning how to read and to write. *How* you read, and what you talk about before and after reading, are just as important as what you read. Consider the following when reading books to young children:

- **Read the book several times** to yourself before sharing it with children. Mark the places at which you would like to pause and ask questions or explain unfamiliar words.
- **Talk about the book cover.** Point out the title, author, and illustrator and talk about what they do. Look at and talk about the art.
- **Create a context.** Share a related personal experience, look at the pictures together, or ask children to predict what might happen in the story.
- **Read slowly** so children can understand and enjoy the rhythm of the words and explore the pictures. Hold the book so everyone can see it.
- **Add drama** to your reading by using different voices and simple props. Don't be afraid to be silly or dramatic!
- **Invite children to join in** on repeating lines and phrases such as, *I'll huff and I'll puff, and I'll blow your house in!*
- **Point to the illustrations** to clarify the meaning of unfamiliar words.

- **Use facial expressions, movements, and gestures** to demonstrate the meaning of action words.
- **Ask open-ended questions** after reading to help children think about, remember, and discuss the story. Encourage them to connect the story to their lives. Remember to pause for at least 10 seconds after asking a question to give children time to think about their answer.

The Three Rs of Preschool: *Rhythm, Rhyme, and Repetition*

Rhyming and singing are great fun. They are also wonderful ways for children to hear the rhythms and patterns of language and to play with words and practice their sounds—important steps to learning to read. Rhythm, rhyme, and repetition make words memorable. The songs and poems children learn by heart today will help them learn to read the words in books tomorrow.

- **Sing a song or recite a poem a few times** before inviting the children to join in.
- **Add movements and gestures** to demonstrate the actions in a song or poem. Invite children to clap or sway to the rhythm.
- **Identify rhyming words.** As you sing a song or recite a poem, emphasize the rhyming words by chanting or singing them in a softer voice or louder voice.
- **Print the words to the song or poem** on a chart. You may want to add pictures for key words: *Twinkle, twinkle little* ★.
- **Invite children to find familiar words and letters** on the song or poem chart.
- **Sing favorite songs** over and over again.

The Literacy Scope and Sequence

Although all children develop at their own rate and in their own way, every child needs to develop the following essential literacy skills:

Oral Language: Listening and Understanding	■ Listens to others with understanding ■ Listens attentively to stories, poems, and songs ■ Uses active listening and viewing ■ Recognizes environmental sounds ■ Listens to and follows directions ■ Develops varied and complex vocabulary ■ Listens to music ■ Listens to the sounds produced by musical instruments
Oral Language: Speaking and Communicating	■ Uses language to express actions ■ Identifies common objects and interprets pictures ■ Uses language for conversation and to communicate information, experiences, ideas, thoughts, feelings, opinions, needs, wants, and questions ■ Retells a familiar story ■ Uses language to recall a sequence of events ■ Develops and uses new vocabulary ■ Uses positional words in proper context ■ Speaks in simple sentences
Book Appreciation and Knowledge	■ Listens to and discusses stories (realistic and fantasy) ■ Listens to and discusses nonfiction and concept books ■ Learns how to handle, care for, and turn the pages of a book ■ Selects theme-related books to "read" alone or with other children ■ Draws pictures based on a story ■ Joins in the reading of familiar/predictable/pattern books ■ Seeks information from nonfiction texts
Story Comprehension	■ Understands the literal meaning of a story ■ Predicts an outcome and/or what will happen next in a story ■ Connects information from a story to life experiences ■ Differentiates reality from fantasy ■ Interprets illustrations ■ Develops awareness of cause and effect ■ Uses experiences to understand characters' feeling and motivations ■ Retells or acts out stories in dramatic play ■ Discusses story elements (character, setting, plot) ■ Compares and contrasts characters, settings, and events ■ Understands that stories have a beginning, middle, and end

Phonological and Phonemic Awareness	■ Listens to and identifies sounds in words (phonemes) ■ Listens to rhyming words ■ Recognizes rhyming words ■ Generates rhyming words ■ Understands that different words begin with the same sound (alliteration) ■ Distinguishes words in a sentence ■ Listens to and distinguishes syllables in words by clapping, stomping, or finger tapping ■ Listens to and begins to notice beginning sounds in words ■ Begins to notice ending sounds in words ■ Identifies initial sound in words ■ Segments, blends, and deletes syllables in compound words ■ Listens to and begins to blend beginning and ending sounds in words (onset and rime) ■ Listens to and begins to blend three- and four-phoneme words ■ Begins to become familiar with onomatopoeia (words that have a sound that imitates or suggests its meaning, such as *quack*, *hiss*, or *woof*)
Concepts of Print	■ Understands that a book has a title, author, and illustrator ■ Identifies the book author and illustrator ■ Locates the book title ■ Understands that English is read from left to right ■ Understands that English is read from top to bottom ■ Holds a book correctly (right side up) ■ Recognizes local environmental print ■ Understands that print conveys meaning ■ Recognizes the association between spoken and written words ■ Recognizes that letters are grouped to form words ■ Recognizes that words are separated by spaces ■ Recognizes familiar words ■ Understands the different functions of forms of print, such as signs, letters, lists, menus, and messages
Alphabet Knowledge and Letter Recognition	■ Begins to recognize letters ■ Recognizes his or her first name in print ■ Understands that the alphabet is made up of letters that each have a different name ■ Distinguishes letter shapes (straight line, curvy line, slanted line, and so on) ■ Associates names of letters with their shapes ■ Notices the beginning letters in familiar words ■ Identifies the first letters in words ■ Associates names of letters with their sounds
Beginning Writing	■ Experiments with a variety of writing tools and materials ■ Dictates stories or experiences ■ Represents stories, ideas, and experiences through scribbles, shapes, drawings ■ Writes for many purposes (signs, labels, stories, messages) ■ Attempts to write his or her name

Setting Up the Classroom—Checklist

The way you arrange your physical space greatly influences how children play, work, and learn. Following is a checklist to help you create an environment that supports children as they learn about language and the world of print and books:

- [ ] Is the children's work displayed at their eye level around the room?
- [ ] Are the children's names written in different places around the room? (on cubbies, helper chart, and so on)
- [ ] Is environmental print displayed at the children's eye level?
- [ ] Is there an alphabet chart displayed at the children's eye level?
- [ ] Are topic-related posters and wall displays placed where children can easily see and talk about the pictures?
- [ ] Are art supplies and other materials labeled?
- [ ] Are chairs and other furniture arranged so children can talk and play together?
- [ ] Is the classroom space divided into small learning centers?
- [ ] Is each learning center labeled with words and/or pictures that children can understand?
- [ ] Is there a variety of writing tools (paper, pencils, markers, crayons, and so on) in each learning center?
- [ ] Are theme-related books available in the learning centers?
- [ ] Are books in the library center easy for children to see and to reach?
- [ ] Is a variety of fiction and nonfiction books located in the library center? Are books that reflect the children's racial and ethnic backgrounds available, as well as books from diverse cultures?
- [ ] Is a CD or tape player in the area? Are there different types of musical recordings for children to listen and move to during the day?

Glossary

alliteration: repeating the same sound at the beginning of words, as in *Sally sells seashells by the seashore*

alphabet knowledge: being able to name and write the 26 letters of the alphabet

blending: putting together individual sounds to make words (I'm *thinking of a word that names an animal. It has these sounds: /p/ /i/ /g/. What's the word?)*

characters: the people or animals in a story

concepts of print: children's understanding of the different ways we use written language—as in letters, recipes, labels, and stories—as well as the way we write and read print (Example: Printed words are separated by spaces; words are read from left to right and from top to bottom.)

environmental print: the written letters and words we see every day in our homes and neighborhoods that we recognize from the pictures, colors, and shapes that surround them. Examples include food and clothing labels, store logos, and road signs.

fiction: stories, essays, articles, and books that tell a made-up story, such as storybooks, fairy tales, and folktales

literacy: the skills and activities involved in speaking, listening, reading, and writing

making predictions: using information that they already know to guess what a story will be about or what will happen next

modeling: showing children how to perform a task or skill before asking them to complete it on their own

nonfiction: stories, essays, articles, and books that give information or facts about a subject, including biographies and concept books (books about colors, shapes, sizes, and so on)

onset and rime: Onset is the initial consonant sound(s) in a syllable; rime is the part that contains the vowel and all that follows it. In the word *cat*, /c/ is the onset and /at/ is the rime. In the word *bat*, /b/ is the onset and /at/ is the rime.

open-ended questions: questions that cannot be answered with a yes or no answer; for example: Ask, *What part of the story did you like best?*

phonemic awareness: the ability to hear and identify the individual sounds in *spoken* words. When the children hear the individual /m/, /o/, and /p/ sounds that make up the word *mop*, they are developing phonemic awareness. [In *Wild About Group Time*, the *letter* is written in quotation marks ("m"), while the *sound of the letter* is written between two slashes (/m/).]

phonics: a skill that matches *written* letters and words with the sounds they make. A child that looks at the printed word *cat* and sounds it out is using phonics. Children need a solid foundation in phonological awareness before they learn phonics.

phonological awareness: a broad range of listening skills—from being able to hear and recognize sounds in the environment to paying attention to and manipulating the individual sounds in words. Rhyming, singing, and clapping the syllables in words are examples of activities that build phonological awareness.

picture walk: turning the pages of a book from the beginning to end and asking children to look at and talk about the illustrations. Picture walks before reading help prepare children for listening. Picture walks after reading help children retell the story.

plot: what happens in the beginning, middle, and end of a story

print-rich environment: a classroom that displays words and letters that are meaningful to children in places where children can see and interact with them

retell: to tell a story in your own words and in the correct order or sequence

rhyme: the repetition of the ending sound of a word, as in Jack and *Jill* went up the *hill*

scaffolding: helping children learn a new skill step by step and gradually removing support as children become able to perform the skill on their own

segmenting: taking spoken words apart sound by sound. Clapping the parts or syllables in words and names is an example of segmenting (*A-bi-yo-yo*; *Ben-ja-min;* and so on).

setting: where and when a story takes place

shared reading: when you read aloud a Big Book or chart with large print and encourage the children to read along on parts they can remember or guess

shared writing: when the children dictate their stories or ideas for you to write

spoken or oral language: the language we use to talk and listen

story structure: the way stories are organized into a beginning, middle, and end

syllable: a word part that contains a vowel sound. The word *dog* has one syllable. The word *an-i-mal* has three syllables.

vocabulary: knowing the meaning of the words we use when we speak, listen, read, and write

word play: playing with the beginning, middle, and ending sounds of words for fun and to learn how words work

CHAPTER 1

Families

Talking with the children in your classroom about their families is a wonderful way to learn about the children and for them to learn about one another. As the children talk about their families and home life, they learn new words and concepts and discover similarities and differences between themselves and others.

Setting Up the Room

- Fill the walls of your room with photographs of the children and their families. Ask family members to bring in family photographs (see Family Letter, page 38), or take photographs of the children and their families (with their permission) at drop-off or pick-up time.

- Create a family poster for each child: Fill each family poster with photographs of that child's family and label each photograph with the names of the people in the picture. Display these family posters at the children's height. Update the posters throughout the year. The posters will help comfort the children when they feel lonely and miss their families. The posters will also help the children begin to recognize and appreciate the ways that families are alike and different.

- Make a class chart of the things the children like to do with their families. Ask the children to complete the sentence: *I like to ____________ with my (family member)*. Encourage a wide variety of responses. Create a class chart by writing each child's response, one directly below the other, as in the following example. Set off each child's name from the rest of the sentence by writing it in a different color.

  Brianna likes to read with her grandfather.
  Jonvante likes to cook with his father.
  Kayla likes to play hide-and-seek with her brother.
  Michael likes to sing with his mother.

Read the chart together. Have each child read his sentence with you as you touch each word with your finger or a pointer. Ask each child to come up to the chart and touch his name.

Family Letter

Prepare and make photocopies of the Family Letter on page 38 that explains this topic. Give the letter to parents at pick-up time before you begin the topic.

"Here We Are Together"

Literacy Skill Focus
Name Recognition

Vocabulary

match
name(s)
recognize
sing
together

Materials

index cards or card stock
markers
photos, stickers, stamps, or simple pictures (optional)

What Children Will Learn

1. To recognize their names in print
2. To sing with others
3. To match the same names

Related Themes

All About Me
Feelings

Preparation

Use the index cards or card stock to create two name cards for each child in the group.

What to Do

- Begin group time with "Here We Are Together," a greeting song that helps the children recognize their names in print.
- Before singing the song, give each child a name card with his name on it. The name cards can have photos, stickers, stamps, or simple pictures that help the children recognize their names.
- Hold up one name card at a time from your matching set of name cards. Ask, *Whose name is this?* Help each child make the match. You may also want to say the letters in the child's name as you point to them on the name card. Continue until every child has two matching cards.
- Next, tell the children that you are going to sing a song that has everyone's name in it. Sing "Here We Are Together" (on the next page). Point to each child as you sing his name.

Here We Are Together
(Tune: "Have You Ever Seen a Lassie?")
Here we are together, together, together,
Here we are together, together again.
Here's Asante
and Zoe
and William
and Jevonte
and Brianna (*keep going until you name all the children*)
Here we are together, together again.

- Invite the children to sing the song with you.

Simplify It

Use one set of name cards. Hold up one name card at a time, say the name on the card, and then give the card to the child whose name is on the card.

Add a Challenge

Use two sets of cards. Give each child a name card with his name on it. Hold up one card from the second set. Ask, *Whose name is this?* After the child identifies his name, ask him to say the letters in his name.

Assessment

To assess each child's learning, consider the following:
1. Is the child able to recognize his name?
2. Is the child able to name the first letter in his name?
3. Is the child able to sing along with the rest of the group?

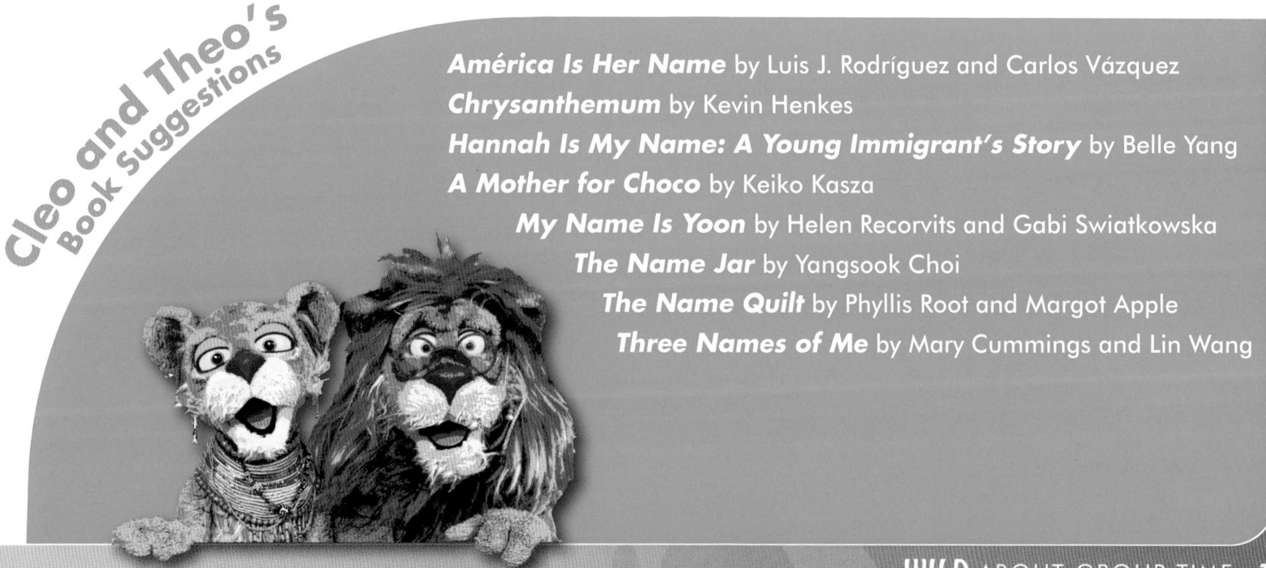

Cleo and Theo's Book Suggestions

América Is Her Name by Luis J. Rodríguez and Carlos Vázquez
Chrysanthemum by Kevin Henkes
Hannah Is My Name: A Young Immigrant's Story by Belle Yang
A Mother for Choco by Keiko Kasza
My Name Is Yoon by Helen Recorvits and Gabi Swiatkowska
The Name Jar by Yangsook Choi
The Name Quilt by Phyllis Root and Margot Apple
Three Names of Me by Mary Cummings and Lin Wang

My Family, Your Family

Literacy Skill Focus
Listening and Speaking
Making Connections

Vocabulary

act out
brother
family
father
feel
feelings
grandfather
grandmother
happy
miss
mother
photograph
picture
puppet
sister
story

What Children Will Learn

1. About families
2. Words that describe family relationships—*father, mother, brother, sister, grandmother, grandfather*

Related Themes

All About Me
Feelings

Preparation

Cut out the patterns of the Lion family—Theo, Cleo, Lionel, and Leona. Glue each member of the Lion family onto a tongue depressor to make stick puppets.

Materials

books about families (see suggestions on the next page)
glue
patterns of the *Between the Lions family* (see pages 237–238)
photograph(s) of your family
scissors
tongue depressors

What to Do

- At group time, talk with the children about their families.
- Begin by bringing in photographs of your family to share with the children. Name each family member and his or her relationship to you.
- Invite the children to ask questions about your family. Then ask the children, *Who is in your family? Who takes care of you? Who do you love?*
- Encourage the children to use words that describe their family relationships (for example, *father*, *mother*, *brother*, *sister*, *grandmother*, and *grandfather*).
- Read aloud a nonfiction or fiction book about families. Choose one of the suggestions or one of your favorites.
- Before, during, and after reading the book or books, ask the children questions to help them make connections between the families featured in the book(s) and their families.

- Use the stick puppets to introduce the Lion family to the children—four-year-old Leona, seven-year-old Lionel, and their parents, Cleo and Theo.
- Ask one or more of the children to use the puppets to act out things that their family likes to do or to show how she feels about her family.
- Tell the children that you are going to put the puppets in the Library Center for them to use.
- Throughout the day, continue to talk with the children about their families.

Simplify It

Read one of the suggested books. Use the characters and situations in the book as a way to help the children talk about their families.

Add a Challenge

- Create word cards of family-related vocabulary (*father*, *mother*, *brother*, *sister*, and so on). When a child talks about a family member, ask her to point to the word that describes that family member.
- Suggest that the children use the puppets to act out the storyline of one of the book suggestions.

Assessment

To assess each child's learning, consider the following:

1. Is the child able to name the people in her family?
2. Is the child able to use appropriate family-related vocabulary?
3. Is the child able to relate the storyline in one of the books to her family?
4. Is the child able to use the puppets to tell a story?

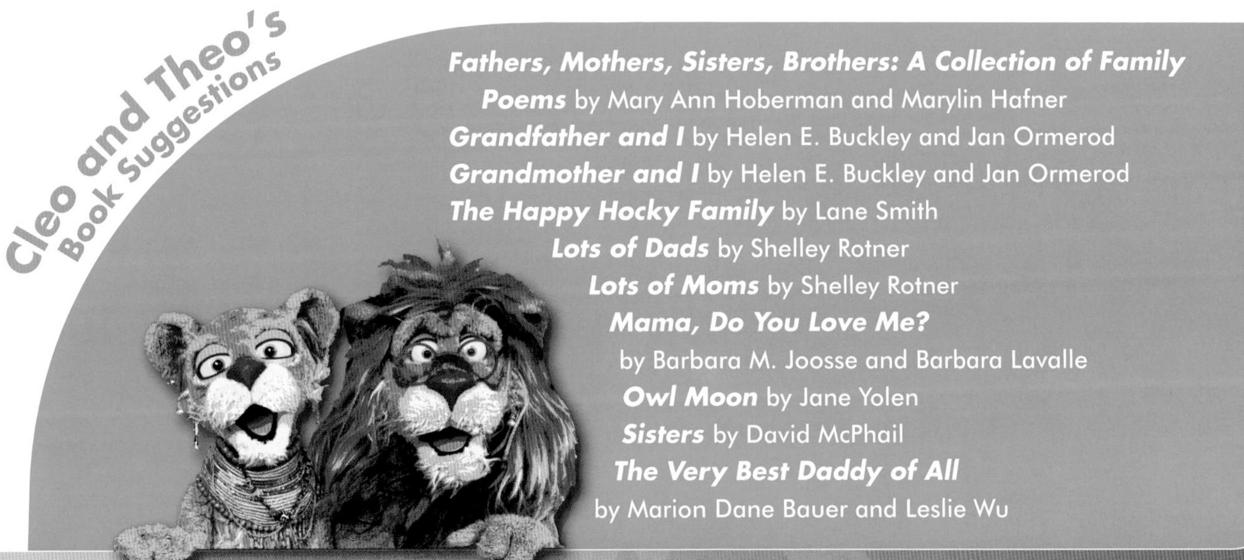

Cleo and Theo's Book Suggestions

Fathers, Mothers, Sisters, Brothers: A Collection of Family Poems by Mary Ann Hoberman and Marylin Hafner
Grandfather and I by Helen E. Buckley and Jan Ormerod
Grandmother and I by Helen E. Buckley and Jan Ormerod
The Happy Hocky Family by Lane Smith
Lots of Dads by Shelley Rotner
Lots of Moms by Shelley Rotner
Mama, Do You Love Me? by Barbara M. Joosse and Barbara Lavalle
Owl Moon by Jane Yolen
Sisters by David McPhail
The Very Best Daddy of All by Marion Dane Bauer and Leslie Wu

Reading *I Miss You, Stinky Face*

Literacy Skill Focus
Listening and Speaking
Phonological Awareness
(Rhythm and Repetition)
Story Comprehension

Vocabulary

astronaut
author
boy
camel
cheetah
family
feelings
happy
hot-air balloon
illustrator
miss
mother
scared

What Children Will Learn

1. About families
2. Words that describe feelings
3. To describe things they like about their families

Related Themes

All About Me
Feelings

Materials

I Miss You, Stinky Face by Lisa McCourt and Cyd Moore
photographs(s) of someone in your family

What to Do

- Remind the children about the conversations the group has had about families.
- Introduce a new topic: *We talked about the people in our families, about the people who take care of us, and about the people we love. Today, we are going to talk about things we like about our families.*
- Show the children a picture of someone in your family and tell the group something you like about him or her. *I like the way my daughter Mimi laughs.* Ask, *What do you like about the people in your family?* Encourage a variety of responses.
- Before you read the book, tell the children the name of the book, the name of the author and illustrator, and the names of the characters in the book.
- To keep the children focused and engaged, provide a focus: *Listen for how the little boy in the story feels about his mother being away.*
- Read the book *I Miss You, Stinky Face.*
- As you read, pause and explain the meaning of unfamiliar words, such as *hot-air balloon, camel, cheetah*, and *astronaut.*
- Ask, *How do you think the boy in the story feels when his mother comes home?*
- Continue to talk with the children about their families throughout the day.

Families

Simplify It

Show the group a photograph of your family and then ask the children if they have ever done what the photograph depicts. For example, if the photograph shows your family eating ice cream, ask the children if they have ever eaten ice cream; or if the photograph shows your daughter swinging on a swing, ask the children if they have ever been on a swing.

Add a Challenge

- Ask the children to describe other things about their families. For example, *What is something that you like about your brother (sister or other family member)? What are some things you do to help at home?*

Assessment

To assess each child's learning, consider the following:

1. Is the child able to say how the boy in the story felt?
2. Is the child able to say what he likes about his family?

Cleo and Theo's Book Suggestions

Brave Georgie Goat: 3 Little Stories About Growing Up by Denis Roche
Families by Ann Morris
Grandfather and I by Helen E. Buckley and Jan Ormerod
Grandmother and I by Helen E. Buckley and Jan Ormerod
Lots of Dads by Shelley Rotner
Lots of Moms by Shelley Rotner
A Mother for Choco by Keiko Kasza
Oh My Baby, Little One by Kathi Appelt and Jane Dyer
Owl Moon by Jane Yolen
The Very Best Daddy of All by Marion Dane Bauer and Leslie Wu
Waddle, Waddle, Quack, Quack, Quack by Barbara Anne Skalak

Reading *I Miss You, Stinky Face Again*

Literacy Skill Focus
Active Listening
Concepts of Print
Parts of a Book
Story Comprehension

Vocabulary

astronaut
author
bicycle
boy
camel
cheetah
dog
dragon
happy
hot-air balloon
illustrator
imaginary
imagination
mama
real
sad
spaceship
title

Materials

I Miss You, Stinky Face by Lisa McCourt and Cyd Moore

What Children Will Learn

1. About books
2. New vocabulary words
3. To talk about preferences
4. To use illustrations to increase understanding of the text

Related Themes

All About Me
Feelings

What to Do

- Show the children the book cover and ask if anyone recognizes the book.
- Point to the words in the title as you read it aloud: *Here's the title, or name, of the book:* I Miss You, Stinky Face.
- Point to the names of the author and illustrator as you read them aloud. *Lisa McCourt is the author of* I Miss You, Stinky Face. *She wrote the story. Cyd Moore is the illustrator. He drew the pictures.*
- Ask the children to name some of the things on the front cover that they see (boy, dragon, bicycle, dog, and so on).
- Read the book slowly and with expression. Use different voices for Mama and Stinky Face.
- Ask the children to listen for how Mama comes home.
- Talk with the children about the story. Ask questions, *How will the mama in the story really come home? What do you think Stinky Face and his mama might do together when she comes home?*
- Show the children pictures from the book as you ask them if they would rather ride on a camel or a cheetah? A hot-air balloon or a spaceship? A pirate ship or a magic dragon?
- Point to the illustrations to help explain the meaning of unfamiliar words, such as *hot-air balloon*, *camel*, *cheetah*, *spaceship*, and *astronaut*.

Simplify It

When you say each new vocabulary word, point to the picture so the children associate the picture of the object with the new vocabulary word.

Add a Challenge

Ask the children to tell the rest of the group the meaning of some of the unfamiliar words in the story, such as *hot-air balloon, camel, cheetah, spaceship,* and *astronaut.*

Assessment

To assess each child's learning, consider the following:

1. Is the child able to understand the storyline?
2. Is the child able to name some of the things on the front cover?
3. Is the child able to communicate preferences?
4. Is the child able to use the illustrations to help understand the story?

Cleo and Theo's Book Suggestions

Brave Georgie Goat: 3 Little Stories About Growing Up by Denis Roche
Families by Ann Morris
If You're Happy and You Know It! by Jan Ormerod and Lindsey Gardiner
If You're Happy and You Know It! by Jane Cabrera
I Love You, Stinky Face by Lisa McCourt and Cyd Moore
Oh My Baby, Little One by Kathi Appelt and Jane Dyer
Waddle, Waddle, Quack, Quack, Quack by Barbara Anne Skalak and Sylvia Long
The Way I Feel by Janan Cain

Rhyming Words

Literacy Skill Focus
Phonological Awareness (Rhyme and Repetition)

Vocabulary

airplane
aunt
brother
bus
father
grandma
grandpa
home
mother
ship
sister
sound
train
trip
uncle

Materials

none needed

What Children Will Learn

1. About different modes of transportation
2. About rhythm and rhyme
3. To sing a song with a group

Related Themes

Sounds
Transportation

What to Do

- Tell the children that they are going to sing a song about going to visit families. Before singing the song, tell the children about a visit you made to a family member who lives far away. Explain how you traveled there.
- Ask the children to talk about visiting members of their family who don't live close by. Ask, *Who did you visit? Who went with you? Where did you go? How did you get there?*
- Sing the following rhyming variation of "Clap Hands, Clap Hands." If you don't know the tune, emphasize the rhythm and the rhyme as you chant the words. Clap your hands to the beat.

Clap Hands, Clap Hands
Clap hands, clap hands
'Til Mommy comes home.
She went on a plane
To visit Aunt Jane.

Clap hands, clap hands,
'Til Grandma comes home.
She went on a bus
To visit Grandpa Gus.

Clap hands, clap hands,
'Til Daddy comes home.
He went on a ship
To visit cousin Skip.
Have a nice trip! (*Wave good-bye.*)

- Invite the children to sing the song and clap along with you.
- Point out some of the rhyming words in the song. Repeat the first verse of the song. Point out that the words *plane* and *Jane* rhyme: *When words rhyme, they sound the same at the end.* Plane *and* Jane *sound the same at the end. It's fun to say rhyming words. Let's say the rhyming words together:* plane, Jane.
- Repeat for the words *bus* and *Gus* in the second verse. Repeat for the words *ship*, *Skip*, and *trip* in the third verse. Point out that the words rhyme because they end with /ip/.
- Say the rhyme with the class, emphasizing the words that rhyme.

Simplify It

Show the children objects or pictures of objects that rhyme like a *hat* and a *cat*. Say the words with the children, emphasizing the sounds at the ends of the words.

Add a Challenge

Ask the children to come up with more words that rhyme with the rhyming words in the song.

Assessment

To assess each child's learning, consider the following:

1. Is the child able to sing with the group?
2. Is the child able to clap in rhythm to the song?
3. Is the child able to recognize words that rhyme?
4. Is the child able to name different modes of transportation?

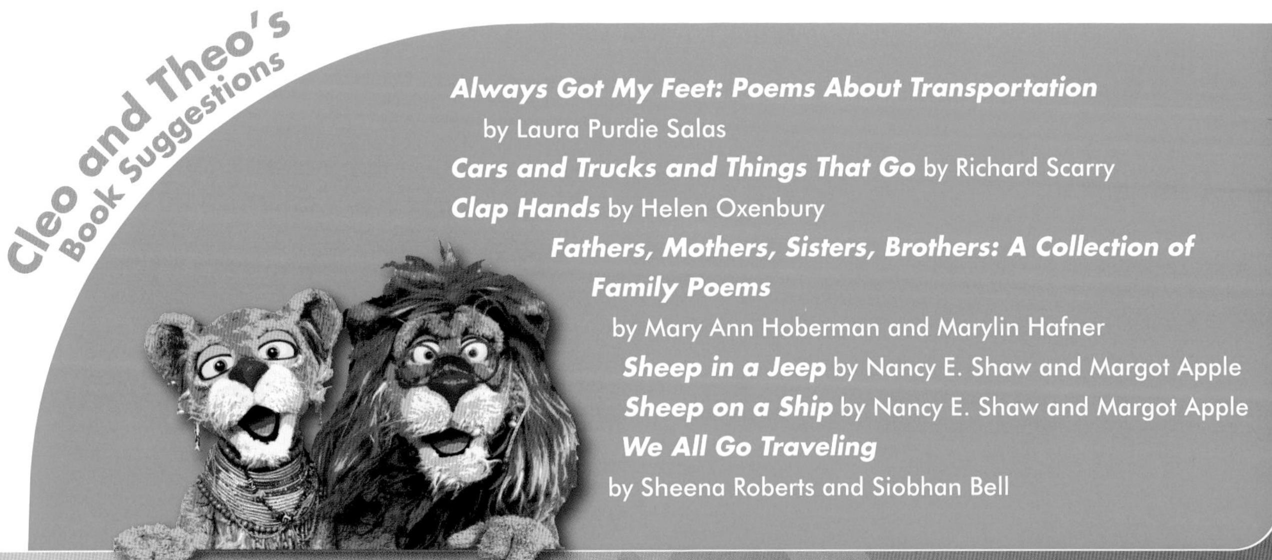

Cleo and Theo's Book Suggestions

Always Got My Feet: Poems About Transportation by Laura Purdie Salas

Cars and Trucks and Things That Go by Richard Scarry

Clap Hands by Helen Oxenbury

Fathers, Mothers, Sisters, Brothers: A Collection of Family Poems by Mary Ann Hoberman and Marylin Hafner

Sheep in a Jeep by Nancy E. Shaw and Margot Apple

Sheep on a Ship by Nancy E. Shaw and Margot Apple

We All Go Traveling by Sheena Roberts and Siobhan Bell

Reading *Owl Babies*

Literacy Skill Focus

Active Listening
Concepts of Print
Listening and Speaking
Parts of a Book
Sequencing
Story Structure
Story Comprehension

Vocabulary

animal	ivy
author	lonely
awake	mommy
baby	night
bird	owls
book	sad
branch	safe
brave	scared
count	sleep
day	swoop
family	title
flap	tree
happy	tree trunk
illustrator	twigs

Materials

Owl Babies by Martin Waddell and Patrick Benson

Note: You may want to shut the shades and dim the lights to create a nighttime atmosphere.

What Children Will Learn

1. About owls
2. About feelings
3. New vocabulary
4. How to recognize repetition in literature

Related Themes

Animals
Feelings

What to Do

- Engage the children in a discussion about families, including animal families. Ask, *Do you think that animals have families, too?* Tell the children that today you are going to read a book about an owl family. In the book, the baby owls miss their mommy, just like Stinky Face misses his mommy in the book, *I Miss You, Stinky Face* by Lisa McCourt.
- Ask, *What do you know about owls? Where do they live? What do you think they like to eat? Do you know that owls are birds that sleep during the day and stay awake at night?*
- Point to the title of the book and tell the children that the name, or title, of the book is *Owl Babies*. Point to the names of the author and the illustrator as you read them aloud.
- Read *Owl Babies* with expression, using your voice to show Bill's growing fear and longing for his mother. Ask the children to listen for how the baby owls feel. Point to the owl babies as you read their names: Sarah, Percy, and Bill.
- Invite the children to chime in on Bill's repeating line in the story.
- Use the pictures to talk about the meaning of any words the children may not know, such as *tree trunk*, *twigs*, *branch*, and *ivy*. Use your arms and body to demonstrate the meaning of *swooped* and *flapped*. Have the children imitate your motions.

- Talk about the story with the children. Ask questions such as, *Did you like the story? What was your favorite part? How do the owl babies feel when they wake up and their mommy is gone?* (sad, lonely, scared)
- Show the children the picture of the owl babies in the dark woods. Reread the first sentence on the page and then ask, *How do you think the owl babies feel? What do you think they are scared of? How do the owl babies feel when their mommy comes home?* (happy, safe)

Simplify It

As you read the book, ask the children to point to the owls on the pages of the book.

Add a Challenge

Ask the children to act out the meaning of some of the words in the book, such as *tree trunk, branch, bird, owl, swoop,* and *flap*.

Assessment

To assess each child's learning, consider the following:

1. Is the child able to say the repeating line in the book?
2. Is the child able to say what she learned about owls?
3. Does the child know the meaning of the new words in the book?

Animal Babies by Harry McNaught
Baby Owl by Aubrey Lang and Wayne Lynch
Brave Georgie Goat: 3 Little Stories About Growing Up by Denis Roche
The Littlest Owl by Caroline Pitcher and Tina Macnaughton
A Mother for Choco by Keiko Kasza
Owl Moon by Jane Yolen
Owls by Gail Gibbons
Owls by Adrienne Mason and Nancy Gray Ogle

"Three Owl Babies"

Literacy Skill Focus

Compare and Contrast
Listening and Speaking
Phonological Awareness (Rhythm, Rhyme, and Repetition)
Recall and Retell
Vocabulary

Vocabulary

alone
aunts
baby
brave
brother
compare
cousins
daddy
different
family
grandma
grandpa
happy
home
lonely
mommy
owls
puppet
same
scared
sister
tree
uncles
wait
wish

Materials

Owl Babies by Martin Waddell and Patrick Benson

Lion stick puppets (see the activity on page 20)

What Children Will Learn

1. About owls
2. To sing a new song
3. About same and different
4. New vocabulary

Related Themes

Feelings
Same and Different

What to Do

- Remind the children about the book *Owl Babies*. If necessary, read the story again.
- Singing songs about books and stories helps the children to recall and retell the story and practice new vocabulary. Sing "Three Owl Babies" with the hand motions. Have the children repeat each line after you and then sing the song together.

Three Owl Babies
(Tune: "Five Little Ducks")
Three owl babies sitting in a tree, *(Hold up three fingers.)*
Sarah, Percy, and Bill make three. *(Hold up three fingers, one at a time.)*
But where, oh, where can their mommy be? *(Shrug shoulders.)*
She'll be back soon. Just wait and see.

Wait and see.
Wait and see.
She'll be back soon.
Just wait and see.

Three owl babies feel all alone.
They wish and wish for their mommy to come home.
Look, there she is! She's flying through the trees. *(Extend arm and point finger.)*
Hoot. Hoot. Hoot. They're a happy family.

Happy family.
Happy family.
Hoot. Hoot. Hoot.
They're a happy family.

- Show the children a picture of the owl family from *Owl Babies*. Ask them to identify the different members of the owl family: the mother, sister (Sarah), and two brothers (Percy and Bill).
- Display the Lion family puppets and help the children identify the family members. Ask, *How are families the same? How are they different?* Point out that the owl family has two brothers and one sister and the Lion family has one brother and one sister. The Lion family has a father and the owl family doesn't.

Simplify It

Focus on how the families are the same. Once the children master this concept, ask them how the families are different.

Add a Challenge

Ask the children to dictate or write a story about the owl family or the Lion family in *Between the Lions*.

Assessment

To assess each child's learning, consider the following:

1. Is the child able to sing the song?
2. Is the child able to make the appropriate hand motions?
3. Is the child able to understand the concepts of *same* and *different*?

Cleo and Theo's Book Suggestions

Baby Owl by Aubrey Lang and Wayne Lynch
Brave Georgie Goat: 3 Little Stories About Growing Up by Denis Roche
Fathers, Mothers, Sisters, Brothers: A Collection of Family Poems by Mary Ann Hoberman and Marylin Hafner
The Littlest Owl by Caroline Pitcher and Tina Macnaughton
Lots of Dads by Shelley Rotner
Lots of Moms by Shelley Rotner
A Mother for Choco by Keiko Kasza
Owl Moon by Jane Yolen
Owls by Adrienne Mason and Nancy Gray Ogle
Owls by Gail Gibbons

Family Stories

Literacy Skill Focus
Listening and Speaking
Storytelling

Vocabulary

aunts
baby
brother
compare
cousins
daddy
different
family
grandma
grandpa
home
mommy
puppet
same
sister
uncles

Materials

crayons and markers
journals, one for each child (optional)
paper
stapler
tape

What Children Will Learn

1. About the families of the children in the class
2. How to take turns
3. New vocabulary

Related Theme
Storytelling

Preparation

On the day before you plan to introduce this Family Stories group time, ask the children to draw pictures of their family. Help the children write their names on their pictures. Save the drawings so the children can use them to dictate their family stories. Have the children look at the family pictures that they drew. Invite the children to tell you a story about their families. Write their words on paper or in a journal as the children dictate their stories to you. Read the story back to each child. Ask, *Did I leave out any words? Do you want to add anything?* Help the children write their names on their stories. Display the pictures and stories prominently in the classroom for the children (and families) to see. Consider binding the pictures and stories together to make a class book of family stories.

What to Do

- Display the children's family pictures and family stories (see preparation above).
- Discuss the children's pictures and encourage the children to talk about the people (and pets) in their pictures. Engage the children in a discussion about their drawings with comments and questions. Say, *I like your drawing. Where are you in the picture? Who is next to you?*

- Invite the children to share their pictures and stories. Make connections between the children's stories: *Aaron's story is about going to the playground with his grandma. Who else has a story about going to the playground?*
- Encourage the children to ask one another questions about their pictures and their stories.

Simplify It

Ask the children to say one thing about the family picture they drew.

Add a Challenge

Ask each child to describe another child's family picture or story.

Assessment

To assess each child's learning, consider the following:

1. Is the child able to remember his classmates' family stories?
2. Is the child able to use new vocabulary appropriately?

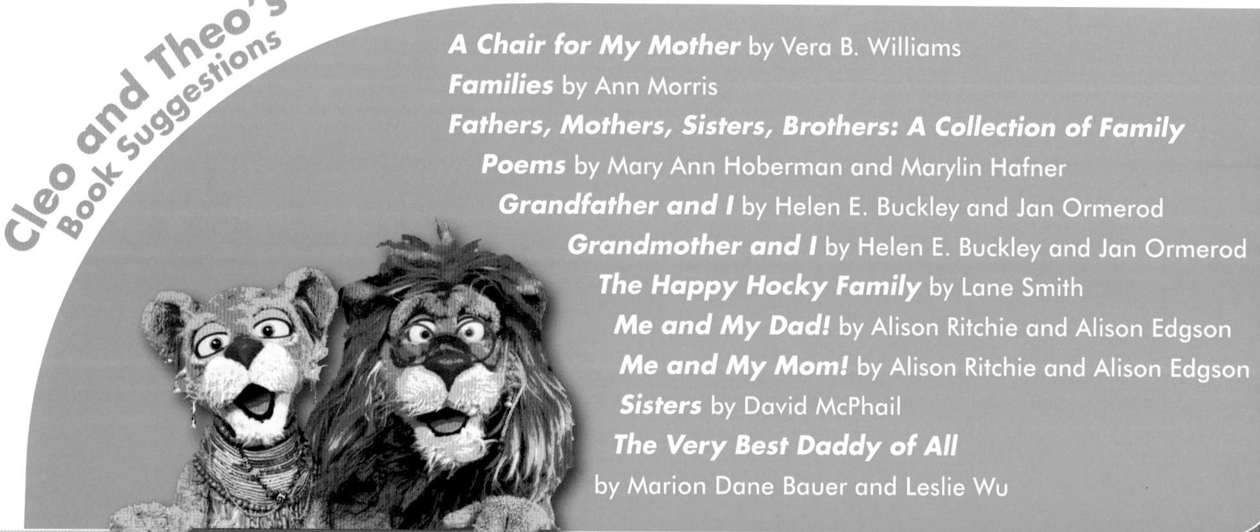

Cleo and Theo's Book Suggestions

A Chair for My Mother by Vera B. Williams
Families by Ann Morris
Fathers, Mothers, Sisters, Brothers: A Collection of Family Poems by Mary Ann Hoberman and Marylin Hafner
Grandfather and I by Helen E. Buckley and Jan Ormerod
Grandmother and I by Helen E. Buckley and Jan Ormerod
The Happy Hocky Family by Lane Smith
Me and My Dad! by Alison Ritchie and Alison Edgson
Me and My Mom! by Alison Ritchie and Alison Edgson
Sisters by David McPhail
The Very Best Daddy of All by Marion Dane Bauer and Leslie Wu

Swooping and Flapping

Literacy Skill Focus

Active Listening
Listening and Speaking
Story Comprehension
Vocabulary

Vocabulary

action
baby
family
flap
happy
home
mommy
repeat
swoop

Materials

Owl Babies by Martin Waddell and Patrick Benson

What Children Will Learn

1. To act out the meaning of words
2. New vocabulary
3. Information about owls

Related Themes

Feelings
Same and Different

What to Do

- Invite the children to participate as you read the story by acting out some of the action words with their bodies and by chiming in on the repeating lines.
- Have the children:
  - Close their eyes tightly when the owl babies wish their mommy would come home.
  - Use their bodies to show how the owl mommy *swoops* through the trees to her babies.
  - Use their bodies to show how the owl babies *flap* their wings, dance, and bounce up and down when their mommy comes home.
- Talk about the story with the children. Ask questions such as, *Why do you think the owl mommy leaves the tree house? Where do you think she goes? How do owl mommies get food for their babies?* (They go hunting.) *How do our mommies or daddies get food for us?*

Families

Simplify It

Model how to act out *swoop* and *flap* and then ask the children to copy your actions.

Add a Challenge

Ask, *What did you find out about owls from reading this book?* (Owls eat mice. Owls fly. Owls hunt.) Display nonfiction books about owls in the Library Center (see Cleo and Theo's Book Suggestions). Ask the children what they want to know about owls. Respond by saying, *That's a great question. Maybe we can find the answer to your question in this book about owls. Let's see!*

Assessment

To assess each child's learning, consider the following:

1. Is the child able to act out *swoop* and *flap*?
2. Can the child tell you a fact about owls?

Cleo and Theo's Book Suggestions

Baby Owl by Aubrey Lang and Wayne Lynch
The Barn Owl by Sally Tagholm and Bert Kitchen
Owl Moon by Jane Yolen
Owls by Adrienne Mason and Nancy Gray Ogle
Owls by Gail Gibbons

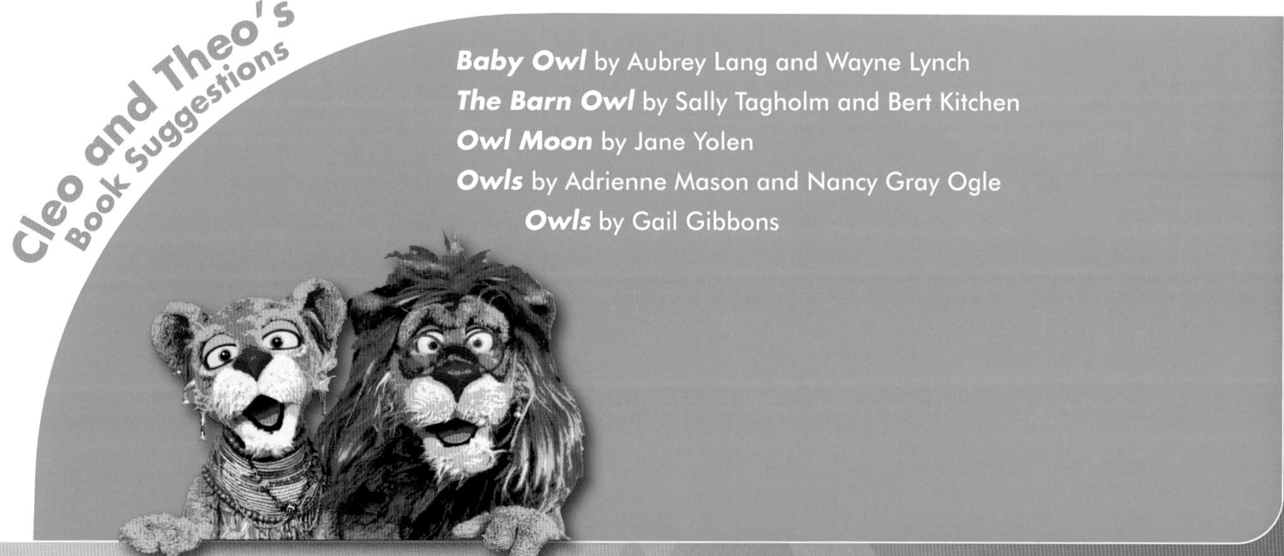

Muffins on Monday

Literacy Skill Focus
Phonological Awareness (Alliteration, Beginning Sounds)

Vocabulary

alliteration, beginning, letter, listen, make, mama, Monday, morning, muffins, my, same, sound

Materials

none needed

What Children Will Learn

1. About the sound /m/
2. To listen carefully

Related Theme
Sounds

What to Do

- Ask the children to listen to the words as you say this sentence: *My mama makes muffins on Monday morning.*
  Note: Consider writing the sentence on chart paper. Highlight each letter "M" by writing it in a different color.
- Prompt the children to say the sentence with you, emphasizing the /m/ sound at the beginning of the words.
- Then invite the children to say the sentence with you faster and faster.
- Identify the /m/ sounds in each word. Tell the children that *alliteration* is the repetition of the same beginning sound in two or more words.

Simplify It

Say each word in the sentence and then ask the children if the word begins with the /m/ sound.

S	M	T	W	Th	F	S
	1	2	3	4	5	6
7	8	9	10	11	12	13
14	15	16	17	18	19	20
21	22	23	24	25	26	27
28	29	30	31			

Add a Challenge

Say the sentence again slowly, pausing between each word. Give the children letter "Mm" cards and have them hold up the letter card when they hear a word that begins with the /m/ sound.

Mm

Assessment

To assess each child's learning, consider the following:

1. Is the child able to notice the alliteration?
2. Is the child able to say the sentence faster and faster?

Cleo and Theo's Book Suggestions

If You Give a Moose a Muffin by Laura Joffe Numeroff and Felicia Bond

Lots of Moms by Shelley Rotner

Mama, Do You Love Me? by Barbara M. Joosse and Barbara Lavalle

A Mother for Choco by Keiko Kasza

Owl Moon by Jane Yolen

Violet's Music by Angela Johnson

Note to Families About the Topic of Families

FAMILY LETTER

Date ____________________

Dear Families,

At group time, we are talking about our families and how we feel when we are together and apart. We are discovering the ways families are alike and different as we draw pictures, read books, sing songs, and recite poems about all kinds of families.

Here are some things that you can do at home with your child:

- Look at family photographs with your child. Talk about the people in each photograph.
- Sing the song "If You're Happy and You Know It" with your child. (The words to the song are printed below. If you do not know the tune, just say the words with enthusiasm.)
- At bedtime (or anytime), read a favorite story or talk about something that you and your child like to do together.

If you can, please send one or more family photographs to school with your child. We will use the photos to make a family poster that your child can look at when he or she misses you.

Thank you!

If You're Happy and You Know It

If you're happy and you know it, clap your hands. (*Clap twice.*)
If you're happy and you know it, clap your hands. (*Clap twice.*)
If you're happy and you know it, then your face will surely show it. (*Smile and point to face.*)
If you're happy and you know it, clap your hands. (*Clap twice.*)

Verse 2: If you're happy and you know it, stomp your feet. (*Stomp feet twice.*)
Verse 3: If you're happy and you know it, shout, "Hurray!" (*Shout, "Hurray!"*)
Verse 4: If you're happy and you know it, do all three. (*Clap hands; stomp feet; shout, "Hurray!"*)

CHAPTER 2

Feelings

This topic helps the children in your classroom learn to use language to name, understand, and express their feelings as they talk about what it means to feel afraid, brave, safe, and loved, as well as other emotions they feel when they have to share something or someone they love.

Setting Up the Room

- Fill the walls of your room with photographs of the children and grownups showing different emotions in various situations (for example, a child crying during a thunderstorm; a grandparent or parent embracing a child; the children laughing as they play together; the children fighting over a toy). Label each picture with the emotion it portrays.

- Using magazine pictures, clip art, or images from the Internet, create a "Feelings" chart (see the example on page 239) with faces that express different emotions (happy, sad, angry, excited, worried, scared, frustrated, jealous, proud, silly, and other feelings). Label the feeling that each picture depicts. Talk to the children about each feeling. *Have you ever felt this way? Point to the face that shows how you feel today.*

- Label and display pictures and/or photographs of different kinds of dogs. Place plush dogs in the Library, Pretend, and Play Centers. Encourage the children to look at and describe the pictures and to hold and play with the plush dogs.

  Ask parents to bring in photographs of family pets. Use the photographs to create an "Our Pets" display, or make a "Pets" collage with pictures and/or photographs of different kinds of pets (turtles, canaries, cats, dogs, hamsters, iguanas, and so on.). Encourage the children to look at the photographs and talk to each other about the pets they have or would like to have.

Family Letter

Prepare and make photocopies of the Family Letter on page 60 that explains this topic. Distribute the letter at pick-up time before you begin the topic.

"Good Morning to You"

Literacy Skill Focus
Listening and Speaking
Phonological Awareness (Rhyming, Rhythm, Repetition)
Vocabulary

Vocabulary

afraid
brave
clowns
fear
feeling
names
scared
spiders
thunderstorm

Materials

chart paper
"feeling face" pictures from the Feelings Chart (see page 239)
markers

What Children Will Learn

1. To sing a song
2. To identify their feelings

Related Themes

All About Me
Sounds

What to Do

- Begin the day with a greeting song such as "Good Morning to You." Invite the children to sing along with you.

Good Morning to You
Good morning to you!
Good morning to you!
We're all in our places
With bright shining faces.
Oh, this is the way to start a great day!

- After singing, greet each child by name and ask how she is feeling this morning. The children can point to the feeling-face picture that best describes how they feel (see page 39, Setting Up the Room).
- Explain that today you are going to talk about things that make people afraid. Emphasize that everyone, including grownups, feels afraid sometimes. Tell the children about something you are afraid of. *Sometimes I feel afraid when I watch a scary movie, even though I know it is just a movie and not real. Do you ever feel scared when you are watching a movie or a TV show?* Ask children to talk about their fears. *What are you afraid of? Are you afraid of thunderstorms?*

- Create a Scary Things class chart. Write the question, *What are we afraid of?* on a large sheet of chart paper. Read aloud the question as you touch each word. Begin by saying something you are afraid of and writing it below the question on the chart. Then ask the children to name things that they find scary. Encourage a variety of responses.
- Write the children's responses on the chart and read aloud the complete list. Save the chart to refer to during this topic.

Teacher Tip: Some children may be reluctant to talk about their fears because they worry that other children will make fun of them. Encourage the children to be sensitive to the feelings of others. You can also explain that sometimes it's smart to be afraid: *It's smart to be afraid of fire, because fire can hurt you. Being afraid often helps us to be safe and careful.*

Simplify It

If it is too difficult for the children to identify what they are afraid of, ask them to talk about things that they don't like, which might lead to a discussion about not liking something because it is scary.

Add a Challenge

Ask the children to draw a picture of how they feel that day.

Assessment

To assess each child's learning, consider the following:

1. Is the child able to sing the song?
2. Is the child able to identify her emotions?

Cleo and Theo's Book Suggestions

Feelings by Aliki
The Feelings Book by Todd Parr
Lots of Feelings by Shelley Rotner
The Owl Who Was Afraid of the Dark by Jill Tomlinson and Paul Howard
The Way I Feel by Janan Cain
Wemberly Worried by Kevin Henkes
When I Feel Angry by Cornelia Maude Spelman and Nancy Cote
Yesterday I Had the Blues by Jeron Ashford Frame and R. Gregory Christie

Reading *Not Afraid of Dogs*

Literacy Skill Focus
Active Listening
Listening and Speaking
Parts of a Book
Predicting
Story Comprehension
Using Illustrations
Vocabulary

Vocabulary

afraid
author
brave
dog
expression
fear
illustrator
scared
snakes
spiders
thunderstorm
yell

Materials

Not Afraid of Dogs by Suzanna Pitzer and Larry Day

What Children Will Learn

1. The meaning of the word *brave*
2. That authors write books and illustrators draw the pictures for books

Related Themes

Animals
Pets

What to Do

- Tell the children that today you are going to read a book about a very brave boy. Ask the children what *brave* means. After they respond, explain that you are brave when you are not afraid. You are also brave when you do something even though you feel scared or afraid. For example: *Firefighters are very brave. They fight fires to save people, even though fire is dangerous and they can get hurt.*
- Say, *Daniel, the boy in the book I am going to read, is very brave. He's not even afraid of thunderstorms!* Talk about the loud noises we hear in the sky during thunderstorms. Ask, *Have you ever heard thunder? It can be very scary!*
- As you underline the words with your finger, read aloud the title and the names of the author and illustrator. Tell the children that Suzanna Pitzer is the author, the person who wrote the book. Larry Day is the illustrator, the person who drew the pictures. Ask the children to look carefully at the cover illustration. As you point to Daniel, say, *This is Daniel. He's not afraid of spiders, snakes, or thunderstorms. Daniel is afraid of something, though. Can you guess what he is afraid of? What makes you think that?*
- Read the book slowly and with expression. Use different voices for the characters. Change your tone when Daniel yells and when his voice softens.

Feelings

- As you read, ask the children to look carefully at the illustrations to see if they can tell how Daniel feels about dogs. Pause at the following places and ask the children to tell you how they think Daniel is feeling:
  - *When he first sees Bandit on his mother's lap*
  - *When he first discovers Bandit in the bathroom*
  - *When he picks up and holds Bandit in the bathroom*
  - *When he snuggles with Bandit in bed*
- Talk about the story with the children. Ask questions such as:
  - *Did you like the story? What was your favorite part?*
  - *In the beginning of the story, how does Daniel feel about dogs?*
  - *At the end of the story, how does Daniel feel about dogs?*
  - *Have you ever felt afraid of a dog?*

Simplify It

Ask the children to point to pictures that show Daniel feeling brave and feeling scared.

Add a Challenge

Ask the children to describe a time when they were brave.

Assessment

To assess each child's learning, consider the following:

1. Is the child able to understand what it means to be brave?
2. Is the child able to understand what authors and illustrators do?

Cleo and Theo's Book Suggestions

Dogs by Gail Gibbons

Give a Dog a Bone: Anthology of Dog Poems by Joanna Cole and Stephanie Calmenson

How Much Is That Doggie in the Window? by Iza Trapani and Bob Merrill

May I Pet Your Dog? The How-to Guide for Kids Meeting Dogs (and Dogs Meeting Kids) by Stephanie Calmenson and Jan Ormerod

My Dog Is Lost by Ezra Jack Keats and Pat Cherr

My Dog Rosie by Isabelle Harper

Nobody's Diggier Than a Dog by Susan Campbell Bartoletti and Beppe Giacobbe

"Where, Oh, Where Has My Little Dog Gone?"

Literacy Skill Focus
Phonological Awareness (Rhyming, Rhythm, Repetition)
Vocabulary

Vocabulary

ears
expression
fear
long
short
song
tail

Materials

Not Afraid of Dogs by Suzanna Pitzer and Larry Day
pictures of dogs

What Children Will Learn

1. To sing a song about dogs
2. To use descriptive words

Related Theme
Animals

What to Do

- Tell the children that you are going to sing a song about a child who is looking for his lost dog.
- Sing "Where, Oh, Where Has My Little Dog Gone?"

Where, Oh, Where Has My Little Dog Gone?
Where, oh, where has my little dog gone?
Where, oh, where can he be?
With his ears cut short and his tail cut long,
Oh, where, oh, where can he be?

- Show the children the dog in *Not Afraid of Dogs* and other pictures of dogs.
- The song describes a dog "with his ears cut short and his tail cut long." Talk with the children about how they think the dog looks.

Simplify It

Sing one line of the song at a time. Ask the children to repeat each line after you sing it.

Add a Challenge

Hide pictures of dogs in the classroom and ask the children to find the dogs that are hiding in the room.

Assessment

To assess each child's learning, consider the following:

1. Is the child able to sing the song?
2. Is the child able to describe how the dog in the song looks?

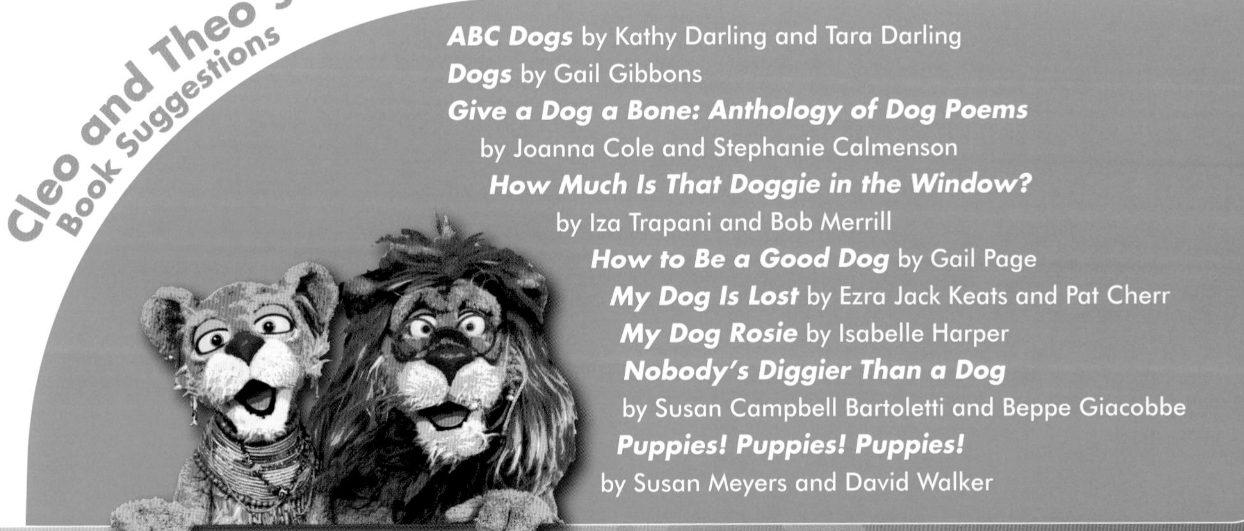

Cleo and Theo's Book Suggestions

ABC Dogs by Kathy Darling and Tara Darling

Dogs by Gail Gibbons

Give a Dog a Bone: Anthology of Dog Poems by Joanna Cole and Stephanie Calmenson

How Much Is That Doggie in the Window? by Iza Trapani and Bob Merrill

How to Be a Good Dog by Gail Page

My Dog Is Lost by Ezra Jack Keats and Pat Cherr

My Dog Rosie by Isabelle Harper

Nobody's Diggier Than a Dog by Susan Campbell Bartoletti and Beppe Giacobbe

Puppies! Puppies! Puppies! by Susan Meyers and David Walker

Bingo Tongue Twister

Literacy Skill Focus
Letter Recognition
Phonological Awareness
(Alliteration, Beginning Sounds, Rhythm, and Repetition)

Vocabulary

Bandit
Bingo
bone
bring
names
sing
sound
tongue twister
verse

Materials

chart paper
markers

What Children Will Learn

1. About tongue twisters
2. About alliteration
3. About fast and slow

Related Themes

Animals
Sounds

What to Do

- Have fun trying to say this tongue twister: *Bring Bingo Bandit's bone.*
- Repeat the words slowly, emphasizing the /b/ sound at the beginning of the words. Invite the children to say the sentence with you faster and faster. Then say the sentence slower and slower, emphasizing the /b/ sound again.
- Say, *I notice something interesting about the words in this tongue twister. They all begin with the same /b/ sound. The names* Bingo *and* Bandit *both begin with the /b/ sound. The words* bring *and* bone *begin with the /b/ sound, too. Belinda and Barry, your names also begin with the /b/ sound!*
- Tell the children you are going to teach them a fun song about a dog named Bingo.
- Write the words to the song (following) on chart paper. Write each letter of *Bingo* in a different color and in large, capital letters.

Bingo
There was a farmer who had a dog
And Bingo was his name-o.
B-I-N-G-O
B-I-N-G-O
B-I-N-G-O
And Bingo was his name-o.

Verses
(2) clap-I-N-G-O
(3) clap-clap-N-G-O
(4) clap-clap-clap-G-O
(5) clap-clap-clap-clap-O
(6) clap-clap-clap-clap-clap

- Point to the name *Bingo* on the chart. Touch each letter in Bingo's name as you say it aloud.
- Sing the first verse of the song. Then invite the children to sing it with you, shouting out the letters *B-I-N-G-O* as you point to them on the chart.
- Sing the song again. This time have the children clap as they sing each letter in Bingo's name.
- Point to the letter "B" and ask the children to tell you the first letter in Bingo's name. Explain that this time you are going to sing the song a little bit differently. Ask the children to carefully watch what you do.
- Cover the letter "B" with a piece of cardboard. Then sing the second verse. Instead of singing the letter "B," clap once before singing the letters *I-N-G-O*. Invite the children to sing the second verse with you. Repeat the process for the third, fourth, fifth, and sixth verses.

Simplify It

Sing the song one day and then have fun with the tongue twister on another day.

Add a Challenge

Ask the children if they know any tongue twisters such as "Peter Piper picked a peck of pickled peppers," "She sells seashells by the seashore," "Mom shops for Pop's socks," and "Mixed biscuits."

Assessment

To assess each child's learning, consider the following:

1. What did the child learn about tongue twisters?
2. Was the child able to learn the song?

Cleo and Theo's Book Suggestions

Fox in Socks by Dr. Seuss

May I Pet Your Dog? The How-to Guide for Kids Meeting Dogs (and Dogs Meeting Kids) by Stephanie Calmenson and Jan Ormerod

My Dog Is Lost by Ezra Jack Keats and Pat Cherr

Nobody's Diggier Than a Dog by Susan Campbell Bartoletti and Beppe Giacobbe

Oh, Say Can You Say? by Dr. Seuss

Six Sick Sheep: 101 Tongue Twisters by Joanna Cole

Who Took My Bone?

Literacy Skill Focus
Environmental Sounds
Follow Directions
Listening

Vocabulary

bone	hide
dog	identify
game	listen
guess	turn

Materials

bone (real, plastic, or paper)

What Children Will Learn

1. Listening skills
2. To play a game

Related Themes

Animals
Pets

What to Do

- Teach the children this listening game to help them identify sounds.
- Ask the children to pretend that they are dogs. Ask for a volunteer to be "Bandit" and to sit with his back to the rest of the children.
- Say, *Bandit, here's your bone. I'm putting it behind you. One of your doggie friends is going to take your bone and say something. When I tell you, turn around and guess who took your bone. Listen very carefully to the voice so you can pick out the friend who took your bone.*
- Select a child to quietly take the bone from behind Bandit's back. Have the child sit down and hide the bone behind her back and say, "I took your bone. Woof! Woof!" Have the other children also put their hands behind their back.
- Signal Bandit to turn around and ask, "Who took my bone?" Give Bandit three guesses.
- Repeat this game during the week to make sure every child gets a turn to be Bandit and the dog that takes the bone.

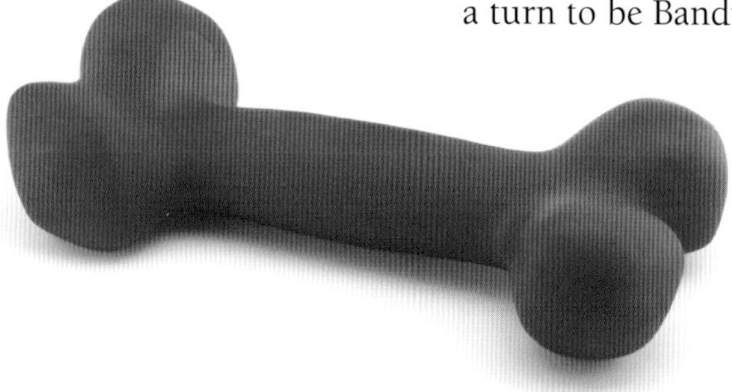

Simplify It

Hide the bone somewhere in the classroom. Ask the children to find the bone by giving them hints about where it is hidden.

Add a Challenge

Ask one child to hide the bone in the classroom and then give the rest of the children hints about where the bone is hidden.

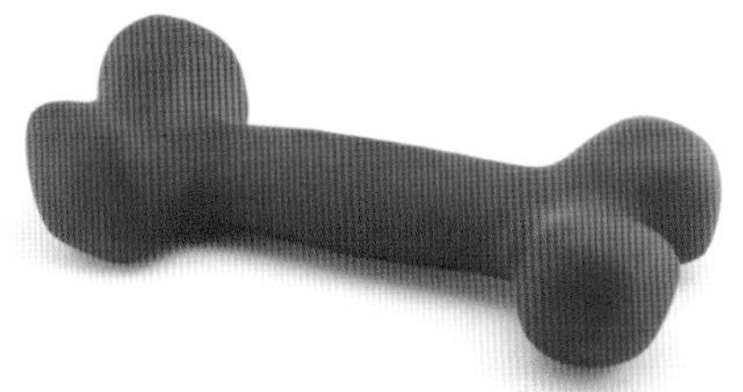

Assessment

To assess each child's learning, consider the following:

1. How well was the child able to identify the other children's voices?
2. Was the child able to play the game and wait for a turn?

Cleo and Theo's Book Suggestions

ABC Dogs by Kathy Darling and Tara Darling

Dogs by Gail Gibbons

Give a Dog a Bone: Anthology of Dog Poems by Joanna Cole and Stephanie Calmenson

How to Be a Good Dog by Gail Page

The Last Puppy by Frank Asch

My Dog Is Lost by Ezra Jack Keats and Pat Cherr

My Dog Rosie by Isabelle Harper

Nobody's Diggier Than a Dog by Susan Campbell Bartoletti and Beppe Giacobbe

Puppies! Puppies! Puppies! by Susan Meyers and David Walker

It's Okay to Feel Afraid

Literacy Skill Focus
Active Listening
Listening and Speaking
Phonological Awareness (Rhythm and Repetition)
Vocabulary

Vocabulary

afraid
body
brave
heart
petrified
pound
scared
shake
shiver
synonym
terrified
thunder
tremble

Materials

Scary Things chart (see the group time activity on pages 40–41 and the chart on page 54)

What Children Will Learn

1. About how we express being afraid
2. About dogs
3. To sing a song about being frightened
4. About synonyms

Related Themes

Animals
Pets

What to Do

- Talk with the children about feeling afraid.
- Display the Scary Things chart from "Good Morning to You" (page 40) and review the things the children are afraid of. Then talk to the children about how our bodies act when we are afraid. Say, *When I watch a scary movie, my heart starts to pound very fast, just like Daniel's heart pounds when he sees Bandit in the bathroom.* (Pat your heart with your hand a few times quickly.) *Sometimes I feel like I'm shaking.* (Pretend to tremble or shiver.) Ask the children, *How does your body feel when you are afraid? What does your body do when you hear thunder?*
- Talk about the meaning of the word *synonym*. Synonyms are words that mean the same thing or almost the same thing. *Afraid* and *scared* are synonyms. They mean the same thing.
- Tell the children you are going to teach them a song about feeling frightened. Before singing the song, remind the children that *frightened* means the same thing as *afraid* and *scared*. Say, *Pretend you are frightened of the dark. Show me, with your body, how you feel. Are you trembling and shaking? Is your heart beating really fast?*
- Sing "I'm Feeling Frightened." Add hand and body motions and facial expressions to help the children remember the words. Then invite children to sing along with you and add the movements.

I'm Feeling Frightened
(Tune: "You Are My Sunshine")
I'm feeling frightened, so very frightened.
My heart is beating (*Pat hand over heart in quick succession.*)
So very fast.
My hands are shaking, (*Shake hands.*)
My legs are quaking. (*Shake legs.*)
I don't like this feeling I have.

I'm feeling happy, so very happy.
I have a smile (*Smile.*)
From ear to ear. (*Touch each ear.*)
I feel like skipping,
I feel like singing.
I hope that you are happy, too.

Simplify It

Talk with the children about things that make them happy.

Add a Challenge

Ask the children to act out feelings with their bodies and their faces.

Assessment

To assess each child's learning, consider the following:

1. Is the child able to say what makes him feel frightened?
2. Is the child able to sing the song with the class?
3. Is the child able to understand the meaning of the word *synonym*?

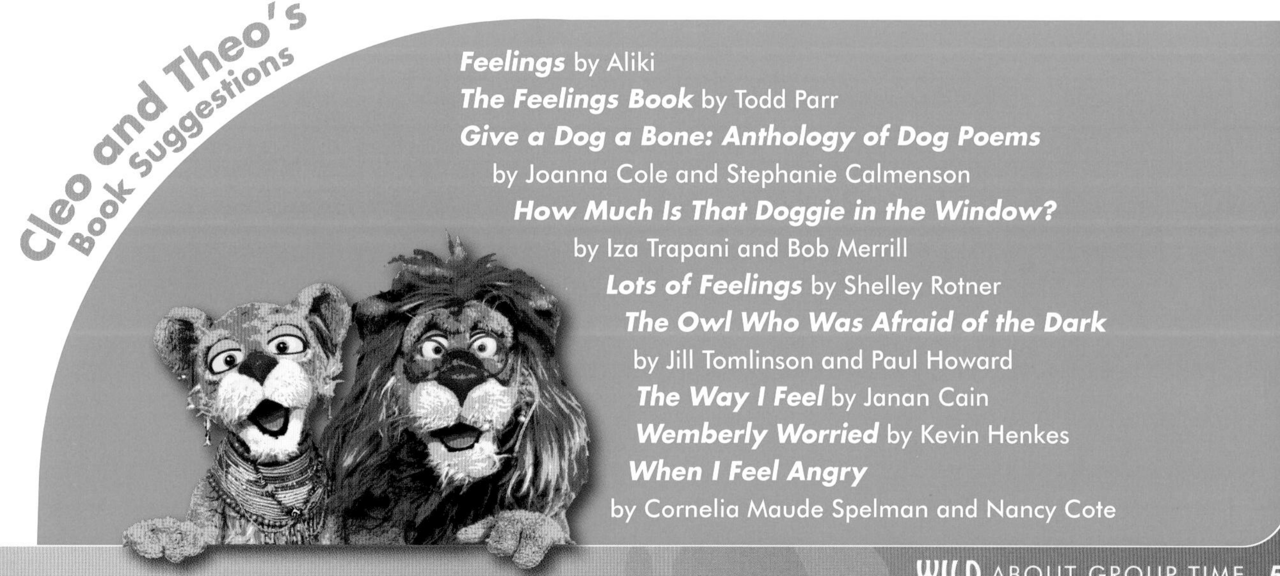

Cleo and Theo's Book Suggestions

Feelings by Aliki
The Feelings Book by Todd Parr
Give a Dog a Bone: Anthology of Dog Poems by Joanna Cole and Stephanie Calmenson
How Much Is That Doggie in the Window? by Iza Trapani and Bob Merrill
Lots of Feelings by Shelley Rotner
The Owl Who Was Afraid of the Dark by Jill Tomlinson and Paul Howard
The Way I Feel by Janan Cain
Wemberly Worried by Kevin Henkes
When I Feel Angry by Cornelia Maude Spelman and Nancy Cote

Feeling Safe and Loved

Literacy Skill Focus

Active Listening
Concepts of Print
Listening and Speaking
Parts of a Book
Story Comprehension
Vocabulary

Vocabulary

author
brother
calm
far
happy
illustrator
jealous
lap
lullaby
near
safe
sister
snug
snuggle
warm

Materials

globe or map of North America

On Mother's Lap by Ann Herbert Scott and Glo Coalson

What Children Will Learn

1. About feeling safe and loved
2. About families
3. About life in a different climate
4. About authors and illustrators

Related Themes

Families
Opposites

What to Do

- Say, *We have been talking about feeling afraid. Today we are going to talk about a different feeling.* Share memories of how you felt when you sat in your mother's, grandmother's, or caregiver's lap when you were a child: *When I was little, after we were ready for bed, my brother and I would climb into my mother's lap and talk about what we did that day. Then she would read us a story. We felt warm and happy. We felt safe and snug. We felt loved.*
- Introduce the book: As you underline the words with your finger, read aloud the title and the names of the author and illustrator. Tell the children that Ann Herbert Scott is the author, the person who wrote the book. Glo Coalson is the illustrator, the person who drew the pictures. Say, *This book is about a boy named Michael. Michael's favorite place to be is on his mother's lap, rocking back and forth, back and forth, in a big rocking chair.*
- Open the book to the title page. Ask the children what they see: *What is the weather like? Do you think Michael and his family live where we do? Why or why not?*
- Explain that Michael and his mom live in a part of the world that has a very cold and long winter. On a globe or map, show the children their home state. Then point to Alaska, where

Michael and his family live. Unless you live in or close to Alaska, say, Michael does not live *near* where we live. He lives very *far* away. Talk about some of the things the children can see that are different from where they live, such as the clothing, the dog sled, and the ice fishing.

- Read aloud the story in a quiet, soothing voice. After you finish reading the story, ask questions such as:
  - *How do you think Michael feels when he's on his mother's lap in the rocking chair?*
  - *How do you think Michael feels when his mother says she thinks his baby sister would like to rock too? Why do you think so?*
  - *How do you think Michael feels when all three are rocking together? Why?*

Simplify It

Read the book and then talk with the children about how they think Michael feels.

Add a Challenge

Have the children sit in a circle. Ask, *What do you have when you are sitting down that you don't have when you stand up?* (a lap) Have the children stand up and "lose" their laps.

Assessment

To assess each child's learning, consider the following:

1. Is the child able to describe what it means to feel safe and loved?
2. Is the child able to talk about the climate in places such as Alaska?

Cleo and Theo's Book Suggestions

A Baby Sister for Frances by Russell Hoban and Lillian Hoban
Feelings by Aliki
The Feelings Book by Todd Parr
In My Family/En mi familia by Carmen Lomas Garza
Lots of Feelings by Shelley Rotner
The Way I Feel by Janan Cain
Wemberly Worried by Kevin Henkes
When I Feel Angry by Cornelia Maude Spelman and Nancy Cote
Yesterday I Had the Blues by Jeron Ashford Frame and R. Gregory Christie

I Feel Better

Literacy Skill Focus
Listening and Speaking
Vocabulary

Vocabulary

afraid, brainstorm, brave, bugs, chart, dark, fear, monsters, overcome, petrified, scared, smart

Materials

Scary Things chart (see example to the right and the activity on pages 40–41)

What Children Will Learn

1. To identify their fears and to overcome them
2. To take turns listening and speaking

Related Theme

Friends

What to Do

- Display the Scary Things chart (see example below). Review some of the things the children are afraid of.

What are we afraid of?
Keisha is afraid of scary movies.
Mike is afraid of spiders.
Davon is afraid of fires.
Micah is afraid when she hears loud noises.
Kayla is afraid of thunderstorms.
Sam is afraid of clowns.
Jake is afraid of monsters.

- Ask, *What can you do when you feel afraid?* Talk about a strategy you have used to overcome something you are afraid of: *Sometimes when I'm afraid of the dark, I sing to myself. The singing helps me feel better, and I'm not so scared anymore.*

- Choose examples of scary things from the chart and ask the children to brainstorm ways to deal with their fears. *What can you do if you are afraid of dogs (the dark, monsters, bugs)?* Encourage a variety of responses, including holding someone's hand and talking to a grownup. Give the children positive feedback. *That's a great idea! That would be a very smart thing to do.*

Simplify It

Ask the children to tell you about one time when they were scared. *What happened? How did you feel? Did someone help you?*

Add a Challenge

Suggest that the children make up a story about a child who was afraid of something and what the child did to overcome his fear.

Assessment

To assess each child's learning, consider the following:

1. Is the child able to identify her fears?
2. Is the child able to suggest ways to overcome her fears?
3. Is the child able to take turns listening to others and speaking at appropriate times?

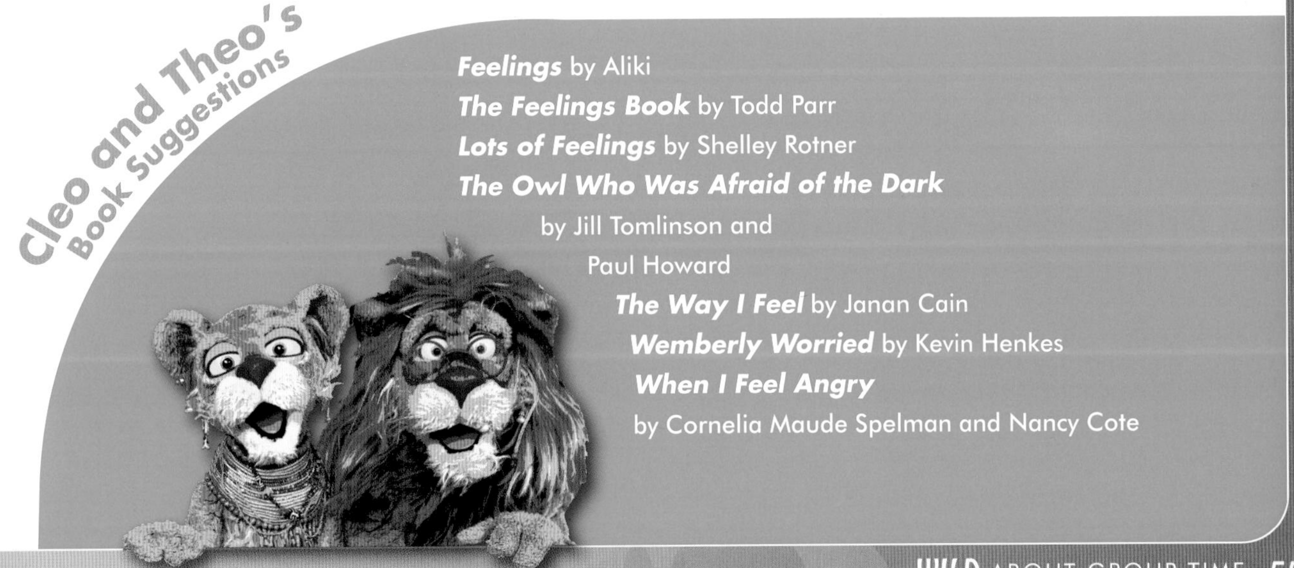

Feelings by Aliki
The Feelings Book by Todd Parr
Lots of Feelings by Shelley Rotner
The Owl Who Was Afraid of the Dark by Jill Tomlinson and Paul Howard
The Way I Feel by Janan Cain
Wemberly Worried by Kevin Henkes
When I Feel Angry by Cornelia Maude Spelman and Nancy Cote

Dogs Get Scared, Too!

Literacy Skill Focus

Active Listening
Book Appreciation
Listening and Speaking
Parts of a Book
Story Comprehension
Vocabulary

Vocabulary

afraid	fear
author	front
back	illustrator
comfort	overcome
cover	petrified
dog	scared

Materials

Not Afraid of Dogs by Suzanna Pitzer and Larry Day

What Children Will Learn

1. That dogs can get scared
2. How to help others when they are scared

Related Themes

Animals
Helping
Pets

What to Do

- As you underline the words with your finger, read aloud the title and the names of the author and illustrator. Ask the children to describe the four dogs on the front and back covers.
- As you read the book, ask the children to listen for what Daniel does to overcome his fear of dogs.
- After reading the page on which Daniel finds Bandit in the bathroom, point to the picture of Daniel. Ask, *How can you tell Daniel is scared in this picture? Yes, he's so afraid he can't move. He's petrified!*
- After reading the page on which Daniel realizes that Bandit is trying to climb into the bathtub because Bandit is afraid of thunder, ask, *Why is Bandit trying to climb into the bathtub? How can Daniel tell that Bandit is scared?*
- Talk about the book with the children. Ask questions such as:
  - *What happens in the bathroom that helps Daniel get over his fear of Bandit?*
  - *What does Daniel do to help comfort Bandit?*
  - *What are some things you can do to help a person who is afraid?*

Simplify It

Ask the children to identify the people and animals in the story that are afraid.

Add a Challenge

Ask the children to tell you other words that mean the same thing as *scared*, such as *petrified*, *terrified*, *afraid*, *frightened*, and so on.

Assessment

To assess each child's learning, consider the following:

1. Is the child able to understand that dogs can be scared?
2. Is the child able to suggest ways to help people when they are scared?
3. Does the child understand the new vocabulary word—*petrified*?

Cleo and Theo's Book Suggestions

Feelings by Aliki

The Feelings Book by Todd Parr

Give a Dog a Bone: Anthology of Dog Poems by Joanna Cole and Stephanie Calmenson

Lots of Feelings by Shelley Rotner

May I Pet Your Dog? The How-to Guide for Kids Meeting Dogs (and Dogs Meeting Kids) by Stephanie Calmenson and Jan Ormerod

The Way I Feel by Janan Cain

Wemberly Worried by Kevin Henkes

When I Feel Angry by Cornelia Maude Spelman and Nancy Cote

Sharing

Literacy Skill Focus
Concepts of Print
Emotional Awareness
Listening and Speaking
Parts of a Book
Story Comprehension
Vocabulary

Vocabulary

back and forth
change
favorite
jealous
lap
rock
share
sister

Materials

On Mother's Lap by Ann Herbert Scott and Glo Coalson

What Children Will Learn

1. About jealousy
2. About sharing

Related Themes

Friends
Sharing

What to Do

- Show the children the cover of the book *On Mother's Lap*. Ask the children how Michael feels when he is rocking on his mother's lap. Then ask, *How does Michael feel about sharing his mother's lap with his baby sister?* Emphasize that it can be hard to share. At first, Michael doesn't want to share his mother's lap with his baby sister. He feels jealous of his sister. He wants his mother's lap all to himself. But later, when he and his sister are together on his mother's lap, he feels good about sharing.
- Create a relaxing mood by singing the song "Rock, Rock."

Rock, Rock
(Tune: "Row, Row, Row Your Boat")
Rock, rock back and forth
Back and forth together.
Rock, rock back and forth
Back and forth together.

- Invite the children to slowly rock back and forth as you sing. Tell the children you are going to read the story again. Set a listening focus: *Listen for how Michael's feelings change about sharing his mother's lap with his baby sister.*

- Read the book to the children and then encourage them to talk about how they feel about sharing. Ask, *How do you feel when you have to share something or someone you love? How do you feel when you have to share a favorite toy? How do you feel when you see a friend playing with something you want to play with?*
- Talk about the story with the children. Ask questions such as:
  - *Why does Michael say there isn't room on his mother's lap for his baby sister?*
  - *How do you feel when your family does something together?*

Simplify It

After reading the book, ask the children to talk about a time when they felt jealous.

Add a Challenge

Suggest that each child create a story about sharing.

Assessment

To assess each child's learning, consider the following:

1. Is the child able to describe how it feels to be jealous?
2. Is the child able to talk about a time when he shared a favorite toy?

Cleo and Theo's Book Suggestions

Feelings by Aliki
The Feelings Book by Todd Parr
Lots of Feelings by Shelley Rotner
The Owl Who Was Afraid of the Dark by Jill Tomlinson and Paul Howard
Sharing Is Fun by Joanna Cole and Maxie Chambliss
The Way I Feel by Janan Cain
Wemberly Worried by Kevin Henkes
When I Feel Angry by Cornelia Maude Spelman and Nancy Cote
When I Feel Jealous by Cornelia Maude Spelman and Nancy Cote

Note to Families About the Topic of Feelings

FAMILY LETTER

Date ____________________

Dear Families,

In class, we are talking about how we feel when we are afraid of something. One of the books that we are reading is called *Not Afraid of Dogs*. It's about a brave boy who overcomes his fear of dogs. We are learning about dogs, and we are talking, drawing, singing, and writing about our fears and how we can deal with them.

The children are also learning that their feelings can change. Another book that we are reading, *On Mother's Lap*, is about a boy who doesn't want to share his mother's lap with his baby sister. However, when they all sit and rock together, he feels happy.

Here are some things you can do at home with your child:

- Tell your child about a time you felt afraid. What were you afraid of? What did you do to deal with your fears?
- Sing a favorite lullaby to your child at bedtime.
- Visit a pet shop, kennel, or a friend who has a dog. Talk about what the dog looks like. Is it big or small? What color is it? Does it have any special marks? What shape are its ears?
- Talk about safety rules concerning animals. When is it okay to approach an animal, pick it up, or pet it?

Please let us know if your child would like to bring a photo of his or her pet to add to the display.

Thank you!

CHAPTER 3

Friends

This topic highlights the true story of the remarkable friendship between a baby hippo and an aging, giant tortoise. The story teaches the children in your classroom that we can be friends with anyone, no matter how different we think they may be. The children also explore what they can do and say when they have a disagreement or conflict with a friend. New buddy pairs help children develop social skills as they play and learn together.

Setting Up the Room

- Create a Friends Together wall display with new pictures of the children playing and learning together and pictures of animal friends.

- Label and display cutout pictures or photographs of hippos, turtles, and tortoises. Encourage the children to describe each animal and how they are alike and different.

- Create a "Friends" book-browsing box by placing books about hippos, turtles, and tortoises into a box. If possible, include a few children's magazines about animals.

- Make a "Buddy" chart. When assigning buddies, pair the children who are not already good friends. Mix the children by gender, culture, learning style, and/or personality. For example, you might pair a shy child with an outgoing one. Make a "Buddy" chart that shows the names of buddies as paired. Post it at the children's eye level so they can see who their buddy is. Review the chart with the children. Explain that buddy means "a friend, someone you do things with." Buddies share, take turns, and work together.

Teacher Tip: You may want to keep the same buddies together for the week or make new buddy pairs each day. When the children arrive at school, you may want to place matching stickers on each buddy's shirt. Then have the children find their buddy by looking for the matching sticker.

Family Letter

Prepare and make photocopies of the Family Letter on page 82 that explains this topic. Give the letter to parents at pick-up time before you begin the topic.

Two Good Friends

Literacy Skill Focus
Listening and Speaking
Vocabulary

Vocabulary

Africa
different
friend
hippopotamus
hippos
land
tortoise
turtle
water

Materials

Hippos, Turtles, and Tortoises wall display (see Setting Up the Room, page 61)

What Children Will Learn

1. About animal friends
2. About hippos and turtles or tortoises

Related Themes

Animals
Feelings

What to Do

- Tell the children that you are going to show them two different animals that might be friends. Point to a picture of a hippopotamus on the wall display (see page 61). Ask, *Do you know what kind of animal this is?* Explain that a *hippopotamus* is a large animal that lives in Africa. *Sometimes people call them hippos. Hippos have very big noses, or snouts, and very wide mouths. They like water.* Challenge the children to try saying the word *hippopotamus* three times fast! *Hippopotamus, hippopotamus, hippopotamus!*
- Next, point to a picture of a turtle. Ask, *Do you know what kind of animal this is?* Explain that a *turtle* is an animal with a hard, round shell. *When they need to feel safe, turtles can pull their heads, legs, and tails into their shells.* Then, point to a picture of a tortoise. Ask, *Do you know what animal this is?* Explain that some turtles live in water, but a *tortoise* is a kind of turtle that lives on land. *Some tortoises are very big.*
- Say, *Hippos and tortoises are very different animals.* Ask, *Do you think a hippo and a tortoise can be friends? Why or why not?*

Simplify It

Talk with the children about their friends.

Add a Challenge

Create a KWL chart for hippos, turtles, or both by making three columns on a sheet of chart paper. For example, at the top of the first column write "What We Know About Hippos," at the top of the second column write "What We Want to Know About Hippos," and at the top of the third column write "What We Learned About Hippos." Ask the children what they know about hippos. Record their answers in the first column. Ask the children what they want to know about hippos and record their responses in the second column. After reading books about hippos, ask the children what they learned about hippos. Record their responses in the third column.

All About Hippos KWL Chart

What We **K**now about Hippos	What We **W**ant to Know about Hippos	What We **L**earned about Hippos

Assessment

To assess each child's learning, consider the following:

1. What did the child learn about animal friends?
2. What did the child learn about hippos, turtles, and tortoises?

Cleo and Theo's Book Suggestions

Baby Hippopotamus by Patricia A. Pingry

Dog and Bear by Laura Vaccaro Seeger

The Hippopotamus by Christine Denis-Huot and Michel Denis-Huot

Hippopotamus by Patricia Whitehouse

Mama: A True Story by Jeanette Winter

A Mama for Owen by Marion Dane Bauer and John Butler

Nutmeg and Barley: A Budding Friendship by Janie Bynum

Owen & Mzee: Language of Friendship by Isabelle Hatkoff, Craig Hatkoff, Dr. Paula Kahumbu, and Peter Greste

Animal Friends

Literacy Skill Focus

Active Listening
Compare and Contrast
Concepts of Print
Interpreting Illustrations
Listening and Speaking
Predicting
Story Comprehension
Vocabulary

Vocabulary

annoy
bother
different
friend
frustrated
goose
hippo
hippopotamus
polar bear
same
splendid
take care of
tortoise

Materials

globe or map of the world
Owen & Mzee: Best Friends by Isabella Hatkoff, Craig Hatkoff, Dr. Paula Kahumbu, and Peter Greste
A Splendid Friend, Indeed by Suzanne Bloom

What Children Will Learn

1. About differences
2. About friendship

Related Themes

Animals
Feelings

What to Do

- Ask the children to describe what they see on the cover of *Owen & Mzee: Best Friends*. Ask, *Which animal is the hippo? Which is the tortoise?* Point to the words as you read aloud the title. Ask, *Who thought a hippo and a tortoise could be friends? You were right! This is a true story of a baby hippo and an old tortoise that become great friends! What kinds of things do you think the two friends do together?*
- Read the book slowly and with expression. Pause to let the children look closely at the photographs of Owen and Mzee (pronounced Mi-zay) on each page. Ask them to describe what they see and what the two friends do together. Talk about each animal's features and what they are doing on each page.
  Note: Remind the children that *Owen & Mzee: Best Friends* is a true story. Explain that Owen and Mzee met in a nature park. A *nature park* is a place where wild animals can be safe. This nature park is in Kenya, a country in Africa. Show the children Africa, then Kenya, on a world map or globe.
- On the same day or another day, read aloud *A Splendid Friend, Indeed* to the children. The text of the book is spoken by Goose except for on the last two pages. Use a high voice when you read. Change to a deep voice when you read Polar Bear's lines on the final two pages. Have the children notice the bear's expression and body language as the goose continues to interrupt what he is doing. Ask, *How do you think the polar bear feels? How can you tell?*

- After reading the books, ask the children what they think about the stories and if they have any questions about the friends in the two books.

Simplify It

Read and talk about one book at a time.

Add a Challenge

Ask the children to name other books about friends. Talk about these books, including how they are similar to and different from *Owen & Mzee: Best Friends* and *A Splendid Friend, Indeed.*

Assessment

To assess each child's learning, consider the following:

1. Is the child able to describe what it means to be a friend?
2. Is the child able to describe what is similar about the two books and what is different in the two books?

Cleo and Theo's Book Suggestions

Dog and Bear by Laura Vaccaro Seeger
Don't Fidget a Feather by Erica Silverman and S. D. Schindler
It's Mine! by Leo Lionni
Nutmeg and Barley: A Budding Friendship by Janie Bynum
Rabbit's Gift by George Shannon and Laura Dronzek
The Remarkable Friendship of Mr. Cat and Mr. Rat by Rick Walton and Lisa McCue
Sylvie & True by David McPhail
Together by Jane Simmons
Treasure by Suzanne Bloom
Where Are You Going? To See My Friend! by Eric Carle and Kazuo Iwamura
Yes We Can! by Sam McBratney

"The Ballad of Owen and Mzee"

Literacy Skill Focus
Letter Formation
Letter Recognition
Phonological Awareness (Rhythm, Rhyme, and Repetition)
Recall and Retell
Vocabulary

Vocabulary

buddy	home
different	joy
friend	poem
friendship	rhyme
help	sound
hippo	tortoise

Materials

Owen & Mzee: Best Friends by Isabella Hatkoff, Craig Hatkoff, Dr. Paula Kahumbu, and Peter Greste

What Children Will Learn

1. About friends
2. About helping others

Related Themes

Friends
Helping

What to Do

- Tell the children that you are going to recite a poem that tells the story of Owen and Mzee. Recite "The Ballad of Owen and Mzee."

The Ballad of Owen and Mzee
Come listen to a tale about a baby hippo.
Stranded at sea, with nowhere to go.
Along came some rescuers who gave him a new home,
But without any friends, he felt all alone.

They named him Owen and said, "Meet Mzee."
A giant old tortoise showed Owen the way.
A hippo and a tortoise are as different as can be.
Their friendship is a joy for all the world to see.

- Point to pictures of Owen and Mzee in the book as you read the poem. After a few times, invite the children to join in. Explain that joy is when you are very happy.
- Focus on the letter "t" in the word *tortoise*. Ask the children, *How many letter* "t's" *can you find in the word* tortoise?
- Demonstrate how to form a lowercase "t" using two index fingers. Then form an uppercase "T" with your index fingers. Have buddies use their fingers to make both the lowercase "t" and the uppercase "T." Then have buddy pairs use their bodies to make an uppercase "T" on the floor—have one buddy lie straight vertically, while the other lies horizontally at the top of her buddy's head.

Simplify It

Say the poem and then talk with the children about friendship and helping others.

Add a Challenge

Tell the children that the letter "T" makes the /t/ sound. Repeat the word *tortoise*, emphasizing the initial /t/ sound: *tttortoise*. Ask the children to name other words that begin with the same sound.

Assessment

To assess each child's learning, consider the following:

1. Can the child work with a buddy to form the letter "T" and make the /t/ sound?
2. Can the child find the letter "t's" an the word *tortoise* ?

Cleo and Theo's Book Suggestions

Dog and Bear by Laura Vaccaro Seeger
Don't Fidget a Feather by Erica Silverman and S. D. Schindler
It's Mine! by Leo Lionni
Nutmeg and Barley: A Budding Friendship by Janie Bynum
Rabbit's Gift by George Shannon and Laura Dronzek
The Remarkable Friendship of Mr. Cat and Mr. Rat by Rick Walton and Lisa McCue
Sylvie & True by David McPhail
Together by Jane Simmons
Treasure by Suzanne Bloom
Yes We Can! by Sam McBratney

Jambo!

Literacy Skill Focus
Listening and Speaking
Phonological Awareness
(Rhythm and Repetition)
Vocabulary

Vocabulary

Africa	next to
behind	old
country	over
friendship	rescue
globe	stranded
habitat	Swahili
help	underneath
Kenya	wise
map	young

Materials

world map or globe
Owen & Mzee: Best Friends by Isabella Hatkoff, Cray Hatkoff, Dr. Paula Kahumbu, and Peter Gresle, optional

What Children Will Learn

1. About another language and culture
2. About helping others

Related Themes

Feelings
Our World

What to Do

- If necessary, read *Owen & Mzee: Best Friends* to the children before group time.
- Have the children stand in a circle. Wave to them and say, *Jambo.* Jambo *is a word in the Swahili language. People in Kenya, where Owen and Mzee live, speak Swahili.* Remind the children that Kenya is a country in Africa. Show them the continent and then the country on a world map or globe. Ask, *What do you think the word* Jambo *means? Yes, it means "hello."*
- Sing the "Jambo Greeting Song." Invite the children to jump into the middle of the circle when their name is sung. Eventually, all of the children wind up in the middle of the circle.

  Jambo Greeting Song
  (Tune: "Goodnight Ladies")
  Jambo (name of child). (Child jumps into circle.)
  Jambo (name of child). (Child jumps into circle.)
  Jambo (name of child). (Child jumps into circle.)
  We are happy you are here.

- Engage the children in a discussion about Owen and Mzee. Ask, *How old do you think Owen is?* Affirm the children's responses. Say, *Owen was a baby hippo when he was rescued. He was probably not even four years old!* Then ask, *How old is Mzee*? Remind the children that *Mzee* is a Swahili word that means "wise old man." Say, *Mzee is more than 100 years old!* Explain that when you are wise, you are very smart and know many things.

Say, *Owen is very young, and Mzee is very old.* Ask, *Do you have to be the same age to be friends?* Tell the children about a childhood friendship you had with an older adult, or tell them about a friendship you have now with a young child or elderly person. Emphasize the things you enjoy doing together. Then ask the children to think about friendships they have with older people. Remind them that family members can be friends, too. Ask, *Who wants to tell about an older or grownup friend? What is your older or grownup friend's name? What do you like to do together?*

Simplify It

Sing the song and then talk with the children about things that make them happy.

Add a Challenge

Suggest that each child create a story about two unlikely friends.

Assessment

To assess each child's learning, consider the following:

1. What did the child learn about Kenya and where it is located?
2. Is the child able to describe a friendship he has with an older person?
3. Can the child describe what it means to be *wise*?

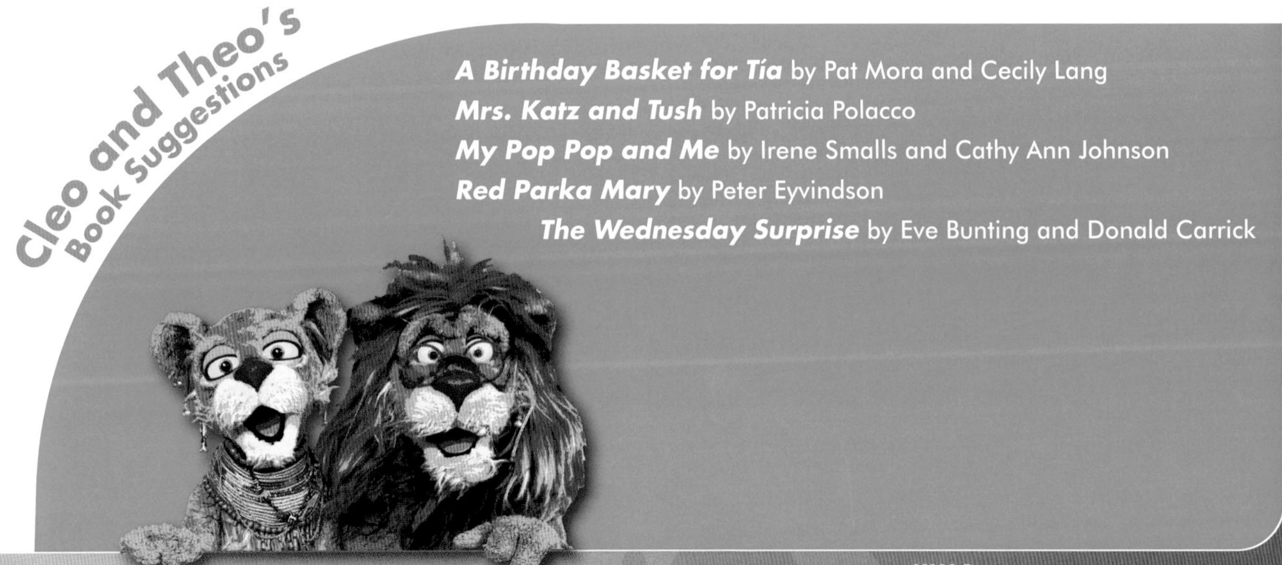

A Birthday Basket for Tía by Pat Mora and Cecily Lang
Mrs. Katz and Tush by Patricia Polacco
My Pop Pop and Me by Irene Smalls and Cathy Ann Johnson
Red Parka Mary by Peter Eyvindson
The Wednesday Surprise by Eve Bunting and Donald Carrick

The Same and Different

Literacy Skill Focus

Active Listening
Compare and Contrast
Concepts of Print (Locating Title)
Letter Recognition
Listening and Speaking
Story Comprehension
Vocabulary

Vocabulary

answer
chart
different
friends
question
same

Materials

Owen & Mzee: Best Friends by Isabella Hatkoff, Craig Hatkoff, Dr. Paula Kahumbu, and Peter Greste

Owen	Mzee
hippo	tortoise
young	old

What Children Will Learn

1. About jealousy
2. About sharing

Related Themes

Feelings
Opposites

What to Do

- Remind the children about the book *Owen & Mzee: Best Friends.* If necessary, read the book again slowly and with expression. Have the children point out which animal is Owen and which is Mzee.
- After reading, ask, *How do you think Owen and Mzee feel about each other? How can you tell?* Open to the next-to-last photo in the book. Ask, *What do you think Owen is doing? Do you think he is giving Mzee a kiss?* Together, give Owen and Mzee a big cheer. *Hip! Hip! Hooray! for Owen and Mzee! Hip! Hip! Hooray!*
- Make a "T" chart (an example appears on this page). Label the left column *Owen* and the right column *Mzee.*
- Say, *Owen and Mzee are very different. Let's make a list of the ways they are different.* Ask, *Who can tell me one way that Owen and Mzee are different? Who can tell me another way?* Write the children's responses on the chart, as shown on the example.
- Display and read aloud the Owen and Mzee T chart. Ask, *What other ways can you think of that Owen and Mzee are different?* Add new observations to the chart. Then ask, *How are Owen and Mzee the same*? (They are both round. They both like being friends.)

Simplify It

On one day, talk about how the two animals are the same, and then on another day discuss the ways they are different.

Add a Challenge

Have the children sit in a circle next to their buddy (see page 61). Sing the first verse of "Rig-a-Jig-Jig." Then signal to one buddy pair to stand up and walk around the circle as you sing the last verse. Repeat until each buddy pair has had a turn.

Rig-a-Jig-Jig
(Tune: "Rig-a-Jig-Jig")
As I was walking down the street,
Down the street, down the street,
A very good friend I chanced to meet.
Hi-ho, hi-ho, hi-ho.

Rig-a-jig-jig and away we go,
Away we go, away we go!
Rig-a-jig-jig and away we go,
Hi-ho, hi-ho, hi-ho.

Note: "Rig-a-Jig-Jig" is a traditional song. If you do not know the tune, there are many CDs available that feature this song such as *Preschool Song and Dance, volume 2* and *Girls Scouts Greatest Hits, Volume 3*. It is also featured on many websites such as songsforteaching.com and kididdles.com.

Assessment

To assess each child's learning, consider the following:

1. Does the child understand how to view the "T "chart?
2. Can the child name similarities and differences between Owen and Mzee?

Cleo and Theo's Book Suggestions

Dog and Bear by Laura Vaccaro Seeger
Don't Fidget a Feather by Erica Silverman and S. D. Schindler
It's Mine! by Leo Lionni
Nutmeg and Barley: A Budding Friendship by Janie Bynum
Rabbit's Gift by George Shannon and Laura Dronzek
The Remarkable Friendship of Mr. Cat and Mr. Rat by Rick Walton and Lisa McCue
Sylvie & True by David McPhail
Together by Jane Simmons
Where Are You Going? To See My Friend! by Eric Carle and Kazuo Iwamura
Yes We Can! by Sam McBratney

"There Once Was a Turtle"

Literacy Skill Focus
Concepts of Print (Directionality, Print Conveys Meaning, Return Sweep)
Phonological Awareness (Rhythm, Rhyme, and Repetition)
Word Recognition

Vocabulary

box
flea
minnow
mosquito
poem
puddle
rhyme
turtle

Materials

chart paper
index card
markers

What Children Will Learn

1. About turtles
2. To recognize the word *turtle*

Related Theme
Animals

Preparation

Write the poem "There Once Was a Turtle" on chart paper.
Write *turtle* on an index card.

What to Do

- Display the poem "There Once Was a Turtle" chart.

  There Once Was a Turtle
  There was a little turtle. *(Make a fist.)*
  He lived in a box. *(Draw a square in the air.)*
  He swam in a puddle. *(Pretend to swim.)*
  He climbed on the rocks. *(Pretend to climb.)*
  He snapped at a mosquito. *(Snap.)*
  He snapped at a flea. *(Snap.)*
  He snapped at a minnow, *(Snap.)*
  And he snapped at me. *(Snap.)*
  He caught the mosquito. *(Clap.)*
  He caught the flea. *(Clap.)*
  He caught the minnow, *(Clap.)*
  But he didn't catch me. *(Wave index finger as if saying no-no.)*

- Point to the words as you read the title aloud.
- Tell the children that there are different kinds of turtles. The turtle in this poem is a snapping turtle. It snaps at a flea, a mosquito, and a minnow (a small fish) because it is trying to eat them. Demonstrate how to make a snapping motion with your hands.

- Chant the poem together with the children, along with the hand motions.
- Chant the poem again. This time, move your finger or pointer under the words, exaggerating slightly the return sweep of your hand to the beginning of the next line.
- Display the index card with the word *turtle* on it. Ask, *What does this word say? Who can find the word* turtle *on the poem chart?*

Simplify It

Recite the poem once with the actions, and then ask the children to do the actions with you as you recite the poem again.

Add a Challenge

Draw a rebus chart of the poem and have the children recite it.

Assessment

To assess each child's learning, consider the following:

1. What did the child learn about turtles?
2. Is the child able to identify the word *turtle*?

Cleo and Theo's Book Suggestions

Hi, Harry! The Moving Story of How One Slow Tortoise Slowly Made a Friend by Martin Waddell and Barbara Firth

Lucille Lost: A True Adventure by Margaret George, Chris Murphy, Bob Dacey, and Debra Bandelin

The Tortoise and the Jackrabbit by Susan Lowell

Turtle Splash: Countdown on the Pond by Cathryn Falwell

Good Friends

Literacy Skill Focus
Concepts of Print (Directionality, Print Conveys Meaning, Spaces Between Words)
Listening and Speaking
Vocabulary

Vocabulary

chart
friend
good
help
list
take care of

Materials

chart paper
markers

What Children Will Learn

1. About what good friends do
2. About writing

Related Themes

Feelings
Sharing

What to Do

- Ask the children to remember Owen and Mzee. Ask, *Is Owen a good friend to Mzee? Is Mzee a good friend to Owen? What makes Owen and Mzee good friends?* Say, *Owen and Mzee take care of each other. That's what good friends do.*
- Tell the children about a good friend of yours. Emphasize what your friend says and does that makes him or her a good friend. Then ask the children to think about their friends. Ask, *How do good friends treat each other? How do you treat your buddy? How does your buddy treat you? What are some things that we do to take care of each other at school?*
- On chart paper, write the heading *A Good Friend*.... Read the first two words aloud, then pause and ask the children if they know what the last word says.
- Tell the children you are going to write a list about the things good friends say and do. Have the children complete the sentence "A good friend...." Your list might look the list on the next page.

A Good Friend...
listens to you.
helps you tie your shoe.
smiles.
gives you a hug when you feel sad.
takes turns.
shares.

- As you write, talk about where you begin to write each new line and the spaces you leave between words.

Simplify It

Suggest an action (shares a toy, keeps a toy for herself) and then ask the children if it is something that a good friend might do, or not.

Add a Challenge

Create a "Good Friends in the Classroom" chart that lists things that the children can do to be good friends to each other. When a child does something for a friend, write her name next to that action.

Assessment

To assess each child's learning, consider the following:

1. Is the child able to describe what good friends do?
2. Does the child understand how information is displayed on a chart?

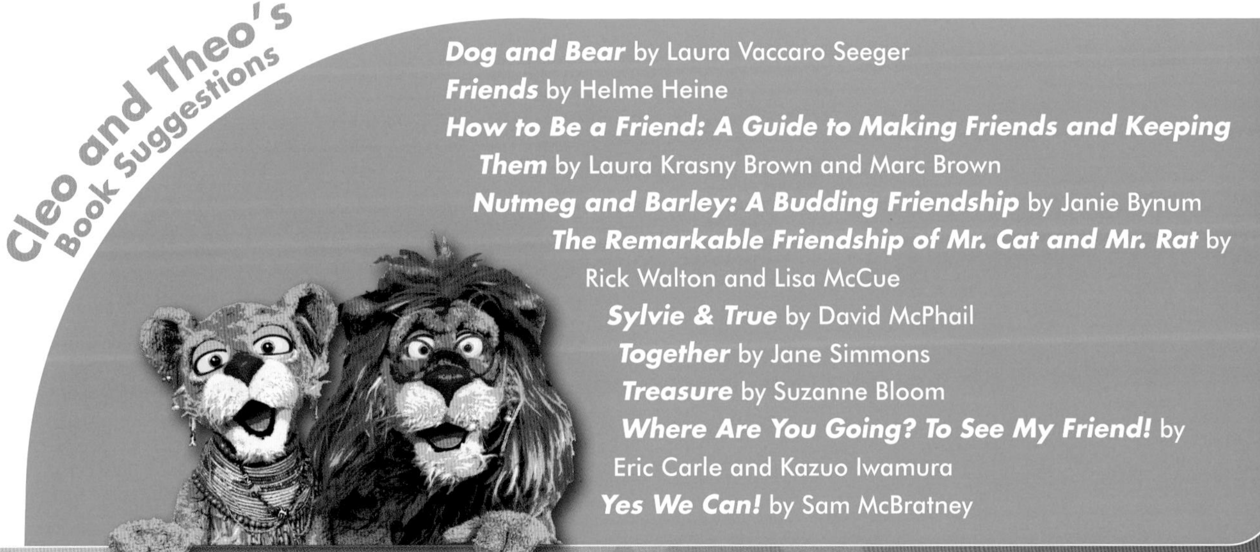

Cleo and Theo's Book Suggestions

Dog and Bear by Laura Vaccaro Seeger
Friends by Helme Heine
How to Be a Friend: A Guide to Making Friends and Keeping Them by Laura Krasny Brown and Marc Brown
Nutmeg and Barley: A Budding Friendship by Janie Bynum
The Remarkable Friendship of Mr. Cat and Mr. Rat by Rick Walton and Lisa McCue
Sylvie & True by David McPhail
Together by Jane Simmons
Treasure by Suzanne Bloom
Where Are You Going? To See My Friend! by Eric Carle and Kazuo Iwamura
Yes We Can! by Sam McBratney

Friendly Conflicts

Literacy Skill Focus
Listening and Speaking
Recall and Retell
Vocabulary

Vocabulary

alone
conflict
dedicate
sister
solution
take turns
together

What Children Will Learn

1. About taking turns
2. About solving conflicts

Related Themes

Animals
Feelings

Materials

bear and goose puppets or stuffed animals, *Between the Lions* Leona and Lionel stick puppets (see pages 237–238), or Kids Preferred *Between the Lions* Lionel and Leona plush puppets or beanies

A Splendid Friend, Indeed by Suzanne Bloom

What to Do

- Ask the children to tell you about Goose and Polar Bear in *A Splendid Friend, Indeed.* If necessary, read the book again. Ask, *At the beginning of the story, how does Bear feel about Goose being around?* Emphasize that at first, Bear wants to be by himself. He wants to read alone, write alone, and think alone. Say, *Sometimes we like to do things with our friends, and sometimes we like to be alone.* Ask, *What are some things that you like to do alone? What are some things that you like to do with a friend?*
- Engage the children in a discussion about resolving conflicts. Say, *Sometimes friends don't always want to do the same thing. Goose wants to be together, and Bear wants to be alone. Goose wants to have a snack, and Bear wants to think.* Ask, *What can you do when your friend doesn't want to do what you want to do?* Encourage a wide variety of responses.
- Emphasize that friends can take turns—first, they can do one thing; and then, they can do another.
- Pose some conflicts that you have seen between the children and talk about possible solutions. For example: One friend wants to play with blocks and the other wants to read. Both friends want to play with the same toy truck. You may want to use puppets to enact the conflicts. For example, hold up the Leona and Lionel stick puppets. Say, *Lionel wants to read* Cliffhanger stories. *Leona wants to hear a* Chicken Jane *story. What do you think they should do?*

Simplify It

Talk with the children about the things that they like to do alone and the things they like to do with other people.

Add a Challenge

Play a listening game with the children to help them hear sounds in sequence and blend them together to make a word. Ask the children to listen carefully and try to guess what or who the mystery friend is. Say /g/ /oose/. Repeat. Ask, *Can you guess our mystery friend?* Show the children the picture of Goose in *A Splendid Friend, Indeed* to confirm that they have guessed correctly. Repeat the process with the word *bear* (/b/ /ear/).

Assessment

To assess each child's learning, consider the following:

1. Is the child able to talk about taking turns?
2. Is the child able to talk about how to resolve conflicts?
3. Can the child recall a conflict and retell what happened and how it was resolved?

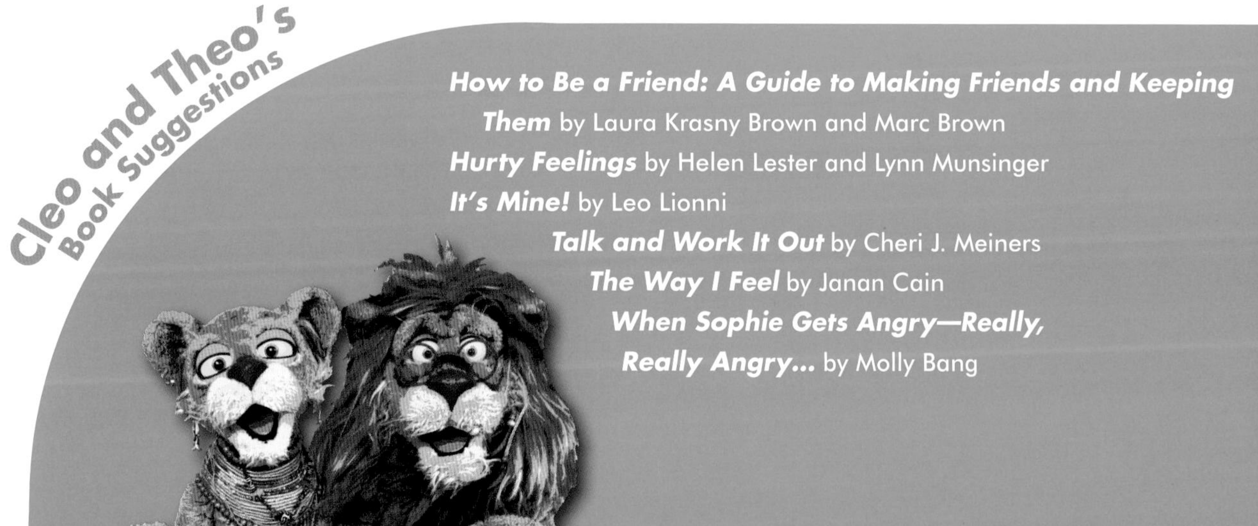

Cleo and Theo's Book Suggestions

How to Be a Friend: A Guide to Making Friends and Keeping Them by Laura Krasny Brown and Marc Brown

Hurty Feelings by Helen Lester and Lynn Munsinger

It's Mine! by Leo Lionni

Talk and Work It Out by Cheri J. Meiners

The Way I Feel by Janan Cain

When Sophie Gets Angry—Really, Really Angry... by Molly Bang

How Do You Feel When...?

Literacy Skill Focus
Active Listening
Listening and Speaking
Making Connections
Story Comprehension (Characters' Feelings)
Vocabulary

Vocabulary

bother
buddy
cover
heart
illustrator
interview
questions
reporter
title

Materials

goose and bear puppets or stuffed animals (optional)
A Splendid Friend, Indeed by Suzanne Bloom
toy or handmade microphone

What Children Will Learn

1. To describe characters in a book
2. To see a situation from another point of view

Related Themes

Feelings
Sharing

What to Do

- Ask a volunteer to locate the title on the book cover. Point to the words as you read the title aloud. Ask, *What kind of friend is a splendid friend?*
- Point out that Bear doesn't say much until the end of the book. **Note**: Set a listening focus: Ask the children to think about what Bear *could* have said when Goose was bothering him. Ask the children to mimic Bear's body movements and facial expressions.
- After you finish reading the book, ask the children questions to help them make connections between the story and their own experiences. Ask:
  - *How do you feel when a friend stops you from doing something?*
  - *How do you feel when a friend takes something you are using?*
  - *What friendly words can you use to tell your friend how you feel?*
- Tell the children to stand next to their buddy. Have one buddy pretend to be Goose and the other buddy pretend to be Bear. Say, *I'm going to be a reporter and interview, or ask questions of, Goose and Bear.* Choose a buddy pair. If available, give one buddy a goose puppet or stuffed animal and the other buddy a bear puppet or stuffed animal. Use a toy or handmade microphone to interview the characters. Remind the children to

answer the questions as if they were Goose or Bear. Ask each buddy a question such as the ones listed below. Then move on to another pair.

- *Goose, tell me about your friend Bear. What do you like about Bear?*
- *Bear, what are some things that you like to do with Goose? What are some things that you like to do alone?*
- *Goose, why did you take Bear's book when he was reading?*
- *Bear, how did you feel when Goose took your book away from you?*

Simplify It

Ask the children to say the names of their friends and then talk about one thing they like to do with each friend.

Add a Challenge

Suggest that the children write or dictate a story about something that Bear and Goose do together.

Assessment

To assess each child's learning, consider the following:

1. Is the child able to describe Bear or Goose?
2. Is the child able to talk about sharing and taking turns?

Cleo and Theo's Book Suggestions

How to Be a Friend: A Guide to Making Friends and Keeping Them by Laura Krasny Brown and Marc Brown
Hurty Feelings by Helen Lester and Lynn Munsinger
It's Mine! by Leo Lionni
Talk and Work It Out by Cheri J. Meiners
The Way I Feel by Janan Cain
When Sophie Gets Angry—Really, Really Angry... by Molly Bang

"Make New Friends"

Literacy Skill Focus

Listening and Speaking
Phonological Awareness (Rhythm, Rhyme, and Repetition)
Vocabulary

Vocabulary

circle
end
friends
friendship
gold
hippo
nature park
new
old
round
silver
tortoise

Materials

none needed

What Children Will Learn

1. About making new friends
2. To recognize rhyming words in songs
3. About circles

Related Theme

Feelings

What to Do

- Engage the children in a discussion about friends.
- Talk with the children about books that feature friends, such as *Owen and Mzee: Best Friends* and *A Splendid Friend, Indeed.*
- Have the children stand in a circle. Talk about how circles are round, and they have no beginning and end points. Tell the children that you are going to sing a song about friendships. The song compares friendships to a circle. Sing "Make New Friends." When you sing the third verse, have the children hold hands.

Make New Friends
(Tune: "Make New Friends")
Make new friends,
But keep the old.
One is silver,
The other is gold.

A circle is round,
It has no end.
That's how long
I will be your friend.

You have one hand,
I have the other.
Put them together, *(Children hold hands.)*
We have each other.

Note: "Make New Friends" is a traditional song. If you do not know the tune, there are many CDs available that feature this song such as *Girls Scouts Greatest Hits, Volume 3*. It is also featured on many websites such as songsforteaching.com and kididdles.com.

Friends

- Engage the children in a discussion about making new friends, like Owen did.

Simplify It

Invite the children to talk about their friends, both new and old.

Add a Challenge

Ask the children to identify the rhyming words in the song (*old/gold* and *end/friend*).

Assessment

To assess each child's learning, consider the following:

1. Is the child able to talk about making new friends?
2. Is the child able to sing the song?

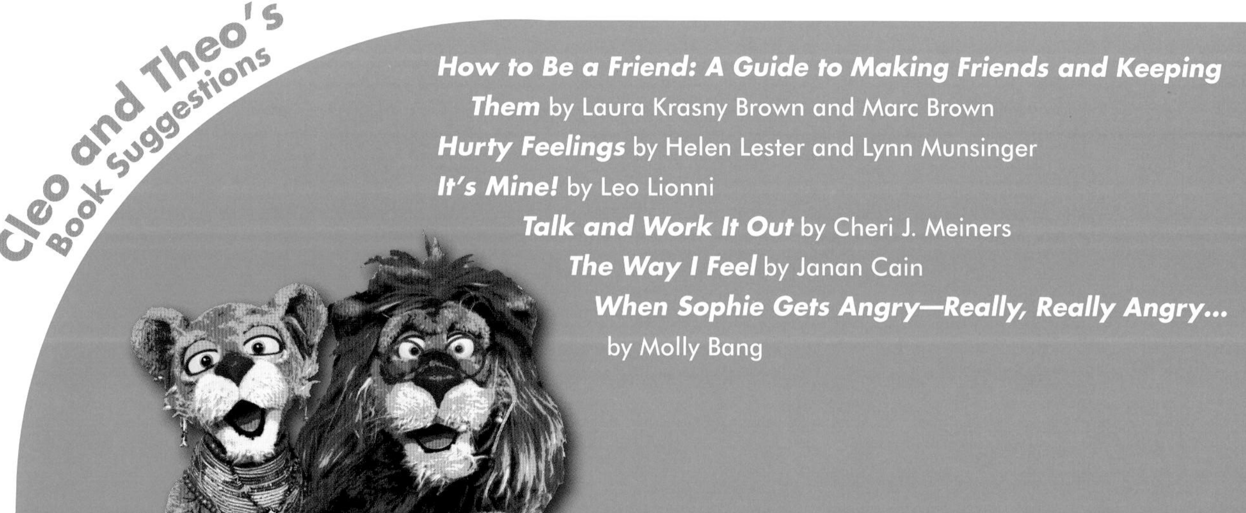

How to Be a Friend: A Guide to Making Friends and Keeping Them by Laura Krasny Brown and Marc Brown

Hurty Feelings by Helen Lester and Lynn Munsinger

It's Mine! by Leo Lionni

Talk and Work It Out by Cheri J. Meiners

The Way I Feel by Janan Cain

When Sophie Gets Angry—Really, Really Angry... by Molly Bang

Note to Families About the Topic of Friends

FAMILY LETTER

Date ____________________

Dear Families,

We are focusing on the topic of friends. One of the books that we are reading is about the amazing friendship between Owen, a baby hippo, and Mzee, a giant, old tortoise. It's a true story! Ask your child to tell you about Owen and Mzee. We are also reading a book about a quiet Bear and his noisy friend Goose. Bear wants to read and write, but Goose keeps interrupting him. Your children are learning that they can be friends with anyone, no matter how different they seem. We are also brainstorming things we can say and do when we have a conflict with a friend.

Here are some things that you can do at home with your child:

- Tell your child about a friendship you have with an elderly person. Talk about the things you enjoy doing together.
- Talk with your child about the things he or she enjoys doing with a grandparent or other favorite grownup.
- Play Follow the Leader with your child. Have your child follow you and copy your movements as you tiptoe, hop, and twirl around the room.
- If you know the song, sing "Make New Friends" (below) with your child. We are singing it in school.

Make New Friends

Make new friends,
But keep the old.
One is silver,
The other is gold.

A circle is round,
It has no end.
That's how long
I will be your friend.

You have one hand,
I have the other.
Put them together, (*Hold hands.*)
We have each other.

- Look for books about animal friends at your local library.

Thank you!

Chapter 4

Houses and Homes

With this topic, the children in your classroom will learn more about themselves and their families by exploring their homes—their source of warmth, love, and security. As they compare and contrast different kinds of houses and building materials, they begin to develop an understanding of cause-and-effect relationships and of similarities and differences. The children will also develop an awareness of the natural world as they learn about animals and animal habitats.

Setting Up the Room

- Create a Houses and Homes wall display. Write the following sentence in large letters: *We live in many different kinds of homes.* Attach pictures of single-family homes, farmhouses, apartment buildings, and other kinds of homes. In addition to houses from the children's neighborhoods, include houses from around the world and those made of different materials, such as wood, stone, adobe, snow, and straw. Ask the children to draw their own home, and add these drawings to the display.

- Create an Animal Habitat wall display with pictures of animals and their homes—nests, hives, caves, shells, cocoons, and other animal homes. Feature animals that the children can see in their neighborhoods, as well as animals the children learn about in books. (You can cut out pictures from magazines such as *Ranger Rick* and *National Geographic*, or you can download images from the Internet.)

- Set up table displays of dried grass, small twigs, and other building materials for the children to explore.

- Create a book-browsing box with different versions of "The Three Little Pigs." Label the box with a picture of the three little pigs so the children can identify the contents and browse on their own. Make a second book-browsing box with fiction and nonfiction books about houses and homes.

Family Letter

Prepare and make photocopies of the Family Letter on page 104 that explains this topic. Give the letter to parents at pick-up time before you begin the topic.

A New "The Three Little Pigs"

Literacy Skill Focus

Imaginative Play
Recall and Retell
Sequencing

Vocabulary

brick
build
house
pig
retell
straw
twigs
wolf

Materials

markers
paper
patterns (three houses, three little pigs, and one wolf) to retell "The Three Little Pigs" (see pages 240–242)
scissors
tongue depressors or felt board or storyboard

What Children Will Learn

1. How to retell a story
2. To listen carefully

Related Themes

Animals
Counting

Preparation

Let the children help you create props to retell the story of "The Three Little Pigs" using the patterns on pages 240–242. Copy the patterns, cut them out, color them, and then attach them to tongue depressors to make stick puppets. If the children are using a storyboard or felt board to retell the story, attach Velcro to the back of the patterns.

What to Do

- Read aloud a traditional version of "The Three Little Pigs" (see Theo and Cleo's Book Suggestions that follow), or retell the story as you remember it from your childhood. Tell the children that "The Three Little Pigs" is a folktale—a story that has been told for many, many years.
- Talk about the story with the children. Ask questions such as:
  - *What material does the first little pig use to build a house?*
  - *What material does the second little pig use?*
  - *What material does the third little pig use?*
  - *If you were going to build a house, what material would you use?*
  - *What material do you think your house is made of?*
- Demonstrate how to retell the story using stick puppets or a storyboard.
- Encourage individual children or small groups of the children to use the materials to retell the story. If necessary, ask questions to help the children retell the story in the correct sequence.

Simplify It

Have the children use the storyboard and props or the stick puppets to retell the story as you read or say it.

Add a Challenge

Create an audiotape of "The Three Little Pigs" by reading aloud a simple version of the story. Have the children contribute the repeating refrains, such as "I'll huff and I'll puff and I'll blow your house down" and "Not by the hair of my chinny-chin-chin." The children will love listening to the story and hearing their voices again and again.

Assessment

To assess each child's learning, consider the following:

1. Is the child able to retell the story?
2. Is the child able to use the props to retell the story?

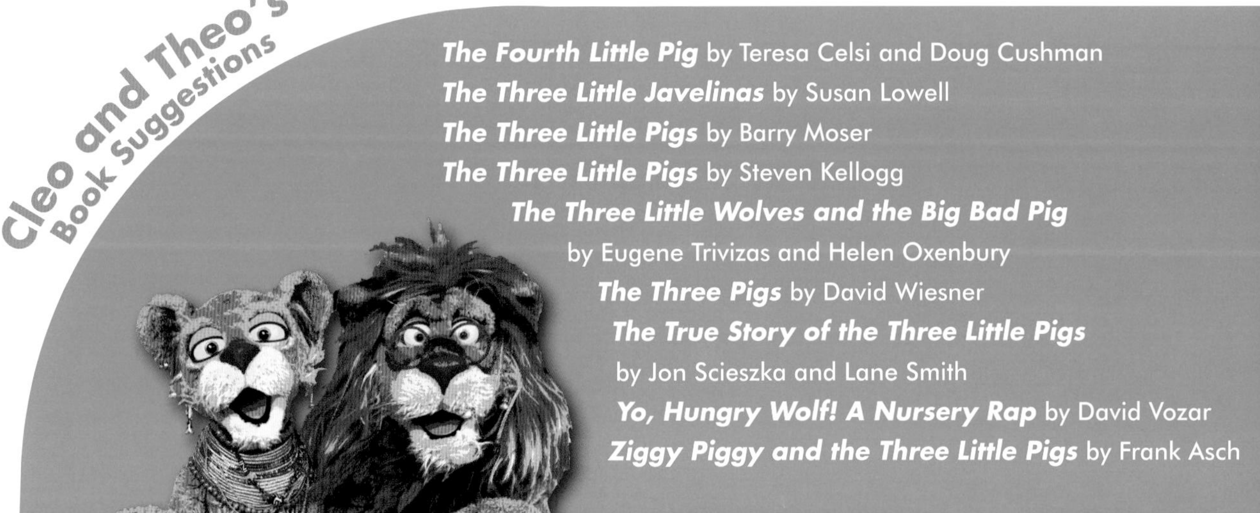

Cleo and Theo's Book Suggestions

The Fourth Little Pig by Teresa Celsi and Doug Cushman
The Three Little Javelinas by Susan Lowell
The Three Little Pigs by Barry Moser
The Three Little Pigs by Steven Kellogg
The Three Little Wolves and the Big Bad Pig by Eugene Trivizas and Helen Oxenbury
The Three Pigs by David Wiesner
The True Story of the Three Little Pigs by Jon Scieszka and Lane Smith
Yo, Hungry Wolf! A Nursery Rap by David Vozar
Ziggy Piggy and the Three Little Pigs by Frank Asch

"I've Been Working on My Straw House"

Literacy Skill Focus
Fine Motor Skills
Following Directions
Phonological Awareness (Rhythm and Repetition)
Sequencing
Vocabulary

Vocabulary

away
brick
day
first
home
house
huff
material
puff
second
single
straw
third
twigs

Materials

none needed

What Children Will Learn

1. How to sing a song
2. To remember the storyline of "The Three Little Pigs"
3. To act out the storyline of "The Three Little Pigs"

Related Theme

Animals

What to Do

- Introduce a song that will help the children remember and retell the story of "The Three Little Pigs."
- Say, *In the first verse, the first little pig builds a house out of straw.* Then ask the children to complete the following sentences: *In the second verse, the second little pig builds a house out of __________. In the third verse, the third little pig builds a house out of ______________.*
- Sing the first verse of the song. Ask the children to join you as you sing it again.
- Sing the second and third verses with the children.

I've Been Working on My Straw House
(Tune: "I've Been Working on the Railroad")
I've been working on my straw (stick, brick) house
Every single day.
I've been working on my straw house
Just to keep the wolf away.
Can't you hear the bad wolf coming,
Can't you hear him huff and puff?
Can't you hear the bad wolf coming?
Hope my house is strong enough!

Wolf is gonna huff,
Wolf is gonna huff.
Wolf is gonna huff and puff.
Wolf is gonna huff,
Wolf is gonna huff,
Wolf is gonna huff and puff.

- Encourage the children to sing and act out the song with their classmates.

Simplify It

Sing one line of the song at a time. Ask the children to repeat each line after you sing it.

Add a Challenge

Ask the children to name the sequence of the types of houses that the pigs built—first straw, then sticks, and then bricks.

Assessment

To assess each child's learning, consider the following:

1. Is the child able to retell or act out the story of "The Three Little Pigs?"
2. Is the child able to sing the song with the class?

Cleo and Theo's Book Suggestions

The Fourth Little Pig by Teresa Celsi and Doug Cushman
Three Little Cajun Pigs by Mike Artell and Jim Harris
The Three Little Javelinas by Susan Lowell
The Three Little Pigs by Barry Moser
The Three Little Pigs by Paul Galdone
The Three Little Pigs by Steven Kellogg
The Three Little Wolves and the Big Bad Pig by Eugene Trivizas and Helen Oxenbury
The Three Pigs by David Wiesner
The True Story of the Three Little Pigs by Jon Scieszka and Lane Smity
Yo, Hungry Wolf! A Nursery Rap by David Vozar
Ziggy Piggy and the Three Little Pigs by Frank Asch

Reading
Alphabet Under Construction

Literacy Skill Focus
Alphabet Awareness
Concepts of Print
Parts of a Book
Vocabulary

Vocabulary

alphabet	materials
author	measuring tape
build	nails
construct	paintbrush
construction	saw
first	second
glue	third
hammer	toolbox
illustrator	tools
letters	

Materials

Alphabet Under Construction by Denise Fleming

What Children Will Learn

1. New vocabulary
2. About tools used in construction
3. About the letters of the alphabet

Related Themes

The Alphabet
Construction

What to Do

- Introduce the book by showing it to the children and touching each word as you read aloud the title. Explain that when something is under construction, it is still being made—it is not yet finished. Give an example: *Nora is building a castle in the Block Center. Her castle is under construction.*
- Ask the children to tell you what they see on the book cover: *What are some things that you see in the mouse's toolbox?* (hammer, saw, paintbrush, glue, nails, measuring tape, etc.) *What do you think the mouse is building or constructing?*
- Explain that *Alphabet Under Construction* is an alphabet book. Say, *In this book, a mouse builds or constructs all the letters of the alphabet using different tools and materials.*
- Explain that Denise Fleming wrote the words and drew the pictures so she is both the author and the illustrator.
- As you read the book, take a "picture walk." Encourage the children to look at the pictures as you turn the pages. Read the letters on each page, emphasizing that there is one letter to a page. Pause every so often to talk about what the mouse is doing and what tools he is using.
- Remind the children that we always say the alphabet in the same order, beginning with "A" and ending with "Z."

Simplify It

Read a few pages a day, focusing on the letter, tools, and pictures on each page.

Add a Challenge

Before you turn a page, ask the children to guess the letter that comes next and what tool the mouse might be using to make the letter.

Assessment

To assess each child's learning, consider the following:

1. Does the child understand the meaning of *construction*?
2. Is the child able to use the new vocabulary words appropriately?

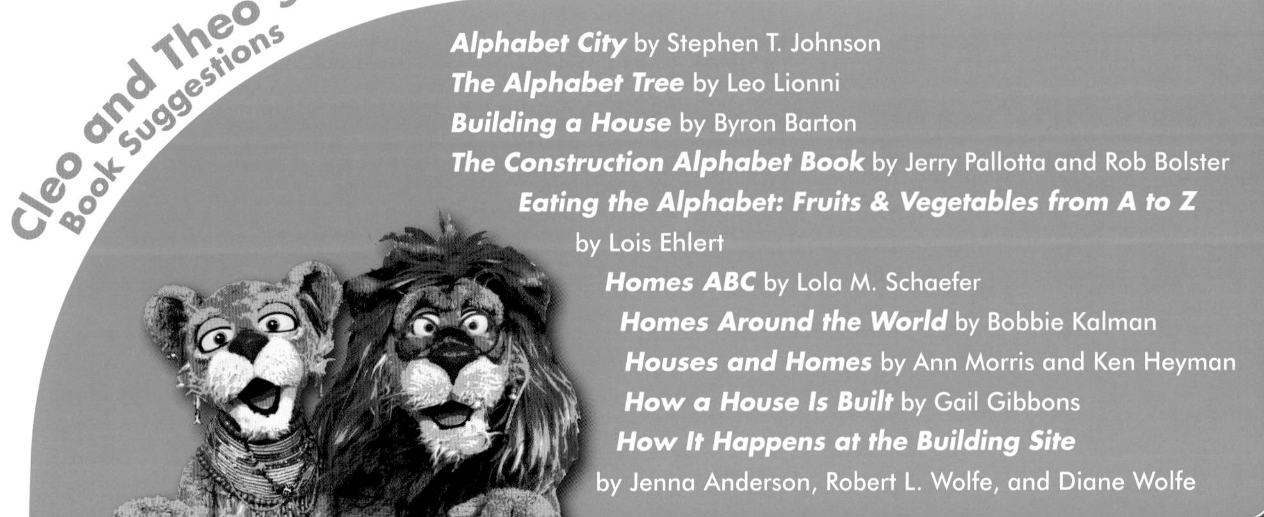

Cleo and Theo's Book Suggestions

Alphabet City by Stephen T. Johnson
The Alphabet Tree by Leo Lionni
Building a House by Byron Barton
The Construction Alphabet Book by Jerry Pallotta and Rob Bolster
Eating the Alphabet: Fruits & Vegetables from A to Z by Lois Ehlert
Homes ABC by Lola M. Schaefer
Homes Around the World by Bobbie Kalman
Houses and Homes by Ann Morris and Ken Heyman
How a House Is Built by Gail Gibbons
How It Happens at the Building Site by Jenna Anderson, Robert L. Wolfe, and Diane Wolfe

Rereading *Alphabet Under Construction*

Literacy Skill Focus

Active Listening
Alphabet Awareness
Concepts of Print
Letter Recognition
Listening and Speaking
Story Comprehension
Vocabulary

Vocabulary

alphabet
airbrush
author
build
construct
construction
dye
first
glue
hammer
illustrator
letters
level
materials
measure
measuring tape
nails
paintbrush
prune
quilt
saw
second
third
tile
toolbox
tools
weld
x-ray

Materials

Alphabet Under Construction by Denise Fleming

What Children Will Learn

1. New vocabulary
2. About tools used in construction
3. About the letters of the alphabet

Related Themes

The Alphabet
Construction

What to Do

- Read the book slowly, pointing to the three words on each page, and then the letter.
- As you read, ask the children to look for the different tools and materials the mouse uses to construct the alphabet.
- Use the illustrations to explain the meaning of unfamiliar words, such as *airbrushes, dyes, levels, measures, prunes, quilts, tiles, welds,* and *x-rays.*
- Read the book again, adding speed and rhythm. Have the children repeat the names of the letters with you, or pause and ask, *Does anyone know the name of this letter? Who has a name that begins with the letter "A"?*
- Talk with the children about the book. Ask questions such as, *What is your favorite letter? Why? What are some of the tools and materials the mouse uses to make the letters of the alphabet? What tools and materials would you use to make (construct) your letter of the alphabet?*

Simplify It

First talk about familiar, everyday construction tools, such as a hammer, a saw, and glue. Teach the children about the new tools one at a time.

Add a Challenge

Name a letter and challenge the children to describe which tools they would use to build it and how they would use the tools.

Assessment

To assess each child's learning, consider the following:

1. Can the child name different letters?
2. Is the child able to use the new vocabulary words appropriately?
3. Can the child tell you what letter her name begins with?

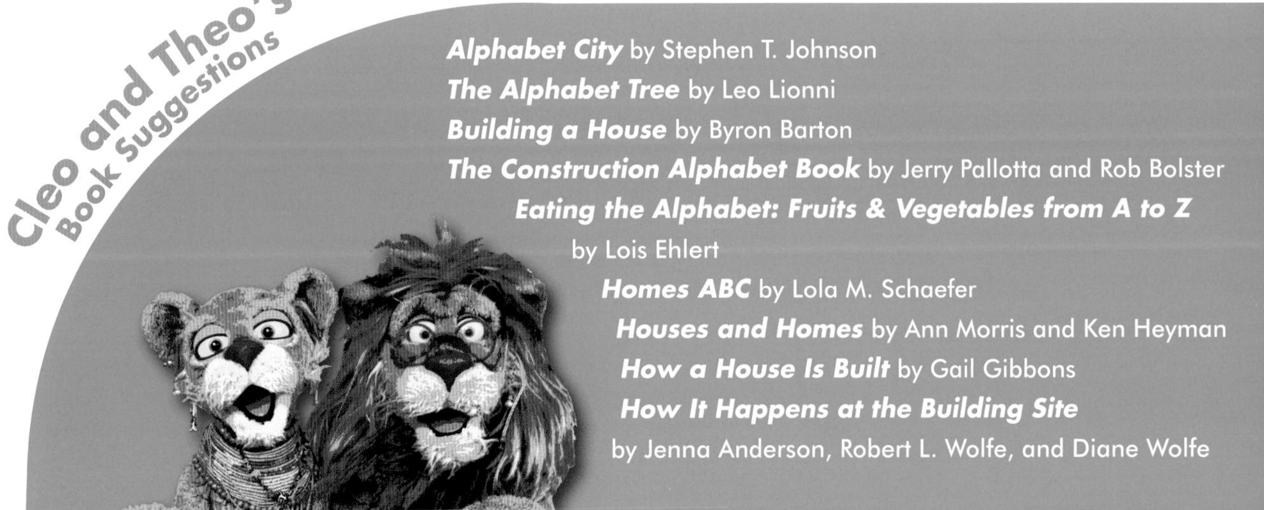

Cleo and Theo's Book Suggestions

Alphabet City by Stephen T. Johnson
The Alphabet Tree by Leo Lionni
Building a House by Byron Barton
The Construction Alphabet Book by Jerry Pallotta and Rob Bolster
Eating the Alphabet: Fruits & Vegetables from A to Z by Lois Ehlert
Homes ABC by Lola M. Schaefer
Houses and Homes by Ann Morris and Ken Heyman
How a House Is Built by Gail Gibbons
How It Happens at the Building Site by Jenna Anderson, Robert L. Wolfe, and Diane Wolfe

"The Three Little Pigs" Sequel

Literacy Skill Focus
Concepts of Print
Sequencing
Story Elements (Setting)

Vocabulary

brick
build
first
house
pig
retell
second
sequel
straw
third
twigs
wolf

What Children Will Learn

1. New vocabulary
2. How to create their own story

Related Themes

Animals
Storytelling

Materials

chart paper
markers
paper

What to Do

- Invite the children to create their own sequel to the story of "The Three Little Pigs." Ask questions to help the children imagine the setting and develop the story, such as:
  - *Do you think the three little pigs live happily every after? Why or why not?*
  - *Where else might the wolf and the three little pigs meet again?*
  - *What does the wolf say and do? What do the pigs say and do?*
  - *How do you want our sequel to end?*
- Compose the story with the children over a few days. At the end of each day, reread what you have written, pointing to each word as you read. Encourage the children to think about what they want to happen next in the story.
- You may want to copy the story onto a large piece of paper or create a class book by writing the story on several pages and having the children illustrate each page. Add a cover with the title and the names of all the authors and illustrators. Bind the pages together.
- Read the book to the children. Include the book in the Library Center for children to enjoy again and again.

Simplify It

Reread the traditional story of "The Three Little Pigs." Stop at an appropriate point in the story and ask, *What do you think happens next?* After listening to what the children have to say, continue reading the story. On the next day, read the story from the beginning, stop reading at another point that is further along in the story and ask, *What happens next?*

Add a Challenge

Suggest that the children make drawings to illustrate the story that the class is creating.

Assessment

To assess each child's learning, consider the following:

1. Does the child understand the meaning of the word *sequel*?
2. Does the child contribute to the class story?

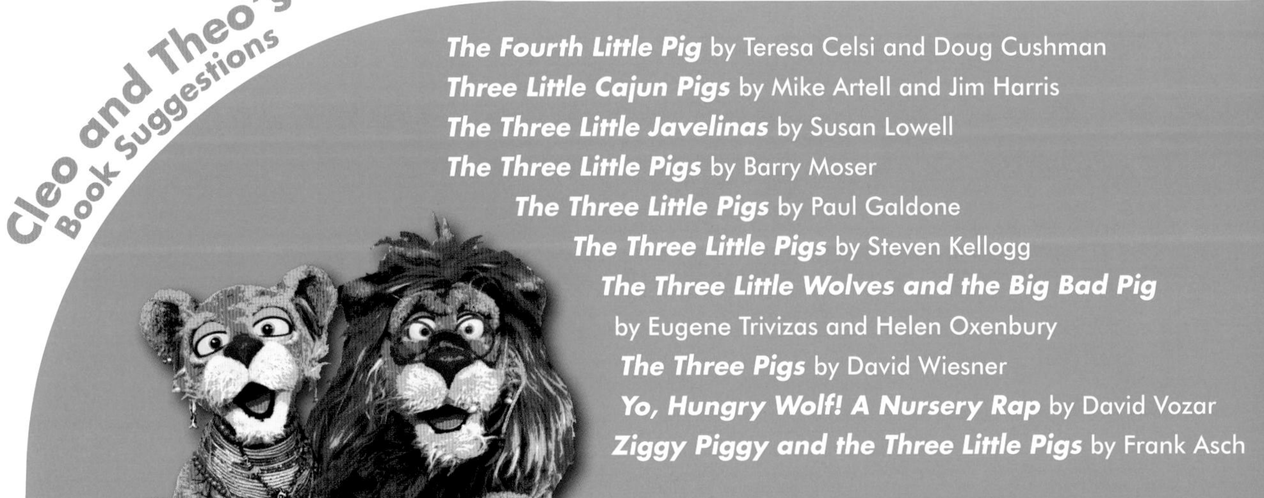

The Fourth Little Pig by Teresa Celsi and Doug Cushman
Three Little Cajun Pigs by Mike Artell and Jim Harris
The Three Little Javelinas by Susan Lowell
The Three Little Pigs by Barry Moser
The Three Little Pigs by Paul Galdone
The Three Little Pigs by Steven Kellogg
The Three Little Wolves and the Big Bad Pig by Eugene Trivizas and Helen Oxenbury
The Three Pigs by David Wiesner
Yo, Hungry Wolf! A Nursery Rap by David Vozar
Ziggy Piggy and the Three Little Pigs by Frank Asch

Reading *Castles, Caves, and Honeycombs*

Literacy Skill Focus

Active Listening
Concepts of Print
Parts of a Book
Phonological Awareness (Rhyming)
Story Comprehension
Vocabulary

Vocabulary

animal
author
bear
chamber
cocoon
den
dune
facts
habitat
honey
honeycomb
illustrator
nest
pit
tidal pool
tree
warren

Materials

Castles, Caves, and Honeycombs by Linda Ashman and Lauren Stringer

What Children Will Learn

1. New vocabulary
2. About the homes that animals live in

Related Themes

Animals
Sounds

What to Do

- Introduce *Castles, Caves, and Honeycombs* to the children. Point to each word as you read the title aloud. Point to the honey and the bees on the cover and explain that a honeycomb is a place in a tree where bees live and make honey. Ask, *Has anyone ever tasted honey? What does it taste like?*
- Read the names of the author and the illustrator and remind the children what an author and illustrator do. Explain that *Castles, Caves, and Honeycombs* tells us true things, or facts, about animals and where they live.
- Ask the children to name the animals they see.
- Use the pictures to explain the meaning of unfamiliar words such as *honeycomb, dune, cocoon, chamber, warren, den, pit,* and *tidal pool.*
- Read the book aloud without pausing so the children can enjoy the rhythm of the rhyming words. Then read the book a second time, pausing to talk about some of the animals and where they live.
- Ask, *Where do animals live? Do they live in houses? Where did the three little pigs live in the story? Do you think that pigs live in houses in real life? Where do you think pigs live?*
- Ask the children to name other animals they know. Talk about where each animal lives. Explain that a *habitat* is a place where a plant or animal lives.
- Show the children pictures of different animals and their habitats.

- Ask a child to name an animal from the book and say where it lives. Turn to the page that features that animal and its home and talk about it with the children:
  - *Have you ever seen a spiderweb? What does it look like? What do you think it feels like?*
  - *What do you think rabbits eat? Why do you think a grassy glen is a good place for rabbits to live?*

Simplify It

Talk about where familiar animals such as birds and squirrels live, and then talk about the homes of more unusual animals.

Add a Challenge

Take a "picture walk" by turning the pages of the book and encouraging the children to look at the pictures. Point out the homes on the three introductory pages (children's playhouse, anthill, and bird's nest). Ask, *Have you ever seen a nest in a tree? An anthill? Have you ever made a playhouse? What did you use to make it?*

Assessment

To assess each child's learning, consider the following:

1. Does the child use the new vocabulary appropriately?
2. Does the child understand why animals live in certain habitats?

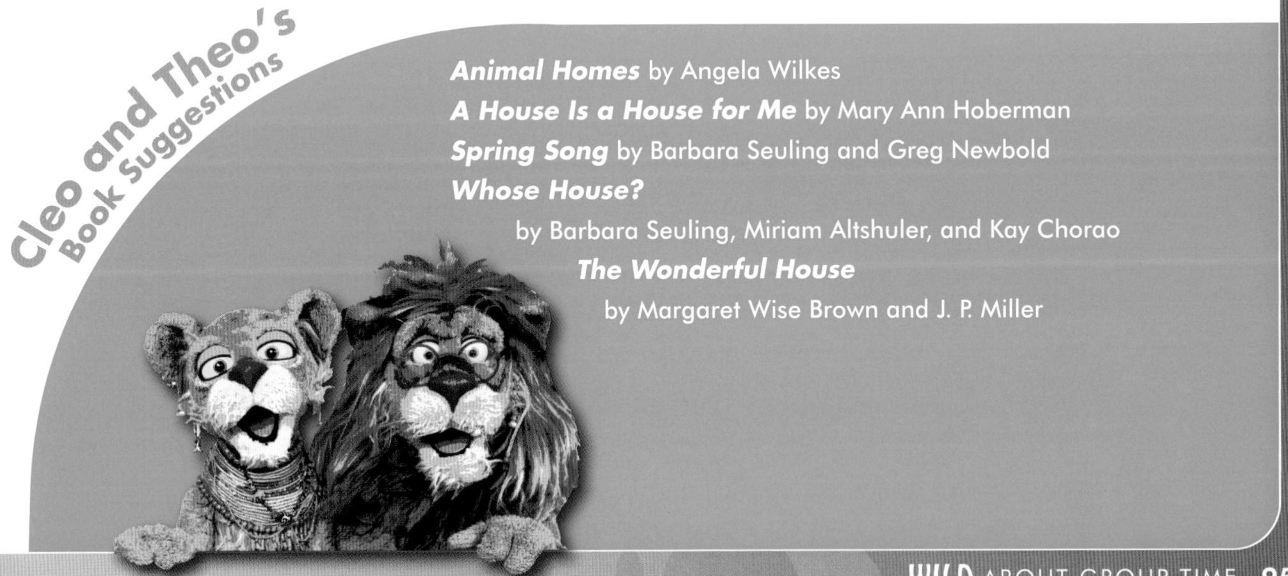

Cleo and Theo's Book Suggestions

Animal Homes by Angela Wilkes

A House Is a House for Me by Mary Ann Hoberman

Spring Song by Barbara Seuling and Greg Newbold

Whose House? by Barbara Seuling, Miriam Altshuler, and Kay Chorao

The Wonderful House by Margaret Wise Brown and J. P. Miller

Rhyming Words

Literacy Skill Focus
Phonological Awareness (Alliteration and Rhyming)

Vocabulary

animal	honeycomb
author	illustrator
bear	nest
chamber	pit
cocoon	rhyme
den	sound
dune	tidal pool
facts	tree
habitat	warren
honey	

Materials

Castles, Caves, and Honeycombs by Linda Ashman and Lauren Stringer

What Children Will Learn

1. New vocabulary
2. About the homes that animals live in
3. About rhyming

Related Themes

Animals
Sounds

What to Do

- Tell the children that one reason that *Castles, Caves, and Honeycombs* is fun to read is because it has rhyming words. Explain that words that rhyme have the same sound at the end.
- Select and read aloud a few passages with rhyming words. Have the children repeat the rhyming words with you.
- Say, *Listen to the words as I read the part of the book about where polar bears live. On this page the words* mound *and* ground *rhyme. Can you say them with me?* mound, ground. *They sound the same at the end—/ound/.*
- Say, *Now listen to the words about a tidal pool. The words* tree *and* sea *rhyme. They sound the same at the end—/ee/. Say the words with me:* tree, sea.
- Read the last line of *Castles, Caves, and Honeycombs*. Point out the rhyming words *hug* and *snug*. Ask the children to repeat the words with you. Say, Hug *and* snug *both sound the same at the end—/ug/.*

Simplify It

Use objects or pictures of simple things that rhyme. For example, show the children a hat and ask them to name something that rhymes with it. (*cat*, *bat*, *mat*, *rat*)

Add a Challenge

- Say, *I'm thinking of an animal that rhymes with the words tree and sea. It makes a buzzzzzzzzzing sound, flies, and makes honey. What is it?* (bee) (If necessary, show the children the picture from the book for support.)
- Say, *I'm thinking of a very small animal that rhymes with hug and snug. It begins with /b/ and crawls on the ground. Can you guess what it is?* (bug)

Assessment

To assess each child's learning, consider the following:

1. Does the child understand the meaning of the word *rhyme*?
2. Does the child recognize rhyming words when you read them aloud?

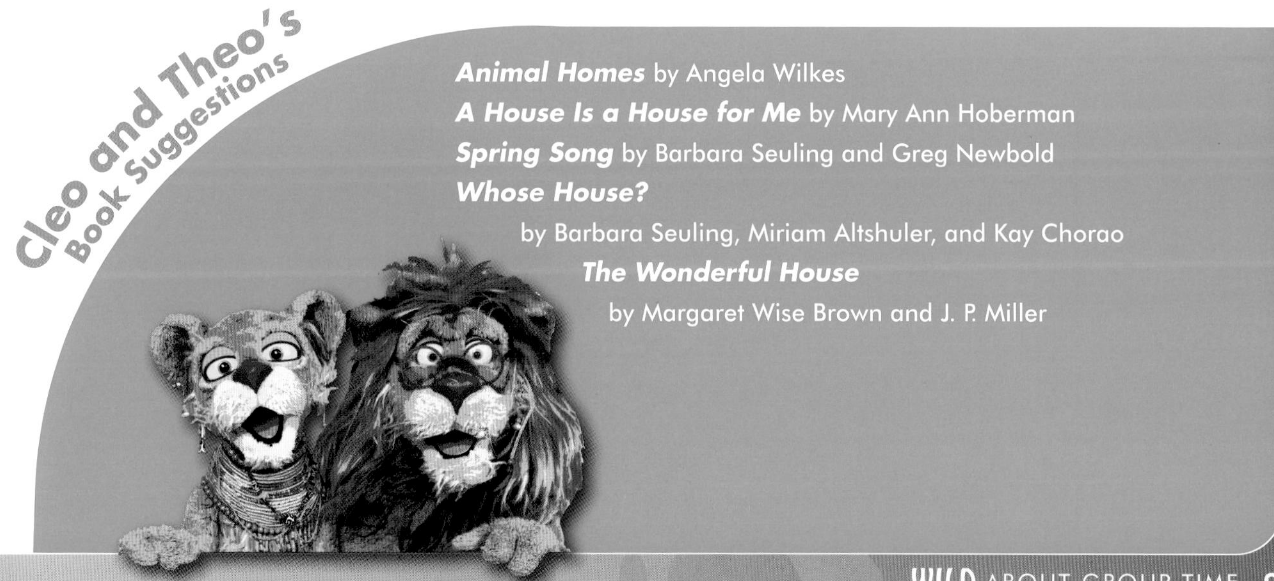

Cleo and Theo's Book Suggestions

Animal Homes by Angela Wilkes
A House Is a House for Me by Mary Ann Hoberman
Spring Song by Barbara Seuling and Greg Newbold
Whose House? by Barbara Seuling, Miriam Altshuler, and Kay Chorao
The Wonderful House by Margaret Wise Brown and J. P. Miller

"The Bear Lives in the Den"

Literacy Skill Focus
Phonological Awareness
Vocabulary

Vocabulary

animal
ant
author
bear
bee
bird
boy
chamber
cocoon
den
dune
facts
girl
ground
habitat
hive
honey
honeycomb
house
illustrator
nest
pen
pig
pit
rhyme
shell
snail
sound
tidal pool
tree
warren

Materials

Castles, Caves, and Honeycombs by Linda Ashman and Lauren Stringer

What Children Will Learn

1. New vocabulary
2. About the homes that animals live in

Related Themes

Animals
Sounds

What to Do

- Tell the children you are going to sing a song about where animals live.
- Show the picture of the wolves in a "secret den" in *Castles, Caves, and Honeycombs.* Ask, *What other animal lives in a den*? (bear)
- Sing the first verse of "The Bear Lives in the Den." Then invite the children to sing along with you.

The Bear Lives in the Den
(Tune: "The Farmer in the Dell")
The bear lives in the den.
The bear lives in the den.
A home for this animal,
The bear lives in the den.

Additional verses:
The bird lives in the nest…
The pig lives in the pen…
The snail lives in the shell…
The ant lives in the ground…
The bee lives in the hive…
The boy (girl) lives in the house…

Simplify It

Sing one line at a time. Ask the children to repeat the line after you sing it.

Add a Challenge

Ask the children to make up additional verses by naming different animals and where they live. Possible verses include, The snake lives in the ground..., The bat lives in the cave..., The whale lives in the sea....

Assessment

To assess each child's learning, consider the following:

1. Does the child understand that animals live in different habitats (homes)?
2. Does the child understand the meaning of the new vocabulary and use words appropriately?

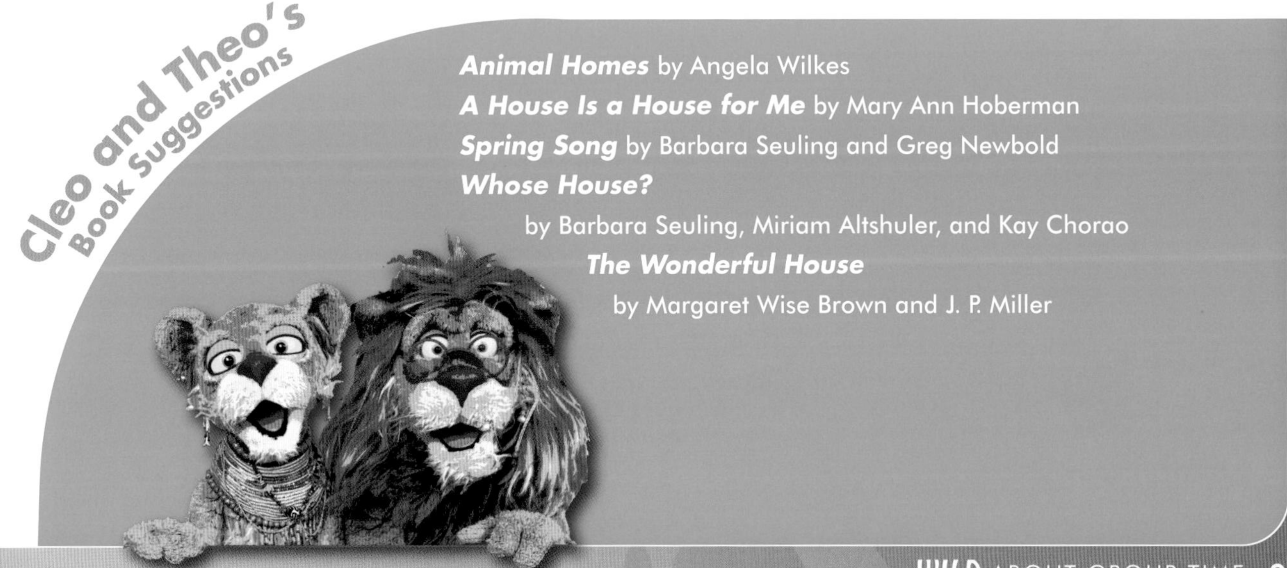

Cleo and Theo's Book Suggestions

Animal Homes by Angela Wilkes
A House Is a House for Me by Mary Ann Hoberman
Spring Song by Barbara Seuling and Greg Newbold
Whose House? by Barbara Seuling, Miriam Altshuler, and Kay Chorao
The Wonderful House by Margaret Wise Brown and J. P. Miller

Home Is a Place to...

Literacy Skill Focus

Active Listening
Listening and Speaking
Phonological Awareness (Rhyming)
Story Comprehension
Vocabulary

Vocabulary

animal
bear
bee
beehive
chamber
cocoon
den
dune
facts
habitat
home
honey
honeycomb
nest
pit
rhyme
rhyming
safe
snug
sound
tidal pool
tree
warren
word

Materials

Castles, Caves, and Honeycombs by Linda Ashman and Lauren Stringer

What Children Will Learn

1. New vocabulary
2. About animal homes
3. About listening and speaking

Related Themes

Animals
Sounds

What to Do

- Remind the children that during group time you have been talking about the homes we live in and the homes animals live in. Ask, *What do you do at home?* Encourage the children to name different rooms in their houses and what they are for. For example, "We cook and eat in the kitchen. We sleep in the bedroom. We wash up in the bathroom."
  Note: Continue to talk to individual children throughout the day about the kinds of things they do at home.
- Ask the children, *What do you think animals do in their homes?* Encourage a variety of responses. Tell the children that you are going to read *Castles, Caves, and Honeycombs* again. Ask the children to look at and listen for the different things that animals do in their homes.
- Pause before reading the second word of a rhyming pair and ask the children to guess the word before you continue. When possible, use the illustrations to help the children guess. You may also want to talk about some of the things the animals are doing in their homes (eating, sleeping, resting, playing).
- Talk about the book with the children. Ask questions such as:
  - *What are some of the things that the animals do in their homes?* (eat, sleep, rest, play)

- Reread the lines at the end of the book about being in a place that is safe and snug. Explain the meaning of the word *snug*: *When you feel snug, you feel warm, cozy, and safe, the way the children in the book feel when they are tucked into their beds. I feel snug when I'm wrapped in my favorite blanket. When do you feel safe and snug?*

Simplify It

Talk about what the children do in their homes and what animals do in their homes, and then ask the children to name some things that both people and animals do in their homes (eat, sleep, play, rest).

Add a Challenge

Ask the children to name other words that rhyme with the words in the book.

Assessment

To assess each child's learning, consider the following:

1. Does the child understand that animals do different things in their homes?
2. Can the child use the new vocabulary words in a sentence?

Animal Homes by Angela Wilkes

A House Is a House for Me by Mary Ann Hoberman

Spring Song by Barbara Seuling and Greg Newbold

Whose House? by Barbara Seuling, Miriam Altshuler, and Kay Chorao

The Wonderful House by Margaret Wise Brown and J. P. Miller

"Go In and Out the Window"

Literacy Skill Focus
Concepts of Print
Phonological Awareness
(Rhythm and Repetition)

Vocabulary

around
before
door
follow
hand
in
leave
London
out
partner
'round
shake
stand
together
village
window

Materials

chart paper
marker

What Children Will Learn

1. To describe the doors and windows in their homes
2. About the importance of working together

Related Theme

Helping

Preparation

Write the song on chart paper.

What to Do

- Introduce "Go In and Out the Window" by asking the children about where they live and talking about the windows and doors in their homes.
- Display the "Go In and Out the Window" song.
- Touch each word with a pointer or your finger as you say the words in the song. Emphasize the rhythm and exaggerate the repeated words.
- Sing the song. Have the children sing each line in unison after you.

Go In and Out the Window

Go 'round and round the village,
Go 'round and round the village,
Go 'round and round the village,
As we have done before.

Go in and out the window,
Go in and out the window,
Go in and out the window,
As we have done before.

Now stand and face your partner,
Now stand and face your partner,
Now stand and face your partner,
As we have done before.

Now follow her to London,
Now follow her to London,
Now follow her to London,
As we have done before.

Now shake his hand and leave him,
Now shake his hand and leave him,
Now shake his hand and leave him,
As we have done before.

- Sing the song again and add actions.
  - Everyone stands in a circle, holding hands up high.
  - Select one or two children to go to the center of a circle of children as the group sings the first verse. These children thread in and out of the circle through the other children's arms as you sing the second verse.
  - The children pick partners by stopping in front of another child as the group sings the third verse. The chosen children follow their partners as they thread in and out of the circle as the group sings the fourth verse.
  - Everyone rejoins the circle. Everyone in the circle moves in one direction as they sing the fifth verse.

Simplify It

Teach the song without the actions. Once the children have learned the song, add the actions.

Add a Challenge

Ask the children to pick a partner. Suggest that they spend the rest of the day together playing and helping each other.

Assessment

To assess each child's learning, consider the following:

1. Is the child able to describe the doors and windows in her home?
2. Is the child able to sing the song and do the actions?

Cleo and Theo's Book Suggestions

Castles, Caves, and Honeycombs by Linda Ashman and Lauren Stringer

A House Is a House for Me by Mary Ann Hoberman

Spring Song by Barbara Seuling and Greg Newbold

Whose House? by Barbara Seuling, Miriam Altshuler, and Kay Chorao

The Wonderful House by Margaret Wise Brown and J. P. Miller

Note to Families About the Topic of Houses and Homes

FAMILY LETTER

Date ______________

Dear Families,

At group time, we are talking about the topic of houses and homes. We are reading a number of books, including the story *The Three Little Pigs*. The pigs build their houses out of straw, sticks, and bricks. We are drawing pictures of our homes, and we are reading books about animals and where they live.

Here are some ways you can participate in this topic by doing activities at home with your child:

- Talk to your child about your home. What is it made of? How many rooms does it have? What does your family do in each room?
- Visit a construction site. Talk to your child about what the construction workers are building. What materials, tools, and machines are they using?
- Help your child have fun by building a playhouse out of sheets, pillows, blankets, or a large cardboard box. Pretend to eat a meal in it.
- Look outside for animals. Talk to your child about the places animals live and the kinds of homes that they build. What materials do they use? How do they build them—with their feet, hands, paws, beaks, or mouths?

Thank you!

Colors

CHAPTER 5

This topic allows the children to develop color recognition skills through hands-on activities, games, stories, and songs that encourage them to match, identify, and name colors. The children learn how to mix two primary colors to make a new color and write poems about the colors they see around them.

Setting Up the Room

Decorate your room with a rainbow of colors! Create wall displays featuring different colors, such as a collection of pictures of red foods (strawberries, apples, cherries, grapes) and green foods (lettuce, peas, broccoli, pears). As you progress with the topic, fill the walls with the children's artwork, color poems, and color charts. Encourage the children to use color words to describe the objects they see on the walls and around the room.

Color Book-Browsing Box

Set up a browsing box with fiction and nonfiction books about color. Create a colorful label for the box. Show the children the label so they know where to locate and return the color books.

Family Letter

Prepare and make photocopies of the Family Letter on page 126 that explains this topic. Give the letter to parents at pick-up time before you begin the topic.

Color Collage

Literacy Skill Focus
Vocabulary

Vocabulary

arrange
collage
color words (*red, green, blue, and so on*)
glue
paste
shape words (circle, square, triangle)

Materials

construction paper
crayons
glue
markers
materials for collage (crepe paper, buttons, pictures from magazines)
red paint and paintbrushes
red glitter
red objects (small blocks, buttons, milk caps, toys)
red ribbon
shapes cut out of red construction paper

What Children Will Learn

1. To make a collage
2. About different colors

Related Themes

Art
Math

What to Do

- Explain and model the process of making a collage. Say, *A collage is a piece of art made by gluing different objects and shapes onto a piece of paper. Today we will make a red collage using only red objects.*

- Think aloud as you select red objects and shapes to arrange on a piece of construction paper. *I think this red button would look nice here. I think I'll put this red square here.*
- Once you have arranged your items on the paper, show the children how to glue the objects into place. *I'm turning the button over to put glue on the back side. A little bit of glue in each corner or around the edge will usually make it stick.*
- After you have finished gluing objects to your collage, show the children how you can add more red color by drawing with red crayons and markers or painting.
- Help the children as they select objects for their collages. When they have completed their collages, ask them to name the different shapes and objects. Help them write their names on their collages.

Simplify It

Let the children create a collage without asking them to name the different shapes and objects.

Add a Challenge

Suggest that the children find objects in the classroom that are red and arrange them into a large array or construction.

Assessment

To assess each child's learning, consider the following:

1. Is the child able to create a single-color collage?
2. Is the child able to name the shapes and objects in her collage?

Cleo and Theo's Book Suggestions

Blue Hat, Green Hat by Sandra Boynton

Chidi Only Likes Blue: An African Book of Colours by Ifeoma Onyefulu

Color Dance by Ann Jonas

Colors Everywhere by Tana Hoban

Mary Wore Her Red Dress and Henry Wore His Green Sneakers adapted by Merle Peek

Moo Moo, Brown Cow by Jakki Wood and Rog Bonner

Of Colors and Things by Tana Hoban

A Rainbow All Around Me by Sandra L. Pinkney and Myles C. Pinkney

Spicy Hot Colors: Colores Picantes by Sherry Shahan and Paula Barragan

Where Is the Green Sheep? by Mem Fox and Judy Horacek

I See Red

Literacy Skill Focus
Color Recognition
Listening and Speaking
Name Recognition
Phonological Awareness
(Rhythm and Repetition)
Vocabulary

Vocabulary

chart
circle
color
describe
find
glad
happily
happy
look
red
sing

Materials

chart paper
glue
index cards
markers
red paper circle

What Children Will Learn

1. To sing a song
2. To identify red objects

Related Themes

All About Me
Friends

Preparation

Use index cards to create a name card for each child.

Before class, put red objects in visible places around the room. Make sure there is one for each child.

What to Do

- Begin group time with a greeting song, such as "Sing, Sing, Sing with Me."

  Sing, Sing, Sing with Me
  (Tune: "Row, Row, Row Your Boat")
  Sing, sing, sing with me,
  Sing out loud and clear.
  Happily, happily, happily, happily,
  We're glad that (child's name) is here.

- Ask the children to hold up their name card when you sing their name. After singing the song once, invite the children to sing along with you.
  Note: Repeat this greeting song for a few days until all the children know the song and can sing it together as a group.
- *Tell the children that they will be learning about the color red. Hold up a red object and ask, What color is this block? Yes, this is a red block. The color of this block is red.*
- Ask the children to look around the room and to raise their hand when they see something red. Ask, *What do you see that is red?* One by one, have the children find a red object and bring it to the circle.

- Prompt the children to describe the object in complete sentences. *(This is a red ball.)*
- Start a color chart together. Hold up a red paper circle and ask, *What color is this? Yes, it's red. I am going to write the word* red *on the red circle*—r-e-d.
- Glue the circle onto a large sheet of chart paper, leaving space for other color circles you will add during the week. You may want to make the chart into a bouquet of colored balloons. Throughout the day, encourage the children to identify red objects.

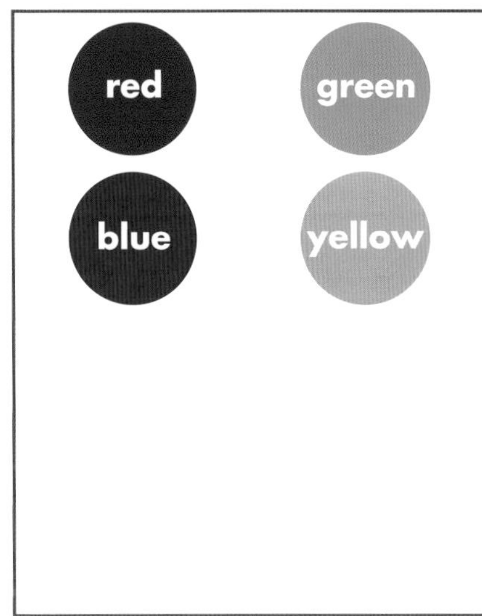

Simplify It

Gather several red items and one item of another color. Ask the children to tell you which object is not red.

Add a Challenge

Encourage the children to find objects that are red and at least one other color. Ask them to name the other colors in the object.

Assessment

To assess each child's learning, consider the following:

1. Is the child able to sing the song?
2. Is the child able to identify red objects in the room?

Cleo and Theo's Book Suggestions

Blue Hat, Green Hat by Sandra Boynton
Chidi Only Likes Blue: An African Book of Colours by Ifeoma Onyefulu
Color Farm by Lois Ehlert
Colors Everywhere by Tana Hoban
Growing Colors by Bruce McMillan
The Lion and the Little Red Bird by Elisa Kleven
Moo Moo, Brown Cow by Jakki Wood and Rog Bonner
Of Colors and Things by Tana Hoban
A Rainbow All Around Me by Sandra L. Pinkney and Myles C. Pinkney
Spicy Hot Colors: Colores Picantes by Sherry Shahan and Paula Barragan

Reading *Who Said Red?*

Literacy Skill Focus

Active Listening
Concepts of Print
Listening and Speaking
Parts of a Book
Prediction
Story Comprehension
Vocabulary

Vocabulary

author, boy, color, cover, girl, high, illustrator, kite, red, sky, story, title

Materials

Who Said Red? by Mary Serfozo and Keiko Narahashi

What Children Will Learn

1. What an author and an illustrator do
2. To identify the characters in a story

Related Themes

Friends
Toys

What to Do

- Show the children the book cover. Point to the words as you read aloud the title, the author, and the illustrator. Review what an author and an illustrator do.
- *Ask the children to describe what they see on the cover. Ask,* What color is the kite? Have you ever flown a kite? What do you think might happen to the kite if you let go of the string?
- Show the title page. Point out that the boy is flying his kite high in the sky. Tell the children that before the story begins, the kite falls from the sky. Say, *The boy can't find it. He asks the girl: "Did you see my red kite?" Instead of saying yes or no, the girl teases the boy and makes believe she didn't hear him. She names all the colors around her. Let's look at the pictures and see what colors she names.*
- Read slowly and with expression. There are two speakers in the story, the boy and the girl. Change your voice to indicate the teasing tone of the girl and the growing impatience of the boy. Point out that the girl is asking the questions. Provide a listening focus: Say, *As you listen to the story, pay attention to who is talking.*
- When you show the red pages, have the children identify the red objects in the illustrations. Repeat the process for each color.
- When you look at the last two pages, ask, *Where does the boy find his kite?*

- After you finish reading the story, talk about it with the children. Ask questions such as:
  - *Did you like the story? What did you like about it?*
  - *In the story, who said, "No, I said red!"—the girl or the boy?*
  - *What are some red things in the story? (Show the pages.)*
  - *What are some other things that are red?*

Simplify It

Read the book and identify the colors of the objects in the book.

Add a Challenge

Distribute red color cards or circles to a few of the children. Say, *If you have the color red, jump up and say "Red!"* Then ask the group, *Who said "red"?* Prompt the children to answer in complete sentences. *Tyrone said "red." Alexa said "red."*

Assessment

To assess each child's learning, consider the following:

1. Is the child able to describe what an author and an illustrator do?
2. Is the child able to identify the characters in the story?

Blue Hat, Green Hat by Sandra Boynton

Chidi Only Likes Blue: An African Book of Colours by Ifeoma Onyefulu

Color Farm by Lois Ehlert

Colors Everywhere by Tana Hoban

Growing Colors by Bruce McMillan

Moo Moo, Brown Cow by Jakki Wood and Rog Bonner

Of Colors and Things by Tana Hoban

A Rainbow All Around Me by Sandra L. Pinkney and Myles C. Pinkney

Spicy Hot Colors: Colores Picantes by Sherry Shahan and Paula Barragan

"A Kite"

Literacy Skill Focus
Concepts of Print
Phonological Awareness (Rhyme)
Vocabulary

Vocabulary

card
chart
color
different
fly
fun
green
kite
poem
red
rhyme
run
sentence
sky

Materials

chart paper
index cards
markers in many colors
sentence chart
sentence strips

Teacher Tip: During this topic, use the colors of the clothing the children are wearing to help organize transitions. *If you are wearing something red, you can line up now to go to the bathroom.*

What Children Will Learn

1. To recite a poem about kites
2. To create a poem

Related Themes

Science
Weather

Preparation

Write each line of "A Kite" on a sentence strip. Cut the first line into two pieces—*A / kite is lots of fun*—so you can insert different color word cards between them. Make a set of color word cards to insert into the poem. Write *red* in red and *green* in green, and so on, so the children can use the chart independently. Assemble and display the sentence strips in a sentence chart. Insert the red word card in the first line. Write the template for the red color poem (see page 113) on a sheet of chart paper.

What to Do

- Tell the children you are going to recite a poem about kites. If appropriate, engage the children in a discussion about their experiences flying kites.
- Recite the poem without referring to the chart.

  A Kite
  A red kite is lots of fun.
  So grab the string and run, run, run.
  Watch it go up in the sky
  Because a kite is meant to fly.

- Recite the poem again, touching each word on the sentence chart with a pointer or your finger. Then invite the children to recite the poem with you.

- Now tell the children that you are going to write a poem together. Today, you are going to write the first part about the color red. Provide a template with a topic sentence at the beginning and a closing statement at the end, such as the one below:

Red

We see red all around us.	Red ______________
Red ______________	and ______________.
And red ___________.	Red. Red. We see red all around us!

- Ask the children to complete the lines by naming red things. Write the words in red on the template.
- Read aloud the verse, touching the words with your finger or a pointer to help the children read the poem.

Simplify It

Either recite "A Kite" or help the children create a poem about the color red.

Add a Challenge

Choose a red object that can be easily seen by the children and describe it using the color word first. *I spy something that is red, round, and can bounce. What is it?* (a ball!) Invite the children to locate a red object and ask an "I Spy" question for the rest of the class to answer.

Assessment

To assess each child's learning, consider the following:

1. Is the child able to recite "A Kite"?
2. Is the child able to contribute to the creation of the "Red" poem?

Cleo and Theo's
Book Suggestions
Brown Bear, Brown Bear, What Do You See? by Bill Martin Jr. and Eric Carle
Chidi Only Likes Blue: An African Book of Colours by Ifeoma Onyefulu
Color Farm by Lois Ehlert
Colors Everywhere by Tana Hoban
Growing Colors by Bruce McMillan
The Lion and the Little Red Bird by Elisa Kleven
Mary Wore Her Red Dress and Henry Wore His Green Sneakers adapted by Merle Peek
Moo Moo, Brown Cow by Jakki Wood and Rog Bonner
Of Colors and Things by Tana Hoban
Spicy Hot Colors: Colores Picantes by Sherry Shahan and Paula Barragan

It's Red! It's Green!

Literacy Skill Focus
Listening and Speaking
Phonological Awareness (Rhyming, Rhythm, and Repetition)
Vocabulary

Vocabulary

chart	green
circle	identify
disagree	look around
disagreement	object
find	red

Materials

black and green markers
color chart (see page 109)
glue
green building block
green objects
green paper circle
red-and-green paper hat (newspaper, red paper, green paper, and tape or glue)

What Children Will Learn

1. To identify objects that are green
2. To sing a song

Related Themes

Clothing
Feelings

Preparation

Before class, put green objects in visible places around the room. Make sure there is one for each child. Display the color chart from "I See Red" on page 109. Make a hat that is green on one side and red on the other. Fold a page of newspaper in half from top to bottom. With the folded edge away from you, fold the upper corners to the center so that they form a point at the top. Fold the bottom edges up, one on each side. Tape or glue red paper onto one side of the hat and green paper onto the other.

What to Do

- Touch the red circle or balloon on the color chart and ask, *What color did we talk about before? Yes, we talked about the color red! Today we will talk about a new color. Hold up a green building block and ask,* What color is this block? Yes, this is a green block. Look around the room. What do you see that is green? *Prompt the children to respond in full sentences.* (I see a green pencil.)
- Hold up a green paper circle and ask, *What color is this? Yes, it is green. I am going to write the word* green *on the green circle*—g-r-e-e-n. Glue the circle onto the color chart. Throughout the day, encourage the children to identify green objects in the room.
- Have the children stand in two lines facing one another. Ask them to take 10 steps backward, leaving a space in the middle. On your head, place a paper hat that is red on one side and green on the other. Look straight ahead and walk in between the two lines of children. Ask, *What color is my hat?* Then change direction and walk back the opposite way. Repeat the question, *What color is my hat?*

- Show the children both sides of the hat. Say, *This is an unusual hat. It's red on one side and green on the other! When I show you this* (red) *side, what color do you think the hat is? When I show you this* (green) *side, what color do you think the hat is?*
- Tell the children you are going to teach them a song about a red/green hat. Sing both verses of the song "Red Hat, Green Hat." Wear the red/green hat as you sing.

Red Hat, Green Hat
(Tune: "Mary Wore Her Red Dress")
Farmer wore a red hat, red hat, red hat.
Farmer wore a red hat
All day long.

Farmer wore a green hat, green hat, green hat.
Farmer wore a green hat
All day long.

Simplify It

Have the children identify green objects in the classroom one day and teach them the song on another day.

Add a Challenge

Divide the class in half. Have one half sing the first verse ("Farmer wore a red hat"), the other half sing the second verse ("Farmer wore a green hat"), and then both groups sing their verses at the same time.

Assessment

To assess each child's learning, consider the following:
1. Is the child able to identify objects that are green?
2. Is the child able to sing the song with the class?

Cleo and Theo's Book Suggestions

Blue Hat, Green Hat by Sandra Boynton
Brown Bear, Brown Bear, What Do You See? by Bill Martin Jr. and Eric Carle
Caps for Sale by Esphyr Slobodkina
Chidi Only Likes Blue: An African Book of Colours by Ifeoma Onyefulu
Color Farm by Lois Ehlert
Growing Colors by Bruce McMillan
Hats, Hats, Hats by Ann Morris and Ken Heyman
Moo Moo, Brown Cow by Jakki Wood and Rog Bonner
My Very First Book of Colors by Eric Carle
Of Colors and Things by Tana Hoban
Spicy Hot Colors: Colores Picantes by Sherry Shahan and Paula Barragan

Rhymes with Fun

Literacy Skill Focus
Concepts of Print
Phonological Awareness (Rhyming)
Vocabulary

Vocabulary

bun
card
chart
color
different
done
fly
fun
green
kite
poem
red
rhyme
run
sentence
sky
sun

Materials

color chart from "I See Red" (pages 108–109)
green word card from "A Kite" (page 112)
sentence chart for "A Kite" (page 112)

What Children Will Learn

1. About rhyming
2. About the color green

Related Themes

Sounds
Toys

What to Do

- Display the sentence chart for "A Kite" (see page 112) and read the poem with the children several times. Say, *Let's change the color of the kite. Let's make it green!* Display the color word cards and ask the children to find the green card. Insert the card in the space in the sentence chart. Touch each word as you read the poem.
- Show the children how they can use the chart on their own. Encourage the children to use this chart independently throughout the day.
- Select a pair of rhyming words from "A Kite" and play a game to help the children hear and recognize rhymes.
- Display the sentence chart for "A Kite." Point to the word *fun* in the first line and the word *run* in the second line. Ask the children to repeat the words with you. Say, *These two words rhyme. They both sound the same at the end: /un/. Say the words with me again:* fun, run.
- Say, *I'm going to say some words. I want you to listen carefully. If the word I say rhymes with the word* fun, *I want you to raise your hand. If it doesn't rhyme with the word* fun, *don't raise your hand.* Say the word *sun.* Ask, *Does* sun *rhyme with* fun? Sun, fun. *They rhyme! Raise your hand!*

- Repeat the process with the words *done* and *bun*. Then repeat with a word such as *red* that doesn't rhyme with *sun*.
  Note: Using a green marker, write a second verse of the class color poem about the color green. Follow the procedure on page 113.

Simplify It

In addition to reading the words on the color word cards, display objects that are the same color as the color word.

Add a Challenge

Play "I Spy" with the color green. Follow the procedure on page 113.

Assessment

To assess each child's learning, consider the following:

1. Is the child able to recognize objects that are green?
2. Is the child able to identify words that rhyme?

Cleo and Theo's Book Suggestions

Blue Hat, Green Hat by Sandra Boynton
Chidi Only Likes Blue: An African Book of Colours by Ifeoma Onyefulu
Colors Everywhere by Tana Hoban
Growing Colors by Bruce McMillan
Mary Wore Her Red Dress and Henry Wore His Green Sneakers adapted by Merle Peek
Moo Moo, Brown Cow by Jakki Wood and Rog Bonner
My Very First Book of Colors by Eric Carle
Of Colors and Things by Tana Hoban
Spicy Hot Colors: Colores Picantes by Sherry Shahan and Paula Barragan

Reading *Mouse Paint*

Literacy Skill Focus

Active Listening
Cause and Effect
Listening and Speaking
Predicting
Story Comprehension
Vocabulary

Vocabulary

author
cover
illustrator
mix
orange
paintbrushes
stir
title
yellow

Materials

Mouse Paint by Ellen Stoll Walsh
plastic container for mixing paint
red and yellow paint

What Children Will Learn

1. About mixing colors
2. About the book *Mouse Paint*

Related Theme

Animals

What to Do

- Hold up a jar of red paint and a jar of yellow paint and ask the children to name the colors. Then ask, *What do you think will happen if we mix red and yellow?* Think aloud as you demonstrate: *First, let's put some red paint in this container. Then let's put some yellow paint in with the red paint, stir them together, and see what happens. What color did we make? When we stir, or mix, red and yellow together, we make orange!* Tell the children that they will have a chance to mix colors and see what happens. *Right now, we are going to read a story about some mice that have lots of fun mixing colors!*
  Note: Add yellow and orange to the color chart, following the procedure on pages 108–109. Throughout the day, encourage the children to identify objects that are yellow and orange.
- Show the children the cover of *Mouse Paint*. Point to the words with your finger as you read aloud the title and the name of the author/illustrator. Review what an author and illustrator do. Ask the children what they see on the front cover.
  - *What are the mice holding?* (paintbrushes)
  - *What are they doing with the paintbrushes?* (painting)
  - *What colors are the mice painting?* (red, yellow, and blue)
- Read slowly and with expression. Point to the red, yellow, and blue jars of paint and the red, yellow, and blue mice when you read about them in the text. Invite the children to predict what colors the mice will make when they mix colors with their feet. Ask, *What color do you think red feet in a yellow puddle will make?*

- After you finish reading the book, talk about it with the children. Ask questions such as:
  - What happens to the mice when they jump into the jars of paint?
  - Why are there puddles of paint on the paper?
  - What do the mice do with the puddles of paint?

  Note: Write a third verse of the class color poem about the color yellow or the color orange. Follow the procedure on page 113.

Simplify It

Enjoy the story without asking the children to predict what will happen.

Add a Challenge

Suggest that the children create color books. Each page features one color. The children draw or glue magazine pictures that feature a color on each page.

Assessment

To assess each child's learning, consider the following:

1. Is the child able to understand how to create different colors by mixing paint?
2. Is the child able to appreciate the storyline of *Mouse Paint*?

Cleo and Theo's Book Suggestions

Brown Bear, Brown Bear, What Do You See? by Bill Martin Jr. and Eric Carle

Chidi Only Likes Blue: An African Book of Colours by Ifeoma Onyefulu

Colors Everywhere by Tana Hoban

Mary Wore Her Red Dress and Henry Wore His Green Sneakers adapted by Merle Peek

Moo Moo, Brown Cow by Jakki Wood and Rog Bonner

My Very First Book of Colors by Eric Carle

Of Colors and Things by Tana Hoban

Spicy Hot Colors: Colores Picantes by Sherry Shahan and Paula Barragan

Color Mixing Chart

Literacy Skill Focus
Active Listening
Listening and Speaking
Phonological Awareness (Rhythm and Repetition)
Story Comprehension
Vocabulary

Vocabulary

chart
color names
dancing
mix
puddle
purple
splashing
stirring

What Children Will Learn

1. How to mix two colors to make a third color
2. To identify objects that are orange, green, and purple

Related Themes

Animals
Colors

Materials

chart paper
markers
Mouse Paint by Ellen Stoll Walsh
red, yellow, orange, blue, green, and purple paper circles

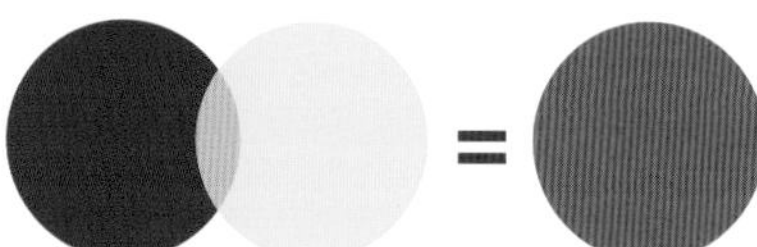

What to Do

- Use the story of *Mouse Paint* to create a simple color mixing chart with the children. Say, *Let's look at the book and see what happens when the mice mix colors by stirring, splashing, and dancing in the puddles of paint.*
- Show the illustration of the red mouse dancing in the yellow puddle. Say, *Here is the red mouse. He is stirring the yellow puddle with his feet. What color does he make?* Turn the page and point to the orange puddle. Wait for the children to answer *orange.*
- Say, *Let's make a chart that shows what happens when we mix colors together.* Overlap a red circle and a yellow circle. Then write an equal sign next to the overlapping circles and place an orange circle next to the equal sign. As you point to the colored circles, ask, *When we mix red and yellow together, what color do we get? Orange!*
- Repeat the process for mixing yellow and blue (green).
- Hold up a red circle and a blue circle and ask the children to name each color. Then ask, *What happens when we mix red and blue? Yes, when we stir or mix red and blue together, we make purple!* Add red and blue = purple to the color mixing chart. **Note**: Throughout the day, encourage the children to identify objects that are the colors orange, green, and purple—colors that are created by mixing other colors.

- Tell the children you are going to teach them a song about mice mixing colors, just like in the book. Point to the color mixing chart as you sing "Mice Mix Colors." As you sing the color words, point to the corresponding colors on the color mixing chart.

Mice Mix Colors
(Tune: "The Wheels on the Bus")
Three little mice mix red and yellow,
Red and yellow,
Red and yellow.
Three little mice mix red and yellow.
Red and yellow make orange.

Additional verses:
Three little mice mix blue and red…
Blue and red make purple.

Three little mice mix yellow and blue…
Yellow and blue make green.

- Invite the children to sing the song with you.

Teaching Tip: Write the words to the song on chart paper. Use colored markers to write the color words. Explain that *red* is written in the color red and so on.

Simplify It

Give the children paint so they can explore mixing two colors.

Add a Challenge

Challenge the children to create color books showing the colors created by mixing two colors together to make orange, green, and purple.

Assessment

To assess each child's learning, consider the following:

1. Is the child able to understand how to mix two colors to create a third color?
2. Is the child able to identify objects in the classroom that are orange, green, and purple?

Cleo and Theo's Book Suggestions

Blue Hat, Green Hat by Sandra Boynton
Brown Bear, Brown Bear, What Do You See? by Bill Martin Jr. and Eric Carle
Chidi Only Likes Blue: An African Book of Colours by Ifeoma Onyefulu
Color Farm by Lois Ehlert
Colors Everywhere by Tana Hoban
Growing Colors by Bruce McMillan
Moo Moo, Brown Cow by Jakki Wood and Rog Bonner
My Very First Book of Colors by Eric Carle
Of Colors and Things by Tana Hoban
Spicy Hot Colors: Colores Picantes by Sherry Shahan and Paula Barragan

"Oh, Do You Know Two Rhyming Words?"

Literacy Skill Focus
Phonological Awareness
(Rhyme)

Vocabulary

black
brown
bug
hug
lug
rhyme
rug
sing
song
sound

Materials

none needed

What Children Will Learn

1. About rhyming
2. To sing a song

Related Theme

Sounds

What to Do

- Sing the song, "Oh, Do You Know Two Rhyming Words?" using the words *rug* and *bug* or *hug* and *lug*. Invite the children to sing the song with you.

Oh, Do You Know Two Rhyming Words?
(Tune: "Oh, Do You Know the Muffin Man?")
Oh, do you know two rhyming words,
Two rhyming words,
Two rhyming words?
Oh, do you know two rhyming words?
They sound a lot alike.

Rug and bug are two rhyming words,
Two rhyming words,
Two rhyming words.
Rug and bug are two rhyming words.
They sound a lot alike.

- Ask, *Do you notice something about the words* rug *and* bug*? They rhyme! They end with the same sound: /ug/.*
- After singing the song, add brown and black to the class color chart, following the procedure on page 108–109.

Teacher Tip: Use this song throughout the year to help the children hear and identify rhyming words.

Simplify It

Sing one line of the song at a time. Ask the children to repeat the line after you sing it. Once they are able to repeat each line correctly, sing the whole song together.

Add a Challenge

Challenge the children to name other words that have the same ending sound of /ug/.

Assessment

To assess each child's learning, consider the following:

1. Is the child able to understand what makes words rhyme?
2. Is the child able to sing the song with the class?

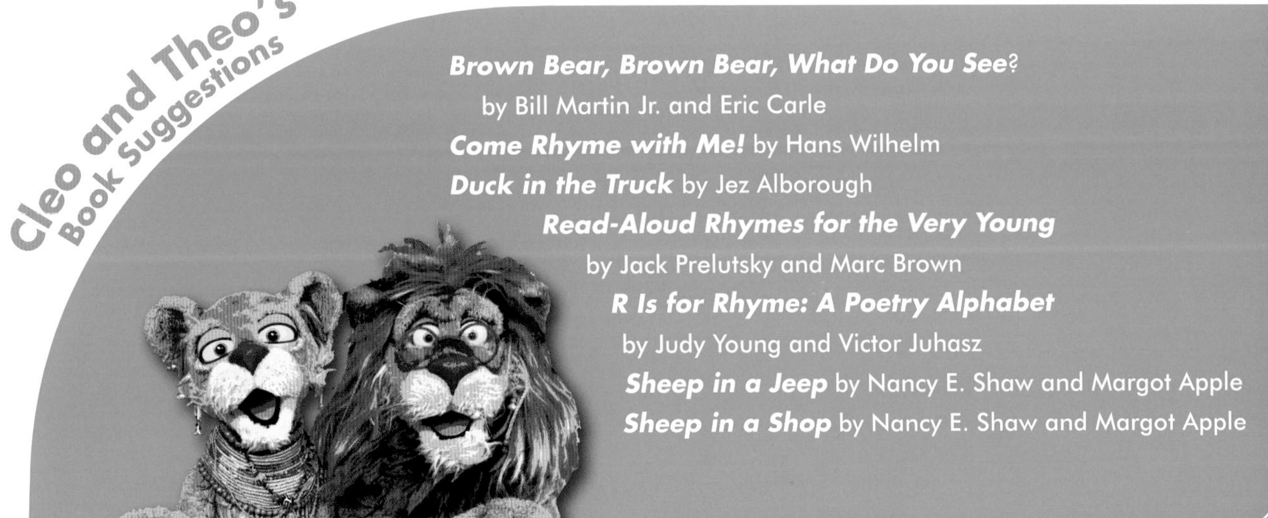

Brown Bear, Brown Bear, What Do You See? by Bill Martin Jr. and Eric Carle

Come Rhyme with Me! by Hans Wilhelm

Duck in the Truck by Jez Alborough

Read-Aloud Rhymes for the Very Young by Jack Prelutsky and Marc Brown

R Is for Rhyme: A Poetry Alphabet by Judy Young and Victor Juhasz

Sheep in a Jeep by Nancy E. Shaw and Margot Apple

Sheep in a Shop by Nancy E. Shaw and Margot Apple

"Traffic Light"

Literacy Skill Focus
Following Directions
Phonological Awareness
(Rhythm and Repetition)

Vocabulary

caution
change
circle
go
green
red
sign
stop
traffic light
warn
yellow

Materials

black construction paper
craft stick
glue
marker
red, yellow, and green paper circles

What Children Will Learn

1. About traffic lights
2. About stop and go

Related Theme

Transportation

Preparation

Make a paper traffic light by gluing red, yellow, and green circles in a vertical line on a rectangle of black construction paper. To make a red/STOP and green/GO sign write "stop" on a red paper circle and "go" on a green paper circle. Glue one paper circle on each side of a craft stick.

What to Do

- Tell the children you are going to teach them a song about the colors of a traffic light.
- Talk to the children about what they know about traffic lights. Ask, *Which color means "go"? Which color means "stop"? What do you think the color yellow tells us to do?* Explain that *yellow* means "caution." *Caution* means "be careful." Yellow warns drivers that the light is about to change colors and to slow down because the next color is red.
- Sing the song "Traffic Light." As you sing, point to the colors on the traffic light.

Traffic Light
(Tune: "The Wheels on the Bus")
The colors on the light turn
Green, yellow, red,
Green, yellow, red,
Green, yellow, red.
The colors on the light turn
Green, yellow, red
All around the town.

- Repeat the song and invite the children to sing the song with you.

- Play a game about traffic lights—Red Light! Green Light! Organize a game of Red Light! Green Light! with the red/STOP and green/GO sign. Point out the word *STOP* on the red side of the sign and the word *GO* on the green side. Explain the rules of the game.
- Have the children stand next to each other. Stand facing them at a distance. Turn your back to the group.
- Say, *One, two, three—green light*, and hold up the green/GO side of the sign to face the children. Indicate that you want the children to walk quickly toward you.
- Say, *One, two, three—red light*, and turn the sign so the red/STOP side faces the children. Instruct children to freeze when they see the STOP sign.
- Turn quickly to look at the children. If you see anyone still moving, tell him or her to return to the starting line.
- Keep playing, alternating between STOP and GO, until someone reaches and tags you. The child who tags you becomes the next traffic cop.

Simplify It

Teach the children the song one day and play the game on another day.

Add a Challenge

Take a walk and look at signs in the neighborhood. Talk about each sign's color, shape, and what it tells us to do.

Assessment

To assess each child's learning, consider the following:

1. What did the child learn about traffic lights?
2. What did the child learn about *stop* and *go*?

Cleo and Theo's Book Suggestions

Blue Hat, Green Hat by Sandra Boynton
Brown Bear, Brown Bear, What Do You See? by Bill Martin Jr. and Eric Carle
Chidi Only Likes Blue: An African Book of Colours by Ifeoma Onyefulu
City Signs by Zoran Milich
Colors Everywhere by Tana Hoban
Moo Moo, Brown Cow by Jakki Wood and Rog Bonner
My Very First Book of Colors by Eric Carle
Of Colors and Things by Tana Hoban
Signs in Our World by DK Publishing
Spicy Hot Colors: Colores Picantes by Sherry Shahan and Paula Barragan

Note to Families About the Topic of Colors

FAMILY LETTER

Date ____________________

Dear Families,

In the classroom, we are learning about the different colors we see around us. We are reading a book about three mice that mix colors. We are having fun mixing colors just like the mice! We are also playing games, acting out stories, singing songs, and reciting rhymes about colors.

Here are some activities you can do with your child:

- Ask your child about his or her favorite color. Tell your child what your favorite color is. Together look for and name things inside or outside your home that are your favorite color and your child's favorite color.
- When you are outside, notice and talk about STOP, SLOW, and other road signs with your child. What color are they? What do they say? What do they tell us to do?
- Play a game of "I Spy" with your child. Look around you and describe something that your child can easily see. Say, *I spy something red that can roll and bounce. What is it?* (ball)

Thank you!

Silly Animal Stories

CHAPTER 6

Cows that type! Seals, snakes, and skunks on a bus! The children in your classroom will have fun hearing about amazing animals that do surprising things. The children will learn about animals and explore the joys of writing as they exchange messages with one another and with the story characters.

Setting Up the Room

- Create a Farm Animals wall display. Include labeled pictures or photographs of cows and other farm animals. Encourage the children to look at the pictures and to name and talk about the animals.

- Add fiction and nonfiction books about cows to your classroom book-browsing box. You may want to create a book-browsing box filled with different versions of *The Wheels on the Bus* and *Old MacDonald Had a Farm* and other songbooks. Label the boxes with words and matching pictures or symbols so children can identify the contents and browse on their own.

- Create a message board and post it where children can easily see and reach it. Write notes to the class and post them on the message board. For example, write a note that says, "Today, we are going to have a special visitor." The message board will help children understand that print conveys meaning and that we use print for different purposes.

- Use milk cartons, shoeboxes, cereal boxes, or stackable crates to make a mailbox for each child. Label the mailboxes with the children's first names. Put notes into the children's mailboxes and encourage the children to write and draw messages to each other. Volunteer mail carriers can deliver messages to the mailboxes each day, or the children can put their messages directly into one another's mailboxes.

Family Letter

Prepare and make photocopies of the Family Letter on page 148 that explains this topic. Give the letter to parents at pick-up time before you begin the topic.

A Surprising Message!

Literacy Skill Focus
Concepts of Print (Functions of Print, Print Conveys Meaning)
Listening and Speaking
Name Recognition
Phonological Awareness (Rhythm and Repetition)
Vocabulary

Vocabulary

cow
farm
furious
message
notes
type
typewriter
verse
write

Materials

chart paper
Click, Clack, Moo: Cows That Type by Doreen Cronin and Betsy Lewin
construction paper
markers

Note: During this topic, you will be writing and reading morning messages from the cows (the main characters in the book *Click, Clack, Moo: Cows That Type*). Write the notes and post them in the classroom before the children arrive.

What Children Will Learn

1. To sing a song
2. That writing a note is a way to communicate

Related Themes

All About Me
Farms

Preparation

Before the children arrive, write the following note on construction paper and hang it where the children can easily find it. (See Message Board on page 127.)

Dear Children,
I hope you enjoy our story today, *Click, Clack, Moo.*
Sincerely,
Cows That Type

What to Do

- Begin group time by singing a greeting song such as "Sing, Sing, Sing with Me" on page 108, "Good Morning to You" on page 40, or another greeting song.
- Talk with the children about the topic—Silly Animal Stories. Say, *We are going to read about cows and other animals that do silly things real animals can't do.* Show the children photos or pictures of cows on the Farm Animal wall display (see Setting Up the Room, page 127). Ask, *What do you know about cows? What do cows do?*
- Write what the children say on chart paper.

- Point to today's note and exclaim, *Look, we have a message! I wonder who it's from. I wonder what it says. Let's read it.* Point to the words as you read the note aloud. Pause and say, *Cows that type! Cows can't type! Cows can't write! This message must be from the cows in the book we are going to read,* Click, Clack, Moo!
- Show the children the cover of the *Click, Clack, Moo: Cows That Type* book and then read it to the children.

Simplify It

Read the children a book about cows (see suggestions below), and then ask the children what they know about cows.

Add a Challenge

Suggest that the children write a note to the cows by either dictating it to you or by writing it themselves.

Assessment

To assess each child's learning, consider the following:

1. Is the child able to sing the song with the class?
2. Is the child able to identify a cow in a picture and tell you a fact about cows?

Cleo and Theo's Book Suggestions

And the Cow Said Moo by Mildred Phillips and Sonja Lamut
Barnyard Banter by Denise Fleming
Cock-a-Doodle-Moo! by Bernard Most
The Cow That Went OINK by Bernard Most
Cows in the Kitchen by June Crebbin
Duck on a Bike by David Shannon
Farmer Duck by Martin Waddell and Helen Oxenbury
Giggle, Giggle, Quack by Doreen Cronin and Betsy Lewin
I Love Animals by Flora McDonnell
Two Cool Cows by Toby Speed
Wild About Books by Judy Sierra and Marc Brown

Reading *Click, Clack, Moo*

Literacy Skill Focus

Active Listening
Concepts of Print
Listening and Speaking
Story Comprehension (Characters' Feelings)
Vocabulary

Vocabulary

clack
click
computer
cow
farm
farmer
feeling
furious
message
moo
noisy
notes
type
typewriter
write

Materials

Click, Clack, Moo: Cows That Type by Doreen Cronin and Betsy Lewin
typewriter, if possible

What Children Will Learn

1. About typing and typewriters
2. About notes and messages

Related Themes

Farms
Feelings

What to Do

- Show the children the cover of the *Click, Clack, Moo: Cows That Type* book and the picture of a typewriter on the title page. Point to the words as you read the title aloud. Talk about what the word *type* means.
- Show the children a real typewriter, if available, or glue a picture of a typewriter onto a box or file folder to make a pretend typewriter. You can also demonstrate how to type on a computer keyboard. Explain that a typewriter is a machine that people use to write. Today most people use computers instead of typewriters.
- Tell the children that in the story, the cows use a typewriter to write notes or messages to the farmer to tell him what they want. Say, *Typewriters are noisy machines. When you type, they make a sound like this*—click, clack, click, clack, click, clack. Model typing and then ask the children to copy you. As they type, have them say "click, clack, click, clack."
- Read *Click, Clack, Moo* to the children. Use different voices for the narrator, the farmer, the cows, and the duck. Invite the children to chime in as you read the repeating phrase in the book.
- Set a listening focus: Ask the children to think about how Farmer Brown feels about what is happening on his farm.

- Talk with the children about the book. Ask questions such as:
  - *Did you like the story? What was your favorite part?*
  - *How do you think Farmer Brown feels when the cows say "No milk" and the hens say "No eggs"?*
  - *I wonder how Farmer Brown feels at the end of the story. He was so furious when the cows asked for electric blankets. How do you think he feels when the ducks ask him for a diving board? Why?*

Simplify It

Spread this activity over two days. On the first day, let the children explore how to use the typewriter and make the keys click; on the second day, read the story to the children.

Add a Challenge

Ask the children to write or dictate a different ending to the story.

Assessment

To assess each child's learning, consider the following:

1. Is the child able to understand how typewriters work?
2. Is the child able to understand the importance of notes and messages?

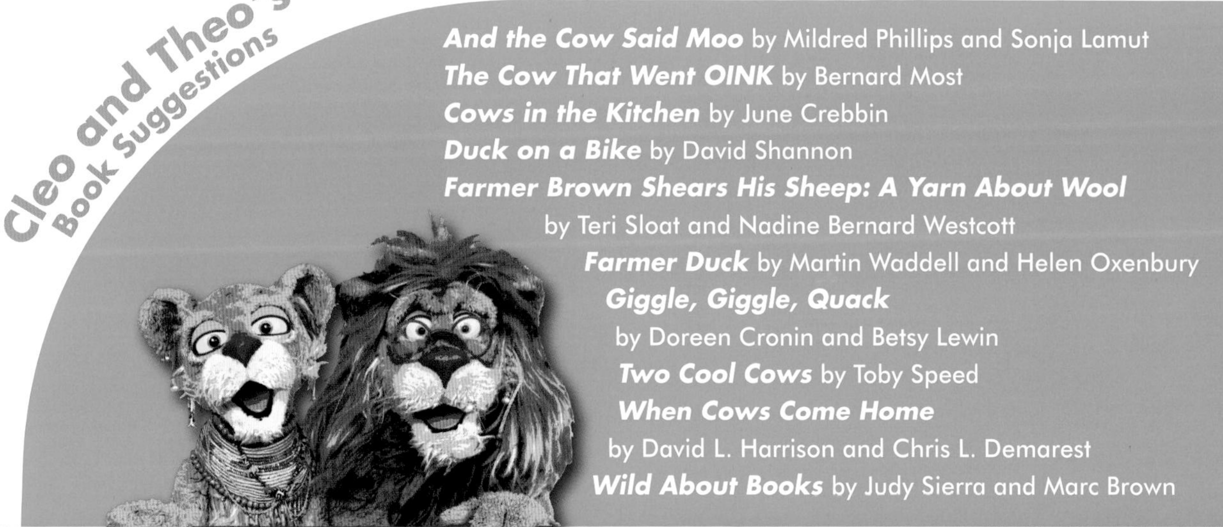

Cleo and Theo's Book Suggestions

And the Cow Said Moo by Mildred Phillips and Sonja Lamut
The Cow That Went OINK by Bernard Most
Cows in the Kitchen by June Crebbin
Duck on a Bike by David Shannon
Farmer Brown Shears His Sheep: A Yarn About Wool by Teri Sloat and Nadine Bernard Westcott
Farmer Duck by Martin Waddell and Helen Oxenbury
Giggle, Giggle, Quack by Doreen Cronin and Betsy Lewin
Two Cool Cows by Toby Speed
When Cows Come Home by David L. Harrison and Chris L. Demarest
Wild About Books by Judy Sierra and Marc Brown

Notes from Cows That Type

Literacy Skill Focus
Concepts of Print (Directionality, Print Conveys Meaning)
Story Comprehension
Vocabulary

Vocabulary

barn
clack
click
computer
cow
demand
diving board
electric blanket
farm
farmer
feeling
furious
greeting
impatient
message
moo
neutral
noisy
notes
pond
strike
type
typewriter
write

Materials

chart paper
Click, Clack, Moo: Cows That Type by Doreen Cronin and Betsy Lewin
markers

What Children Will Learn

1. New vocabulary
2. About feelings

Related Themes

Farms
Feelings

What to Do

- Read aloud *Click, Clack, Moo: Cows That Type* again to the children, focusing on the notes in the books. Pause to read each note from the cows. Point to the words as you read them aloud and explain that the cows typed the note with a typewriter.
- Talk about what each note says. When you read an unfamiliar word, such as *furious*, *demand*, or *strike*, insert a phrase or a sentence that helps the children understand what the word means without interrupting the flow of the story. For example, when the text states that the farmer was "furious," say, *He was very, very angry.* Point to the illustrations in the book to help the children learn the meaning of unfamiliar words such as *barn*, *pond*, and *diving board.*
- Suggest that the children write a note to the cows, telling them what they thought of the story.
- Show the children the cows' note to them (see page 128). Point out that it begins with the greeting *Dear Children*. Explain that this is a way to start a note, letter, or message. Talk about different ways to start notes. Then ask, *How should we start our note to the cows?*
- Write *Dear Cows* or whatever greeting the children choose. Think out loud as you write to emphasize the directionality of the print. *I am going to start writing here at the top of the page, because we start reading at the top of the page. I am going to start on this side of the paper—the left side—because we read from left to right.*

- Ask the children what they want to say about the story. Think aloud as you write. *I'm going to start to write here. Now I've come to the edge of the paper. I need to go back to the other side* (point to left side) *to keep writing.*
- When you finish writing the message, say, *Let's look at the way the cows ended their note to us.* Point to the words as you read, "*Sincerely, Cows That Type.*" Share some other ways of ending a note such as "Love," "Fondly," "Your Friends," and so on. Write the closing that the children choose at the bottom of the note. Tell the children you will give the note to the cows.

Simplify It

Provide examples of notes so the children have more models to follow.

Add a Challenge

Suggest that the children write notes to the farmer.

Assessment

To assess each child's learning, consider the following:

1. Is the child able to use new vocabulary appropriately?
2. Is the child able to understand how the cows and the farmer feel?

Cleo and Theo's Book Suggestions
And the Cow Said Moo by Mildred Phillips and Sonja Lamut
Barnyard Banter by Denise Fleming
Cock-a-Doodle-Moo! by Bernard Most
Cows in the Kitchen by June Crebbin
Duck on a Bike by David Shannon
Farmer Brown Shears His Sheep: A Yarn About Wool by Teri Sloat and Nadine Bernard Westcott
Farmer Duck by Martin Waddell and Helen Oxenbury
Giggle, Giggle, Quack by Doreen Cronin and Betsy Lewin
Two Cool Cows by Toby Speed
When Cows Come Home by David L. Harrison and Chris L. Demarest

Animal Party

Literacy Skill Focus

Concepts of Print (Functions of Print, Print Conveys Meaning)
Differentiating Fantasy from Reality
Listening and Speaking
Story Comprehension
Vocabulary

Vocabulary

author	make-believe
bus	party
fantasy	real
feelings	seal
help	sheep
illustrator	tiger
invitation	transportation

What Children Will Learn

1. About the difference between fantasy and reality
2. About feelings

Related Themes

Celebrations
Feelings
Transportation

Preparation

Before the children arrive, write the following note on construction paper and hang it where the children can easily find it. (See Message Board on page 127.)

Dear Children,
We are glad you liked our story. We heard that there is a big party in town. We would like to go. Do you know how we can get there?
Yours truly,
Cows That Type

Materials

construction paper
markers
The Seals on the Bus by Lenny Hort and G. Brian Karas

What to Do

- Point to another note from the cows posted on the message board. Say, *Look! We have another message! I wonder if it's from those silly cows again. Let's read it.* Point to each word as you read the note.
- Ask the children how they think the cows can get to the party. Say, *I think I know a book that can help our cows. It's a silly story about seals and other animals that ride on a bus to get to a party in town!*
- Show the children the cover of *The Seals on the Bus*. Point to the words as you read aloud the title and the names of the author and illustrator. Ask the children to tell you what they see on the front cover. Then ask, *Have you ever been on a bus? Where did you go? Whom did you sit next to? Did you sit next to a seal?*

- Emphasize the rhythm of the words as you read. Set a listening focus: Ask the children to think about how the people feel about being on the bus with the animals.
- Point to the animals in the illustrations as you read their names. Invite the children to make the sounds of each animal with you.
- Talk about the story with the children. Ask questions such as:
  - *How do you think the people feel about being on the bus with the animals? How can you tell?*
  - *Why do the people on the bus yell, "Help, help, help!"?*
  - *Who is driving the bus in the story? Do real tigers drive buses?*

Simplify It

Talk with the children about one of the animals in the book.

Add a Challenge

Tell the children that the story can be sung like a song. Sing the text to the tune of "The Wheels on the Bus" as you turn the pages and show the illustrations. Invite the children to sing along.

Assessment

To assess each child's learning, consider the following:

1. Is the child able to differentiate fantasy from reality?
2. Is the child able to identify the feelings of the people in the book?

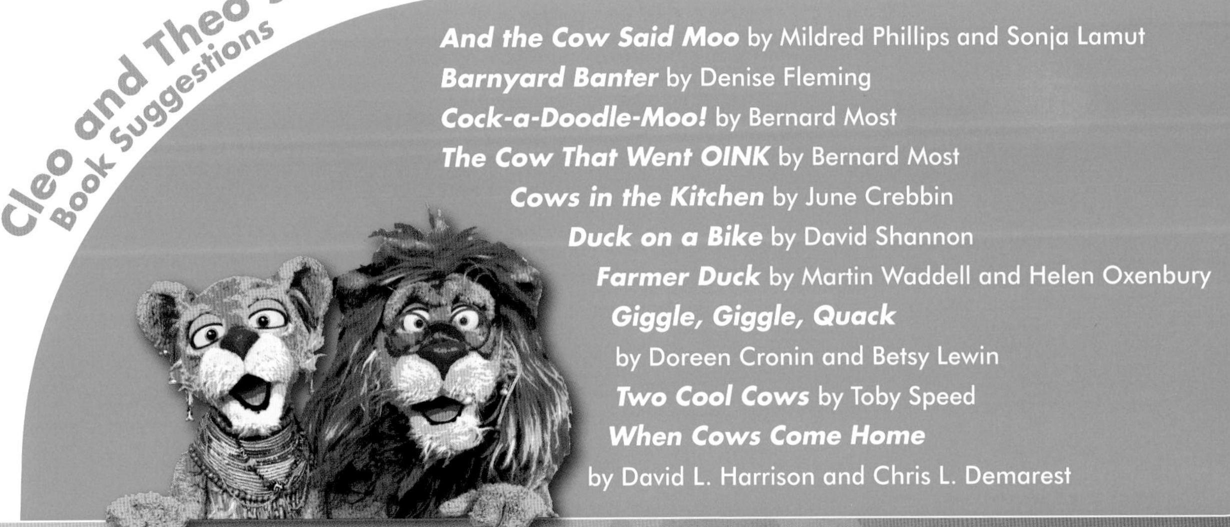

Cleo and Theo's Book Suggestions

And the Cow Said Moo by Mildred Phillips and Sonja Lamut
Barnyard Banter by Denise Fleming
Cock-a-Doodle-Moo! by Bernard Most
The Cow That Went OINK by Bernard Most
Cows in the Kitchen by June Crebbin
Duck on a Bike by David Shannon
Farmer Duck by Martin Waddell and Helen Oxenbury
Giggle, Giggle, Quack by Doreen Cronin and Betsy Lewin
Two Cool Cows by Toby Speed
When Cows Come Home by David L. Harrison and Chris L. Demarest

Real Animals, Silly Animals

Literacy Skill Focus

Differentiating Fantasy from Reality
Listening and Speaking
Phonological Awareness (Beginning Sounds)
Story Comprehension
Vocabulary

Vocabulary

cat	noise
cold	rain forest
cow	seal
curly	sheep
farm	sound
fast	stripe
flipper	sun
hair	swim
live	tiger
look	wool

Materials

photos or pictures (or plastic figures) of cows, seals, sheep, and tigers

The Seals on the Bus by Lenny Hort and G. Brian Karas

What Children Will Learn

1. To differentiate reality from fantasy
2. About the traits of different animals
3. To recognize the sounds of letters

Related Themes

Animals
Sounds

What to Do

- Show the children photos of some of the animals in the book. Talk about the way each animal looks, where it lives, and what noise it makes.
- Show the children a photo of a tiger. Ask, *What animal is this? What noise does it make?* Explain that a tiger is a very large cat with black stripes. Tigers can run very, very fast. Some tigers live in rain forests.
- Show the children a photo of a seal. Ask, *What animal is this? What noise does it make?* Explain that seals often live in the ocean in cold places. They have flippers that they use to swim.
- Show the children a photo of a sheep. Ask, *What animal is this? What noise does it make?* Explain that sheep often live on farms. Their bodies are covered with soft, curly hair called wool.
- Tell the children you are thinking of some other animals that would like to ride on the bus. You are going to give them hints and see if they can guess the animal. Show the children pictures of the animals to confirm their guesses. For example:
  - Say, *I'm thinking of an animal that begins with the /k/ sound.* Ask, *What sound does my animal begin with?* (/k/) *This animal gives us milk and says, "Moo."* Ask, *Can you guess what it is?* (cow)

- Say, *I'm thinking of another animal that begins with the /k/ sound.* Ask, *What sound does my animal begin with?* (/k/) *This animal has soft fur and says, "Meow."* Ask, *Can you guess what it is?* (cat)
- Say, *I'm thinking of another animal that begins with the /k/ sound.* Ask, *What sound does my animal begin with?* (/k/) *This animal wiggles on the ground. It turns into a butterfly. Can you guess what it is?* (caterpillar)

Simplify It

Show the children pictures of animals and ask what they notice about the animals.

Add a Challenge

Play Animal Charades. Have one child choose an animal and act out the way it moves and sounds. Prompt the other children to guess the animal.

Assessment

To assess each child's learning, consider the following:

1. Is the child able to learn about the traits of different animals?
2. Is the child able to differentiate the traits of real animals from the traits of animals in stories?

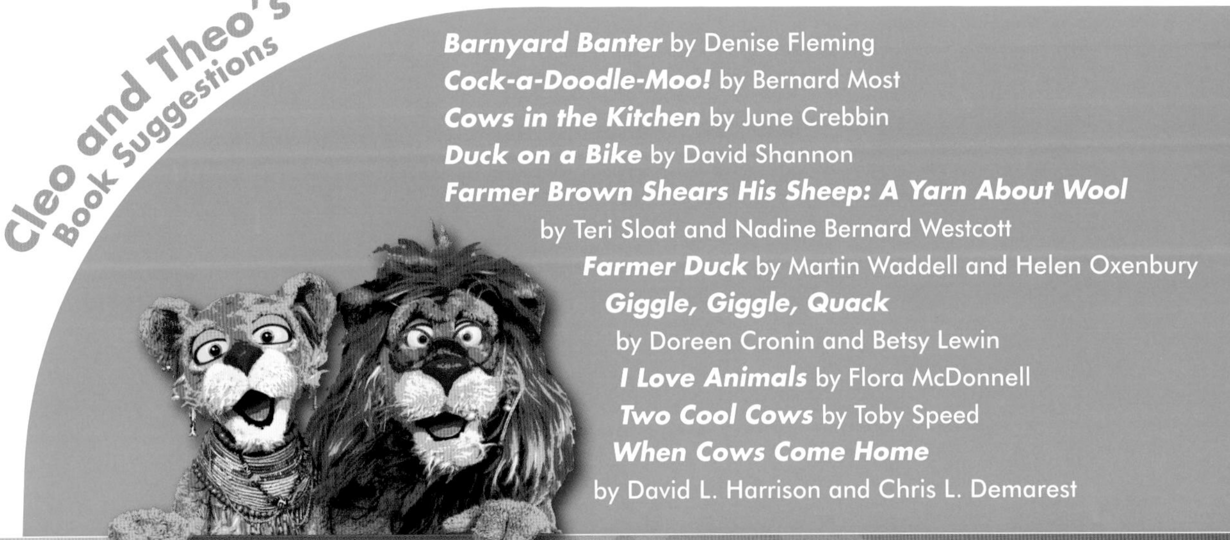

Cleo and Theo's Book Suggestions

Barnyard Banter by Denise Fleming
Cock-a-Doodle-Moo! by Bernard Most
Cows in the Kitchen by June Crebbin
Duck on a Bike by David Shannon
Farmer Brown Shears His Sheep: A Yarn About Wool by Teri Sloat and Nadine Bernard Westcott
Farmer Duck by Martin Waddell and Helen Oxenbury
Giggle, Giggle, Quack by Doreen Cronin and Betsy Lewin
I Love Animals by Flora McDonnell
Two Cool Cows by Toby Speed
When Cows Come Home by David L. Harrison and Chris L. Demarest

Party Invitation

Literacy Skill Focus
Concepts of Print (Directionality, Functions of Print, Print Conveys Meaning)
Listening and Speaking
Vocabulary

Vocabulary

breakfast
celebration
cow
drink
goat
invitation
invite
letter
milk
morning
note
party
sheep
write

Materials

chart paper
markers
The Seals on the Bus by Lenny Hort and G. Brian Karas

What Children Will Learn

1. How to write a party invitation
2. About celebrations

Related Themes
Celebrations
Food

Preparation

Before the children arrive, write the following note on construction paper and hang it where the children can easily see it. (See Message Board on page 127.)

Dear Children,
We had a party and now we are too tired to make milk. What do you drink for breakfast?
Your friends,
Cows That Type

What to Do

- Point to another note from the cows posted on the message board. Exclaim, *Look, here's a third message! I bet it is from those silly cows again.* Point to the words as you read the note.
- Ask, *Does anyone know what animals milk comes from?* (cow, sheep, goat) *How many of you like to drink milk? Raise your hand if you drank milk this morning.* You may want to provide additional background about how cows provide milk.
- Ask the children if they would like to have a party at the end of this topic. Talk about whom to invite and what they would like to do at the party. The children may want to invite their favorite stuffed animals from school and/or home!
- Explain that an invitation is a special kind of letter that asks someone to come to a party or other celebration.

- Ask, *What do you think our invitation should say? What do people need to know about our party?* Emphasize that people need to know what day the party is, what time it is, and where it is. Sometimes it's important to tell people why you are having a party, such as when you are having a birthday party.
- You may want to show the children samples of invitations, including the invitation in *The Seals on the Bus.*
- Ask the children how they would like to begin their invitation. Think aloud about where you start writing. *I'm going to start writing our invitation here, in the top left corner.*
- Point to each word as you read aloud the completed invitation. Ask the children if they want to add anything.
- Talk about how you will post or deliver the invitation.

Simplify It

Show the children many examples of invitations and then talk about what they want their invitation to say.

Add a Challenge

Ask the children to name different events to celebrate with a party.

Assessment

To assess each child's learning, consider the following:

1. Is the child able to write or dictate a party invitation?
2. Does the child know where to begin writing on a page?

Cleo and Theo's Book Suggestions

Bunny Party by Rosemary Wells
Happy Birthday to You, You Belong in a Zoo by Diane deGroat
Noko's Surprise Party by Fiona Moodie
Olive's Pirate Party by Roberta Baker and Debbie Tilley
A Very Special Tea Party by Katharine Holabird and Helen Craig
What a Party! by Sandy Asher and Keith Graves

Click, Clack, Cow

Literacy Skill Focus
Active Listening
Concepts of Print
Letter Recognition
Listening and Speaking
Predicting
Story Comprehension
Vocabulary

Vocabulary

baa
calf
cat
chick
dog
duck
duckling
fair
farmer
hen
horse
letter
lowercase
moo
noise
oink
pig
piglet
quack
sheep
type
typewriter
uppercase

Materials

Click, Clack, Moo: Cows That Type by Doreen Cronin and Betsy Lewin
index card
markers

What Children Will Learn

1. To identify the letter "C"
2. About the different noises that animals make

Related Themes

Animals
Sounds

Preparation

Write the uppercase "C" and lowercase "c" on an index card.

What to Do

- Point to the words as you read aloud the title, *Click, Clack, Moo: Cows That Type*. Say, *I see a lot of letter "C's" in the title. Here are two in the word* Click. *Here are two more in the word* Clack! *Can anyone find another letter "C"? Here it is in the word* Cows. *Look, here's another "C" in the author's last name, Doreen* Cronin.
- Read the book slowly and with expression. Invite the children to supply the repeating phrase in the book.
- Set a new focus: *As I read, look for the different animals that live on Farmer Brown's farm.*
- Talk with the children about the story. Ask questions such as:
  - *What other animals live on Farmer Brown's farm?* (hens, ducks, a horse, a pig, a cat, a dog, sheep)
  - *Why can't the other animals understand the cows?* (They don't speak Moo.)
  - *The cows promised Farmer Brown that Duck would bring him the typewriter. But Duck didn't give Farmer Brown the typewriter, did he? He gave the typewriter to the ducks! I'm wondering if that's fair. What do you think?*

- Suggest that the children imagine that the ducks give the typewriter to other animals on Farmer Brown's farm.
  - Say, *Oh no. The ducks gave the typewriter to the pigs. What noise do the pigs make when they type? Click, clack, oink! What do you think the pigs might ask for?*
  - Say, *Now the sheep have the typewriter. What noises do they make when they type? Click, clack, baa! What do you think the sheep might ask for?*
  - Ask, *Which animal do the sheep give the typewriter to? What noise do they make when they type? What do you think they might ask for?*

Simplify It

Ask the children to name the different animals that live on Farmer Brown's farm.

Add a Challenge

Draw a large letter "C" on the ground outside. Lead the children as they march along the "C" from top to bottom—the way we write the letter. As they march, have the children chant the letter name.

Assessment

To assess each child's learning, consider the following:

1. Is the child able to find an uppercase "C" and a lowercase "c"?
2. Is the child able to make and identify different noises that animals make?

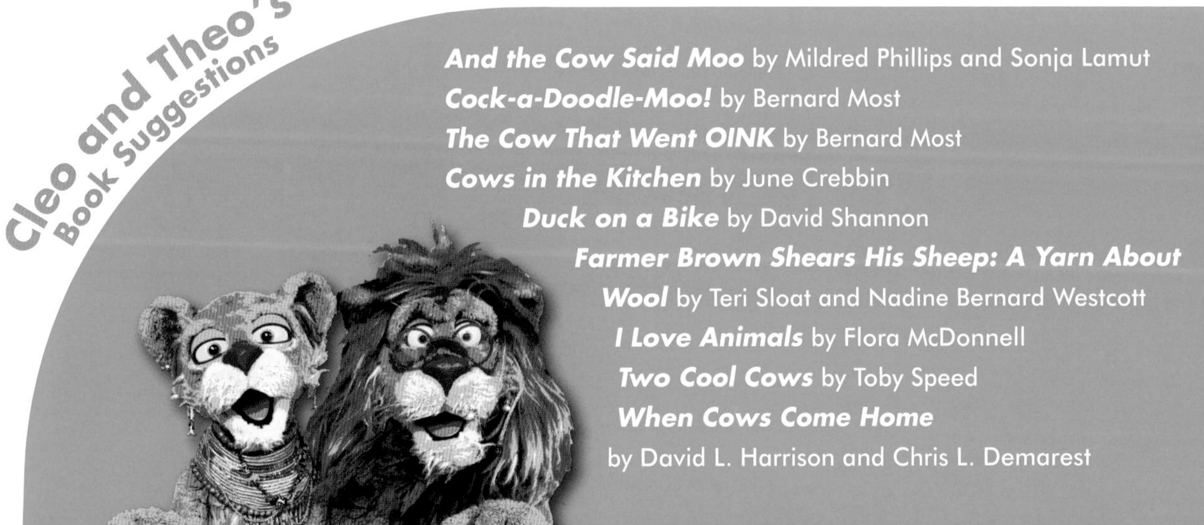

Cleo and Theo's Book Suggestions

And the Cow Said Moo by Mildred Phillips and Sonja Lamut
Cock-a-Doodle-Moo! by Bernard Most
The Cow That Went OINK by Bernard Most
Cows in the Kitchen by June Crebbin
Duck on a Bike by David Shannon
Farmer Brown Shears His Sheep: A Yarn About Wool by Teri Sloat and Nadine Bernard Westcott
I Love Animals by Flora McDonnell
Two Cool Cows by Toby Speed
When Cows Come Home by David L. Harrison and Chris L. Demarest

Farm Animals

Literacy Skill Focus
Listening and Speaking
Phonological Awareness (Rhythm and Repetition, Word Sounds)
Vocabulary

Vocabulary

calf, cat, chick, cow, dog, duck, duckling, farm, farmer, food, grow, hen, horse, milk, noise, pig, piglet, sheep, sound

Materials

Farm Animal wall display (see page 127)

What Children Will Learn

1. About farm animals and baby animals
2. To sing a song with a group

Related Themes

Animals
Farms
Food
Sounds

What to Do

- Ask the children to look at the Farm Animal wall display (see Setting Up the Room, page 127). Talk to the children about what farmers and farm animals do. Say, *Farmers have a very important job. They grow food and raise animals. Many of the animals that live on a farm also have important jobs. The cows' job is to give milk. Farmers sell the cows' milk to grocery stores. That's how we get the milk we drink. What is the hens' job?* (to lay eggs)
- Tell the children that farmers also grow other food that we eat. Ask, *What foods do you think a farmer might grow?*
- Point to each farm animal and ask the children what noise it makes. Say, *A baby pig is called a* piglet. *A baby cow is called a* calf. *A baby hen is called* a chick. Ask, *Who knows what a baby duck is called?* (a duckling)
- Ask each child to choose an animal and practice the noise it makes. Organize the children into their animal groups. For example, group all the ducks together. Then sing "Old MacDonald Had a Farm" and direct the children in an animal chorus.

Old MacDonald Had a Farm
Old MacDonald had a farm. Ee i ee i oh!
And on his farm he had some cows. Ee i ee i oh!
With a moo-moo here,
And a moo-moo there.
Here a moo, there a moo,
Everywhere a moo-moo.
Old MacDonald had a farm. Ee i ee i oh!

Simplify It

Sing about one animal at a time, with the whole class singing the same thing,

Add a Challenge

Add zoo or desert animals to the song. Ask the children to make the noises that these animals might make.

Assessment

To assess each child's learning, consider the following:

1. Is the child able to name some foods that farmers grow?
2. Is the child able to remember the names of some baby animals, such as calf or duckling?
3. Is the child able to sing a song with the group?

Cleo and Theo's Book Suggestions

And the Cow Said Moo by Mildred Phillips and Sonja Lamut
Barnyard Banter by Denise Fleming
Big Red Barn by Margaret Wise Brown and Felicia Bond
Cow by Jules Older and Lyn Severance
Farm Alphabet by Jane Miller
Farmer Duck by Martin Waddell and Helen Oxbury
Farming by Gail Gibbons
I Love Animals by Flora McDonnell
Old MacDonald by Rosemary Wells
Raising Cows on the Koebels' Farm by Alice K. Flanagan and Romie Flanagan

Write Away!

Literacy Skill Focus
Concepts of Print
(Functions of Print)
Letter Recognition
Listening and Speaking
Vocabulary

Vocabulary

brainstorm
chart
crayon
fiddle
friend
invitation
letter
list
marker
name
note
pen
pencil
poem
reason
recipe
shopping list
tools
typewriter
why
write

Materials

chart paper
computer keyboard (or template of keyboard)
construction paper
markers, crayons, pens, pencils

What Children Will Learn

1. About the importance of writing
2. Different instruments that are used for writing

Related Themes

Animals
Communication

Preparation

Before the children arrive, write the following note on construction paper and hang it where the children can easily see it. (See Message Board on page 127.)

Dear Children,
We like to write with a typewriter. What do you like to write with?
Sincerely,
Cows That Type

What to Do

- Point to the note from the cows posted on the Message Board. Exclaim, *Look, we have another note! Those cows sure are busy typing! Let's read it.* Point to the words as you read the note.
- Ask, *What are some things that you write with?* Emphasize there are many kinds of things we write with. Each one has a special name. Invite the children to look around the room and find crayons, markers, pens, pencils, and other things to write with. Collect the writing tools at a table at the front of the room. Demonstrate, or have the children demonstrate, how you write with each one.
- Talk with the children about the different reasons we write. *Remember the invitations we wrote? That's one reason to write. Remember the signs in* Click, Clack, Moo? *That's another reason to write.* Ask, *What are some other reasons to write?*

- Help the children brainstorm a list of things we write, such as our names, a note, a recipe, a poem, a shopping list, an invitation, and a letter to a friend. Say, *We can save our ideas by writing them down. That's another reason to write!* Think aloud as you write the children's ideas on chart paper. Point to each word as you read aloud the completed chart.

Simplify It

Ask the children to write a message or draw a picture for someone in their family.

Add a Challenge

If you have a computer in the room, have the children take turns typing on the keyboard. You can also find keyboard templates online. Print the template, make photocopies, and distribute a template to each child. Ask the children to find the first letter in their name on the keyboard. When the children are able to recognize specific letters, hold up letter cards and ask the children to find that letter on the keyboard.

Assessment

To assess each child's learning, consider the following:

1. Is the child able to understand why writing is important in everyday life?
2. Is the child able to name different things that are used for writing?

Cleo and Theo's Book Suggestions

A Letter to Amy by Ezra Jack Keats
Lots of Letters: From A to Z by Tish Rabe and Kevan Atteberry

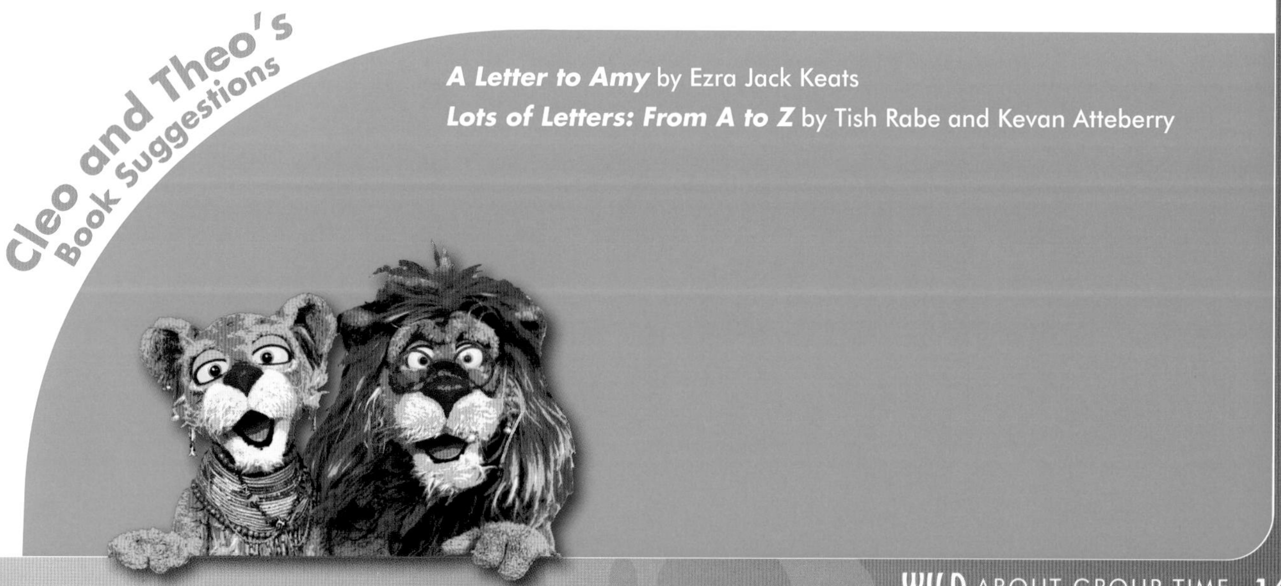

Goodbye!

Literacy Skill Focus
Concepts of Print
Differentiating Fantasy from Reality
Listening and Speaking
Phonological Awareness (Rhythm and Rhyme)
Vocabulary

Vocabulary

cat
chart
cow
dog
fantasy
fiddle
guitar
instrument
music
reality
rhyme
violin

Materials

chart paper
construction paper
markers
picture of a fiddle

What Children Will Learn

1. To begin to distinguish fantasy from reality
2. About musical instruments
3. About rhyming

Related Themes

Communication
Music

Preparation

Write the words to "Hey, Diddle, Diddle" on chart paper. Before the children arrive, write the following note on construction paper and hang it where the children can easily see it. (See Message Board on page 127.)

Dear Children,
We have had fun writing notes to you, but this is our last one. We must go back to the farm. Farmer Brown needs us. Click, clack, moo.
Goodbye,
Cows That Type

What to Do

- Point to the note from the cows posted on the message board. Say, *Who do you think this note is from? Let's read it.* Point to the words as you read. Ask, *Did you like getting notes from the cows? I'm going to miss those silly cows. Are you?*
- Tell the children that you are going to recite a silly nursery rhyme about a cat, a cow, a dog, and a fiddle. Show the children a picture of a fiddle and explain that a fiddle is another name for a violin.

Hey, Diddle, Diddle
Hey, diddle, diddle,
The cat and the fiddle,
The cow jumped over the moon.
The little dog laughed to see such a sight,
And the dish ran away with the spoon.

- Recite the nursery rhyme several times. Tell the children to close their eyes and form a picture about what is happening in the nursery rhyme. Ask, *What did you see when you listened to the words of the poem? What did the cat do? What did the cow do? What did the dish do?*
- Display the poem chart. Tell the children that these are the words to the poem you just recited. Show the children where you will start reading and where you will stop. Point to each word as you recite the poem again. Invite the children to recite each line after you.
- Ask questions to help the children differentiate fantasy from reality. *Can a cat play a fiddle? Do you think a cow can jump over the moon? Does a dish have legs? Does a spoon have legs?*
- Recite the nursery rhyme again. This time, whisper the rhyming words (*diddle/fiddle, moon/spoon*) for emphasis.

Simplify It

Read and sing different versions of "Old MacDonald Had a Farm" or "The Wheels on the Bus."

Add a Challenge

Ask the children to name other words that rhyme with some of the words in the poem. (*What rhymes with* cat *or* dish?)

Assessment

To assess each child's learning, consider the following:

1. Is the child able to distinguish fantasy from reality?
2. Does the child see the humor in the poem?
3. Can the child recognize rhyming words?

Cleo and Theo's Book Suggestions

And the Dish Ran Away with the Spoon by Janet Stevens and Susan Stevens Crummel
Hey Diddle Diddle by Theresa Howell
Old MacDonald by Rosemary Wells
Old Macdonald Had a Farm by Pam Adams
Old MacDonald Had a Farm illustrated by Carol Jones
The Wheels on the Bus by Paul O. Zelinsky

Note to Families About the Topic of Silly Animal Stories

FAMILY LETTER

Date ______________

Dear Families,

We are reading the book *Click, Clack, Moo* about cows that type! The cows write a note to Farmer Brown asking for an electric blanket to keep them warm. We are also reading a book about seals and other animals that go to a party on a bus. (You can sing this story to the tune of "The Wheels on the Bus.")

We are writing messages to each other and learning about the different reasons to write, and we are learning about the letter "C."

Here are some things that you can do at home with your child to reinforce what we are learning at school.

- Write and read a note to your child. Your note might say "I love you," "Let's go for a walk," "Would you like to have pizza for dinner?" or "Thank you for helping me sort the socks."
- Have your child help you write a grocery list.
- Visit a farm or look at a book about farms together. Talk about different farm animals and the noises they make.
- If you know them, sing the songs "Old MacDonald Had a Farm" and "The Wheels on the Bus" with your child.
- Make the letter "C" out of string, yarn, or ribbon.

Thank you!

Helping

CHAPTER 7

This topic lets the children in your classroom explore the themes of helping, cooperation, and teamwork as they enjoy the classic tale of "The Little Red Hen," as well as a modern retelling that gives the story a new twist. The children also practice their counting and rhyming skills while reading about a duck that gets stuck in the muck.

Setting Up the Room

- Create a Community Helpers wall display with labeled pictures or photos of firefighters, police officers, postal workers, nurses, doctors, teachers, librarians, sanitation workers, and other community helpers. Encourage the children to look at the pictures and talk about what community helpers do and what special tools and clothes they use and wear to perform their jobs.

- Display number charts at the children's eye level around the classroom. Encourage children to count the objects on the charts.

- Create a Community Helpers browsing box and a box with different versions of "The Little Red Hen." Label each box with words and a matching picture or symbol so the children can identify the contents and browse on their own.

Family Letter

Prepare and make photocopies of the Family Letter on page 170 that explains this topic. Give the letter to parents at pick-up time before you begin the topic.

Helping Friends

Literacy Skill Focus
Book Appreciation (Genre)
Listening and Speaking
Name Recognition
Phonological Awareness (Rhythm and Repetition)
Predicting
Vocabulary

Vocabulary

flour
grains
grinding
help
learn
mill
name
plant
recognize
sing
wheat

Materials

chart paper
children's name cards
The Little Red Hen (by Byron Barton or another author) or another favorite folktale about helping
markers

What Children Will Learn

1. To recognize their names in print
2. About the importance of helping

Related Theme

Friends

Preparation

Write the words to this call-and-response song on chart paper. Use a different colored marker for the children's parts.

Where Is…?
(Tune: "Where Is Thumbkin?")
Teacher: Where is (name of child)? (Hold up child's name card.)
Teacher: Where is (name of child)? (Hold up child's name card.)
Child: Here I (we) am (are). (Child(ren) stand(s) up as sings.)
Child: Here I (we) am (are). (Child(ren) stand(s) up as sings.)
Teacher: How are you today (name of child)?
Teacher: How are you today (name of child)?
Child: Very well I (we) thank you.
Child: Very well I (we) thank you.
Teacher: Please sit down.
Teacher: Please sit down.

What to Do

- Sing a verse of "Where Is…?" for each child or for two children at a time.
- Hold up the children's name cards as you begin each verse. Help the children who cannot recognize their name in print. *Get ready, Tamara; we will be singing to you next.*
  Note: Repeat this song often so the children learn the names of their friends.

Helping

- After you sing the song, tell the children that today you are going to read a book about a little red hen who asks her friends to help her make bread. Ask, *Have you ever helped someone cook or bake something? Whom did you help? What did you cook or bake? What did you do to help?*
- Read aloud a traditional version of "The Little Red Hen" or another favorite folktale about helping. As you read, ask questions to prompt the children to predict what the characters will say and do.
- After you finish reading the story, talk with the children about it. Ask questions such as:
  - *What does the little red hen do to make the bread?*
  - *How do you think the little red hen feels when her friends won't help her?*
  - *Why do you think the little red hen says that her friends can't eat the bread?*

Simplify It

Ask the children to tell you what they liked about the story.

Add a Challenge

Ask the children to say why they think the animals did not help the little red hen.

Assessment

To assess each child's learning, consider the following:

1. Is the child able to recognize her name in print?
2. Is the child able to learn the importance of helping others?

Cleo and Theo's Book Suggestions

Armadilly Chili by Helen Ketteman and Will Terry
Cook-A-Doodle-Doo! by Janet Stevens and Susan Stevens Crummel
Digger Pig and the Turnip by Caron Lee Cohen and Christopher Denise
The Little Red Hen by Byron Barton
The Little Red Hen by Jerry Pinkney
The Little Red Hen by Paul Galdone
The Little Red Hen and the Ear of Wheat by Mary Finch and Elizabeth Bell
Mañana, Iguana by Ann Whitford Paul and Ethan Long
Rockabye Crocodile: A Folktale from the Philippines by Jose Aruego and Ariane Dewey
With Love, Little Red Hen by Alma Flor Ada and Leslie Tryon

Reading The Little Red Hen (Makes a Pizza)

Literacy Skill Focus
Active Listening
Concepts of Print
Listening and Speaking
Parts of a Book
Predicting
Story Comprehension
Vocabulary

Vocabulary

anchovies
author
chop
describe
dough
grate
illustrator
knead
mix
mozzarella
pepperoni
pickled eggplant
pizza
pound
predict
roll
slice
spread
stir
toppings
tossing

Materials

apron and/or chef's hat (optional)

The Little Red Hen (Makes a Pizza) by Philemon Sturges and Amy Walrod

What Children Will Learn

1. About how to make a pizza
2. About the importance of helping and sharing

Related Themes

Cooking
Food

What to Do

- Tell the children that you are going to read another book about a little red hen. Show the children the book cover. Ask them to describe what they see and to predict what the story will be about. Then read aloud the title, pointing to each word. Ask, *Now, what do you think the story will be about?*
- Read aloud the names of the author and illustrator and ask the children what each did to make the book.

  Note: To set the mood, you may want to wear an apron and/or a chef's hat.
- Set a listening focus—ask the children to listen for what the little red hen does to make the pizza. As you read, use a different voice for each character. Encourage the children to chime in with the repeating phrase that the dog, cat, and duck say.
- Use the illustrations to explain the meaning of unfamiliar words such as *mozzarella*, *anchovies*, *pepperoni*, and *pickled eggplant*.
- Use hand motions to demonstrate the meaning of cooking words such as *stirred*, *mixed*, *kneaded*, *pounded*, *chopped*, *grated*, *sliced*, and *spread*.
- When the little red hen asks her friends if they would like some pizza and if they will help do the dishes, ask the children to predict what the friends will say.

- After you finish reading the story, talk with the children about it. Ask questions such as:
  - *Did you like the story? What was your favorite part?*
  - *Do you think the little red hen should have shared her pizza with her friends, even though they didn't help her make it? Why or why not?*
  - *What would you have done if you were the little red hen? Why?*

Simplify It

To help the children understand the meaning of some of the vocabulary words, display a mixing bowl, a wooden spoon, and a rolling pin. Talk about how the little red hen made the pizza dough. Demonstrate how she mixed the flour and water in the mixing bowl and stirred them together to make the dough. Explain that dough is a mixture of flour and water. Have the children make stirring motions with you. Show the children how to knead dough by pressing and turning a large lump of clay with your hands to form a round shape. Then use a rolling pin to roll the clay flat. If you like, try tossing it in the air like the little red hen did!

Add a Challenge

Ask the children to write a version of this story. How is their version the same, and how is it different?

Assessment

To assess each child's learning, consider the following:

1. Is the child able to learn how to make pizza?
2. Is the child able to understand the importance of helping and sharing?

Cleo and Theo's Book Suggestions

Armadilly Chili by Helen Ketteman and Will Terry
Cook-A-Doodle-Doo! by Janet Stevens and Susan Stevens Crummel
The Little Red Hen and the Ear of Wheat by Mary Finch and Elizabeth Bell
Mañana, Iguana by Ann Whitford Paul and Ethan Long
Pizza at Sally's by Monica Wellington
Pizza Counting by Christina Dobson and Matthew Holmes
Rockabye Crocodile: A Folktale from the Philippines by Jose Aruego and Ariane Dewey
With Love, Little Red Hen by Alma Flor Ada and Leslie Tryon

Pizza Toppings Chart

Literacy Skill Focus
Concepts of Print (Directionality, Print Conveys Meaning)
Letter Recognition
Listening and Speaking
Vocabulary

Vocabulary

answer
chart
different
on top of
pizza
question
same
toppings

Materials

chart paper
markers
paper
scissors

What Children Will Learn

1. To create a chart
2. To understand similarities and differences

Related Themes

Food
Shapes

Preparation

Cut out one very large circle for the chart and enough smaller circles to have one for each child.

What to Do

- Tell the children that they are going to help you create a chart that shows all the different pizza toppings that they like.
- Show the children the illustration of the pizza with all the toppings in *The Little Red Hen (Makes a Pizza)*. Explain that people like different foods on their pizza. We call these foods *toppings* because they are placed on top of the pizza. Help the children name some of the toppings on the little red hen's pizza.
- On a very large, precut circle, write the question, *What pizza topping do you like best?* Think aloud as you write. *I am starting to write here—on the top of the paper—because we read from top to bottom. I am starting here on the left side because we read in this direction—from left to right.* Point to the words as you read aloud the question.
- Ask the children to name their favorite pizza topping or one they would like to try. Write their responses in full sentences under the question.

Priscilla likes cheese.
Kevin likes olives.
Enrique likes mushrooms.

- Point to each word as you read aloud the completed chart. Invite the children to read their sentence with you. Does the class have a shared favorite pizza topping?
- Help the children discover the topping (or toppings) that more than one child likes. *Are there toppings that only one child likes?*

Helping

What pizza topping do you like best?

Priscilla likes cheese.

Kevin likes olives.

Enrique likes mushrooms.

Simplify It

Ask the children to draw a picture of a pizza with their favorite topping on it.

Add a Challenge

Point out that "pizza" begins with the letter "p." Invite the children to find the letter "p" on the chart. How many can they find?

Assessment

To assess each child's learning, consider the following:

1. Is the child able to understand how a chart is constructed?
2. Is the child able to see that some children like the same toppings on their pizza, and others like different toppings?

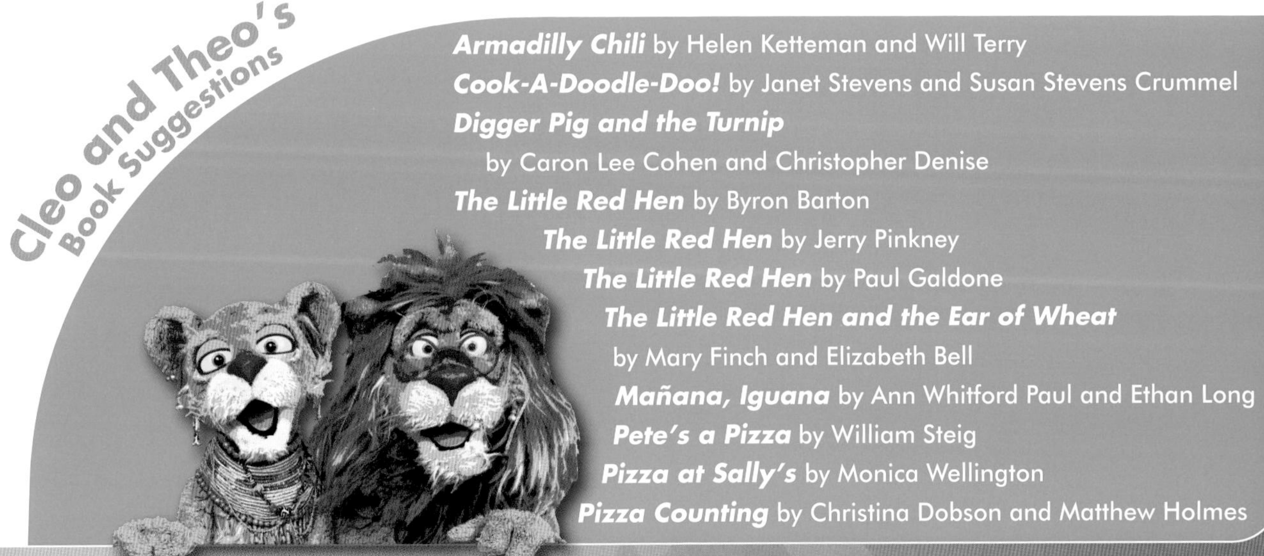

Cleo and Theo's Book Suggestions

Armadilly Chili by Helen Ketteman and Will Terry
Cook-A-Doodle-Doo! by Janet Stevens and Susan Stevens Crummel
Digger Pig and the Turnip by Caron Lee Cohen and Christopher Denise
The Little Red Hen by Byron Barton
The Little Red Hen by Jerry Pinkney
The Little Red Hen by Paul Galdone
The Little Red Hen and the Ear of Wheat by Mary Finch and Elizabeth Bell
Mañana, Iguana by Ann Whitford Paul and Ethan Long
Pete's a Pizza by William Steig
Pizza at Sally's by Monica Wellington
Pizza Counting by Christina Dobson and Matthew Holmes

Environmental Print in *The Little Red Hen (Makes a Pizza)*

Literacy Skill Focus
Concepts of Print
Listening and Speaking
Recall and Retell
Vocabulary

Vocabulary

delicatessen
delicious
dough
flat
flour
grated
hardware store
kneaded
mozzarella
pan
pepperoni
pickled eggplant
pizza slicer
round
sliced
spices
stirred
supermarket
toppings

Materials

The Little Red Hen (Makes a Pizza) by Philemon Sturges and Amy Walrod

What Children Will Learn

1. About environmental print
2. New vocabulary words

Related Themes

Animals
Food

What to Do

- Read aloud *The Little Red Hen (Makes a Pizza)*. Invite the children to chime in on the repeating phrases.
- Linger over each page to allow the children to explore and talk about the fun details in the art. For example, ask the children to talk about what the duck, the dog, and the cat are doing each time the little red hen asks for help.
- Point out and read some of the food labels and other examples of environmental print in the artwork. Point out the name (Biscuits) on the box the dog is wearing. When you read about the pizza's delicious smell when it comes out of the oven, explain that when something smells delicious, it smells so good you can't wait to eat it. When something tastes delicious, it tastes great!
- Ask the children to tell you words that they have noticed in their homes (on cereal boxes, for example) or in their neighborhood (at their grocery store, for example).
- Talk about the different stores (hardware store, supermarket, and delicatessen) and the items the little red hen finds in each. Explain the meaning of unfamiliar words and phrases such as *dough*, *kneaded*, *grated*, and *pickled eggplant*.
- Ask the children to talk about the stores in their neighborhood.

Simplify It

Each time you read the book, focus on helping the children understand one or two new vocabulary words.

Add a Challenge

Read *The Little Red Hen* and *The Little Red Hen (Makes a Pizza)* to the children. Ask questions to help the children compare and contrast the two little red hen stories. Use the illustrations to help the children remember the story details. *Both stories have a little red hen. That's one way the stories are the same. What is another way they are the same?* (In both stories, the little red hen asks her friends to help her make food and her friends don't help her.) *How did the bread taste when it came out of the oven?* (delicious) *How did the pizza taste?* (delicious) Talk about how the stories are different. Ask, *Which book do you like better? Why?*

Assessment

To assess each child's learning, consider the following:

1. Is the child able to connect the environmental print in the story to environmental print in her surroundings?
2. Is the child able to understand the meaning of the new vocabulary words?

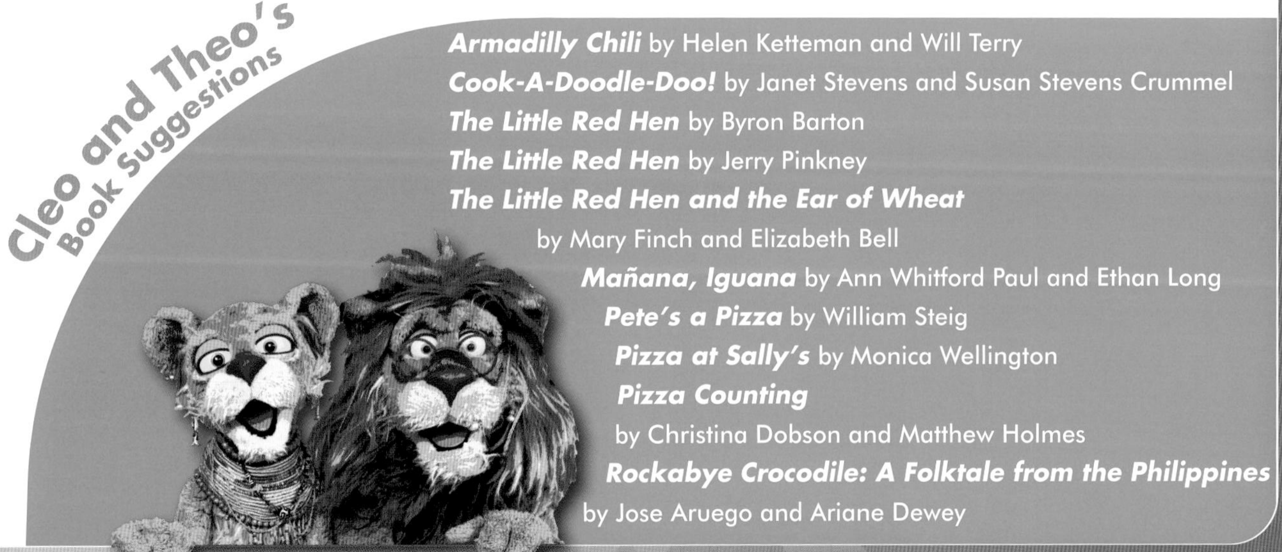

Cleo and Theo's Book Suggestions

Armadilly Chili by Helen Ketteman and Will Terry
Cook-A-Doodle-Doo! by Janet Stevens and Susan Stevens Crummel
The Little Red Hen by Byron Barton
The Little Red Hen by Jerry Pinkney
The Little Red Hen and the Ear of Wheat by Mary Finch and Elizabeth Bell
Mañana, Iguana by Ann Whitford Paul and Ethan Long
Pete's a Pizza by William Steig
Pizza at Sally's by Monica Wellington
Pizza Counting by Christina Dobson and Matthew Holmes
Rockabye Crocodile: A Folktale from the Philippines by Jose Aruego and Ariane Dewey

"What Can We Do to Help Today?"

Literacy Skill Focus
Concepts of Print (Print Conveys Meaning)
Letter Recognition
Listening and Speaking
Phonological Awareness (Rhythm and Repetition)
Vocabulary

Vocabulary

chart
collage
community helper
handprint
help
outline
today
trace
verse

What Children Will Learn

1. How they can help in the classroom
2. How people in the community help them

Related Themes

Friends
Our Community

Preparation

Help the children trace their handprint onto a small square of construction paper or prepare handprints ahead of time, one for each child. Cut out the handprints. Write the words to the song "What Can We Do to Help Today?" on chart paper.

Materials

chart paper
drawing and writing materials
glue or tape
marker, crayon, or pencil
paper
scissors

What to Do

- Ask the children, *What is something you can do to help today?* Write their responses on chart paper. Point to each word as you read the dictation aloud.
- Help the children write their names on their handprints. Use glue or tape to make a collage of all the helping hands.
- Write the title "Helping Hands" in large letters on top of the collage and display it in the classroom. Invite the children to find their hand. Help the children read their sentence on the chart to the group.
- Display the chart paper with the song "What Can We Do to Help Today?" written on it. Tell the children that these are the words to a song. Point to each word as you read the title, "What Can We Do to Help Today?"
- Sing the first verse, pointing to each word as you sing. Sing the song again, inviting the children to join in. Create new verses with the children's names and what they will do to help. (*Jarvis will set the table today. Belinda will feed the turtle today.*)

What Can We Do to Help Today?
(Tune: "Here We Go 'Round the Mulberry Bush")
What can we do to help today?
Help today, help today.
What can we do to help today?
We can help in many ways.

- Explain that there are many people in the community who help us every day. Draw the children's attention to the Community Helpers wall display (see page 149). Talk about how these workers help people in our neighborhoods every day. Ask, *Who are the community helpers in our neighborhood? How do they help us?*

Simplify It

Place in front of you a variety of community helper hats and/or special equipment such as a toy stethoscope. Put on the firefighter hat and say, *I help keep people safe from fires. Who am I?* Repeat for other community helpers and then invite the children to select a hat and say which community helper it belongs to and what that community helper does.

Add a Challenge

Suggest that the children find the letter "Hh" and the word *help* in the song.

Assessment

To assess each child's learning, consider the following:

1. Is the child able to describe what he does to help in the classroom?
2. Is the child able to describe who community helpers are and what they do?

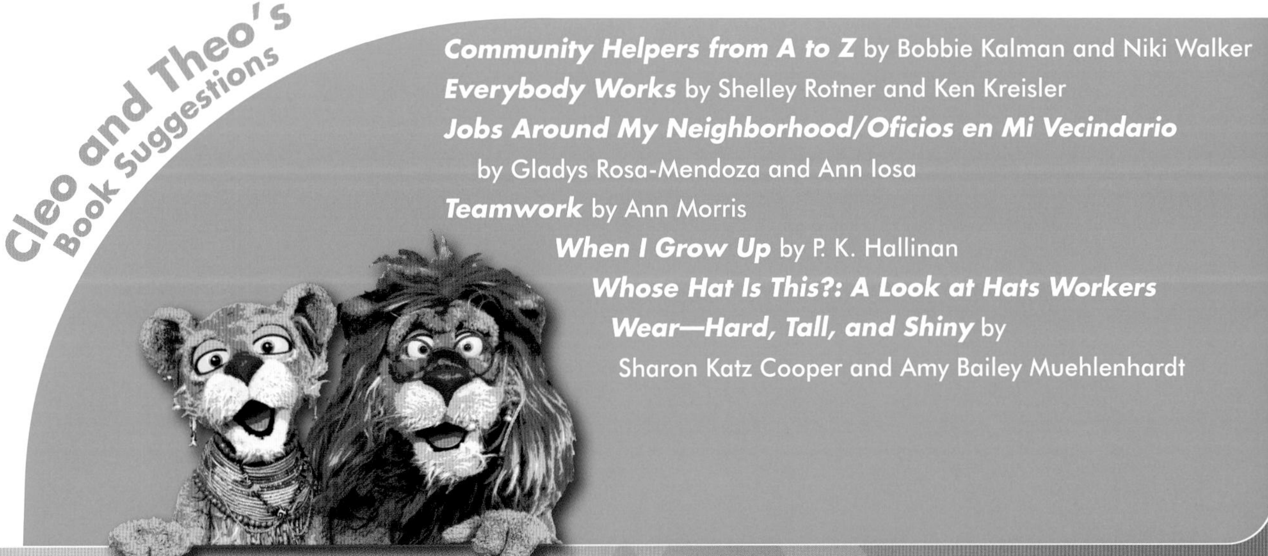

Cleo and Theo's Book Suggestions

Community Helpers from A to Z by Bobbie Kalman and Niki Walker
Everybody Works by Shelley Rotner and Ken Kreisler
Jobs Around My Neighborhood/Oficios en Mi Vecindario by Gladys Rosa-Mendoza and Ann Iosa
Teamwork by Ann Morris
When I Grow Up by P. K. Hallinan
Whose Hat Is This?: A Look at Hats Workers Wear—Hard, Tall, and Shiny by Sharon Katz Cooper and Amy Bailey Muehlenhardt

Who Can Help?

Literacy Skill Focus
Concepts of Print
Making Connections
Parts of a Book
Phonological Awareness (Rhyming)
Predicting
Story Comprehension
Vocabulary

Vocabulary

animal, author, blossom, chirp, cover, creaky, cricket, croaky, dragonfly, friend, gooey, illustrator, leap, marsh, moose, muck, mud, munch, nibble, plod, pond, possum, predict, skunks, slide, slither, snails, spruce, sticky, story, stuck, swish, teamwork, thickets, trails, trunks, whir, zoom

Materials

One Duck Stuck by Phyllis Root and Jane Chapman

What Children Will Learn

1. About ducks and where they live
2. About asking for help

Related Themes

Animals
Friends
Sounds

What to Do

- Tell the children that today you are going to read a story about a duck that asks its friends for help. Ask, *Have you ever asked for help? Whom did you ask? Did they help? What did they do to help you?*
- Show the children the front cover. Point to the words as you read aloud the title and the names of the author and the illustrator. Tell the children that in the story, a duck gets stuck in the muck and asks its animal friends for help. Ask the children to predict how the friends will help the duck.
- Point to the mud on the cover. Tell the children that muck is deep, sticky, gooey mud. Say, *The duck can't get his foot out of the muck: It's stuck! The duck can't move. The duck lives in a marsh. A marsh is wet land near a pond or stream. A pond is a small lake. Ducks and other animals live on or near ponds.*
- Read the book slowly and with expression, emphasizing the rhyming words. Ask the children to listen for how the duck's friends help.
- Encourage the children to call out the duck's refrain before you turn each page.
- Help the children understand all the words in the book:
  - Use the illustrations to clarify the meanings of unfamiliar words such as *marsh*, *moose*, *spruce*, *crickets*, *thickets*, *skunks*, *trunks*, *snails*, *trails*, *possums*, *blossoms*, and *dragonflies*.

Helping

- Use gestures and motions to demonstrate the meaning of words such as *swish, munch, plod, leap, slide, nibble, slither, zooming*, and *whir*.
- Use your voice to demonstrate the meaning of words such as *chirp, creaky*, and *croaky*.

- Show the children the final illustration of the stuck moose. Ask, *What is happening in this picture? What do you think will happen next?*
- Talk with the children about the book. Ask questions such as:
  - *Did you like the story? What was your favorite part?*
  - *What do the friends do to help the duck get unstuck?*
  - *Does this story remind you of another story we have read?*

Simplify It

To help the children internalize the meaning of new words, show them how to act out a few of the words that are new to them.

Add a Challenge

Teach the children about the animals in the book. Say, *Let's look at the pictures in the book to see what animals live in the marsh with the duck.* As you turn the pages, point to the different animals and help the children name them. Talk about animals the children may not be familiar with.

Assessment

To assess each child's learning, consider the following:

1. What did the child learn about ducks?
2. What did the child learn about helping?

Cleo and Theo's Book Suggestions

Armadilly Chili by Helen Ketteman and Will Terry
Cook-A-Doodle-Doo! by Janet Stevens and Susan Stevens Crummel
The Little Red Hen by Byron Barton
The Little Red Hen by Jerry Pinkney
The Little Red Hen by Paul Galdone
The Little Red Hen and the Ear of Wheat by Mary Finch and Elizabeth Bell
Mañana, Iguana by Ann Whitford Paul and Ethan Long
Rockabye Crocodile: A Folktale from the Philippines by Jose Aruego and Ariane Dewey
With Love, Little Red Hen by Alma Flor Ada and Leslie Tryon

Helping Hands

Literacy Skill Focus
Phonological Awareness (Beginning Sounds)
Recall and Retell
Story Comprehension
Story Structure
Vocabulary

Vocabulary

begin
collage
end
first
help
lowercase
next
retell
sentence
start
story
uppercase

Materials

Helping Hands collage (see page 158)
index card
marker

What Children Will Learn

1. To retell a story
2. The importance of working together and helping others

Related Themes

Animals
Food

Preparation

Write the uppercase and lowercase letter "Hh" on an index card.

What to Do

- Help the children retell the story of *The Little Red Hen (Makes a Pizza)*.
- Ask the children questions to help them with their retelling. *How does the story start? What happens next? What do the cat, dog, and duck say? What does the little red hen do next? How does the story end?*
- Engage the children in a discussion about helping.
- Show the children the letter "Hh" index card you created. Have them trace the letters in the air.
- Organize the children into pairs, facing you. Choose a pair to help you demonstrate. Ask each pair to stand side by side with their hands at their sides. then have them take two steps away from each other. Display the letter "H" card and explain that they have made the two lines that go down and up. Say, *Now bend the arm that is closest to your partner. Reach your hand toward your partner and grasp your partner's hand. You've just made an uppercase "H"!*
- Display the Helping Hands collage (page 162). Tell the children that many words on this collage begin with the letter "H." Ask them to find the letter "H" on the collage.

- Ask each child, *What does your helping hand say?* Invite the children to find their hand on the collage and read their sentence to the group. Applaud after each reading. After the last reading, have the class give themselves a hand!

Simplify It

Read a few pages of the book to the children, and then ask the children what comes next.

Add a Challenge

Ask the children to add to the Helping Hands collage.

Assessment

To assess each child's learning, consider the following:

1. Is the child able to retell the story?
2. Is the child able to understand the importance of working together and helping others?

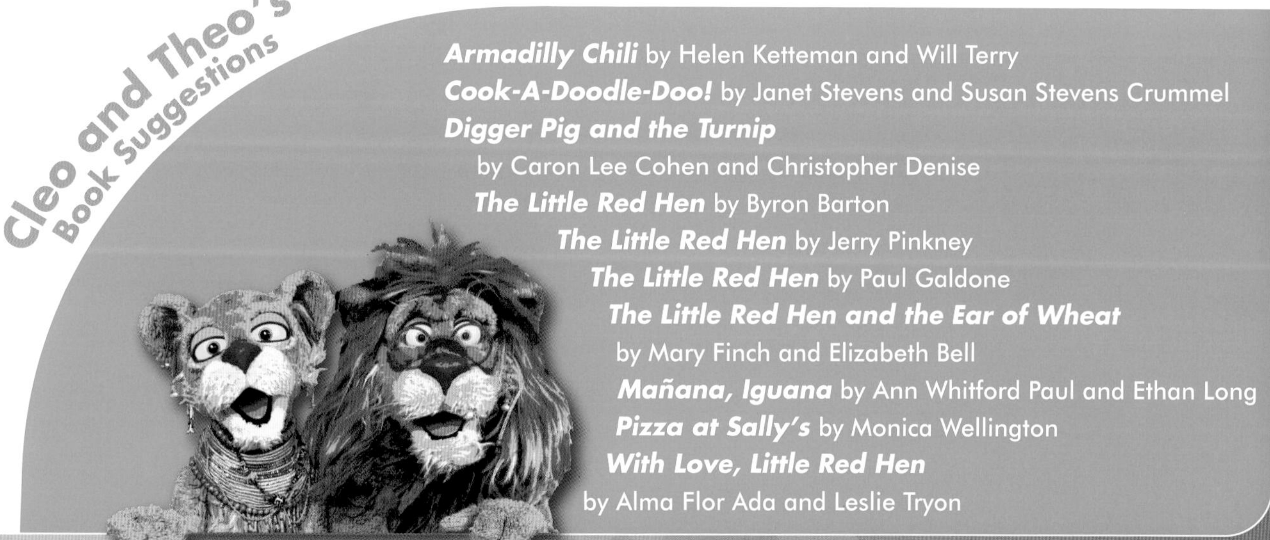

Cleo and Theo's Book Suggestions

Armadilly Chili by Helen Ketteman and Will Terry
Cook-A-Doodle-Doo! by Janet Stevens and Susan Stevens Crummel
Digger Pig and the Turnip by Caron Lee Cohen and Christopher Denise
The Little Red Hen by Byron Barton
The Little Red Hen by Jerry Pinkney
The Little Red Hen by Paul Galdone
The Little Red Hen and the Ear of Wheat by Mary Finch and Elizabeth Bell
Mañana, Iguana by Ann Whitford Paul and Ethan Long
Pizza at Sally's by Monica Wellington
With Love, Little Red Hen by Alma Flor Ada and Leslie Tryon

Reading *One Duck Stuck*

Literacy Skill Focus
Counting
Number Concepts
Story Comprehension

Vocabulary

count
crawl
how many
increase
jump
leap
number
numeral
plod
slide
swim

Materials

chart paper
markers
One Duck Stuck by Phyllis Root and Jane Chapman

What Children Will Learn

1. About counting
2. About the order of numbers when counting

Related Themes
Animals
Counting
Numbers

Preparation

Write the numerals 1–10 on chart paper. Next to each number, make the corresponding number of dots. For example, write 3 and then make three dots next to the number.

1 ●
2 ●●
3 ●●●
4 ●●●●
5 ●●●●●
6 ●●●●●●
7 ●●●●●●●
8 ●●●●●●●●
9 ●●●●●●●●●
10 ●●●●●●●●●●

What to Do

- Explain to the children that *One Duck Stuck* is a counting book. Have the children count to 10 with you as you point to the numerals on a class number chart.
- Explain to the children that as you read the book they should focus their attention on counting the animals in the story.
- Point to the numerals as you say each number and count the animals next to the numeral.

Helping

- Point to the animals in the large illustration and invite the children to count them with you.
- When you are about to turn the page to the three moose, ask, *Last time two animals offered to help, how many animals do you think will offer to help now?* Do this two or three more times during the reading to help the children recognize that each time the animals increase in number.

Simplify It

Focus on the names of the animals and the sounds they make. Add the counting component when the children are ready.

Add a Challenge

Ask the children to count the animals on each page in the book.

Assessment

To assess each child's learning, consider the following:

1. Is the child able to count to 10?
2. Does the child know the sequence of numbers from 1 to 10?

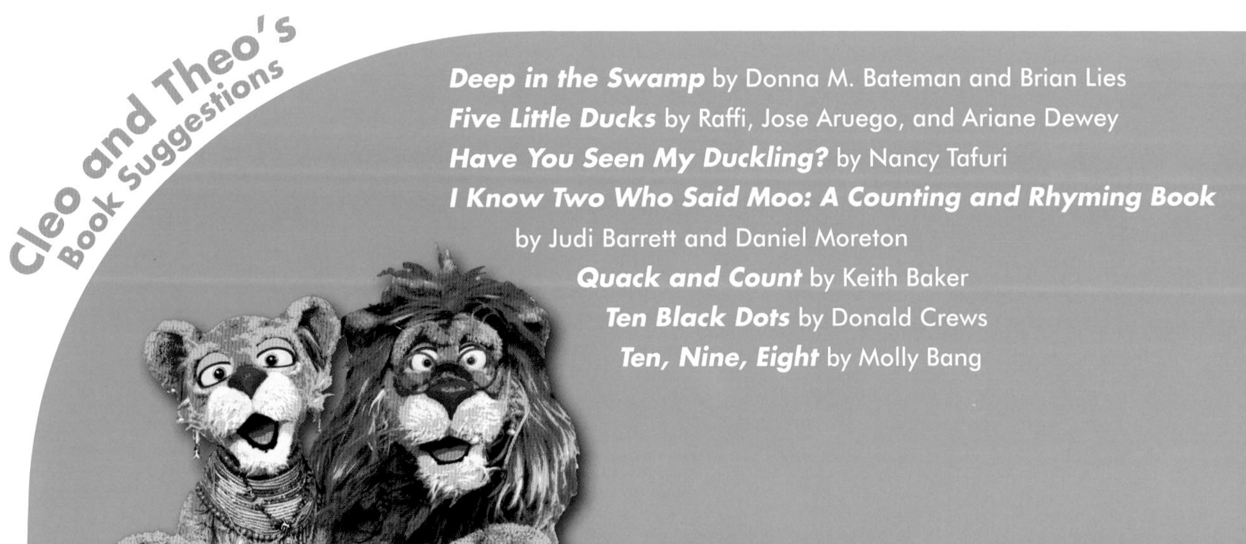

Cleo and Theo's Book Suggestions

Deep in the Swamp by Donna M. Bateman and Brian Lies
Five Little Ducks by Raffi, Jose Aruego, and Ariane Dewey
Have You Seen My Duckling? by Nancy Tafuri
I Know Two Who Said Moo: A Counting and Rhyming Book by Judi Barrett and Daniel Moreton
Quack and Count by Keith Baker
Ten Black Dots by Donald Crews
Ten, Nine, Eight by Molly Bang

Together

Literacy Skill Focus
Phonological Awareness (Rhythm, Rhyme, and Repetition)
Recall and Retell
Story Comprehension
Vocabulary

Vocabulary

clomp
crawl
crickets
dragonflies
duck
fish
frogs
jump
leap
moose
plod
plop
plunk
possums
skunks
slide
slink
slither
slosh
snails
snakes
splish
stuck
swim
teamwork
whir
zing

Materials

none needed

What Children Will Learn

1. About the importance of working together
2. To sing a song with the class

Related Themes

Animals
Sounds

What to Do

- Tell the children you are going to sing a song about *One Duck Stuck*. The song is called "Teamwork." Ask the children if they know what *teamwork* means. Explain that *teamwork* means "when a group works together."
- Sing "Teamwork."

Teamwork
(Tune: "Row, Row, Row Your Boat")

Pull, pull, pull the duck
From the gooey muck.
Together, together, together, together,
The duck is really stuck.

Pull, pull, pull the duck
From the gooey muck.
With teamwork, teamwork, teamwork, teamwork,
We'll get that duck unstuck!
– Splunk!

Pull, pull, and pull some more
Let's all pull the moose.
Together, together, together, together,
We'll work to get it loose.

Pull, pull, and pull some more
Come on let's pull the moose.
With teamwork, teamwork, teamwork, teamwork,
The moose will soon be loose!
– Splunk!

- Invite the children to sing the song with you.
- After singing the song, invite each child to choose an animal from the song or the story and act out how the animal sounds and/or moves. Make sure the children have space to move without bumping into one another.

- Prompt each child (or group of children) in turn to sound and/or move like the animal he chose. Here are the movement and sound words that go with each animal:

duck/stuck/spluck	skunks/crawl/plunk
fish/swim/splish	snails/slide/sloosh
moose/plod/clomp	possums/crawl/slosh
crickets/leap/pleep	snakes/slither/slink
frogs/jump/plop	dragonflies/whir/zing

- At the end, have everyone join hands to pull the duck out of the muck!

Simplify It

Sing the song or act out the movements. Once the children master one part, introduce the other.

Add a Challenge

After the children are familiar with the song, act it out. Have one child be the stuck duck and another child the stuck moose. Organize the rest of the class into two groups—one in a line behind the "duck" and the other in a line behind the "moose." As the children sing the first two verses, have the first group gently pull together until the duck becomes unstuck on the word *splunk*. Sing the last two verses while the second group gently pulls together to release the moose.

Assessment

To assess each child's learning, consider the following:

1. Is the child able to understand the importance of working together?
2. Is the child able to sing the song with the class?

Cleo and Theo's Book Suggestions

Community Helpers from A to Z by Bobbie Kalman and Niki Walker
Everybody Works by Shelley Rotner and Ken Kreisler
Good Bread: A Book of Thanks by Brigitte Weninger and Anne Moller
Kevin and His Dad by Irene Smalls and Michael Hays
Little Nino's Pizzeria by Karen Barbour
Preschool to the Rescue by Judy Sierra and Will Hillenbrand
Subway Sparrow by Leyla Torres
Teamwork by Ann Morris
With Love, Little Red Hen by Alma Flor Ada and Leslie Tryon

Rhyming Fun

Literacy Skill Focus

Phonological Awareness (Rhythm, Rhyme, and Repetition)

Vocabulary

buggy
came back
duck
far away
fish
five
four
frogs
logs
muck
muggy
one
over
sad
skunks
snakes
swish
three
trunks
two
wakes
went out

Materials

none needed

What Children Will Learn

1. To sing a song with the class
2. To recognize rhyming words

Related Themes

Animals
Sounds

What to Do

- Ask the children to listen carefully as you say two words. Say, *If the two words rhyme, quack like a duck*. duck, muck. *Do they rhyme? Yes! Quack!*
- Repeat with the following rhyme pairs from *One Duck Stuck*: *fish/swish, frogs/logs, skunks/trunks, snakes/wakes,* and *muggy/buggy*. Alternate with pairs of words that don't rhyme, such as *cat/dog, car/plane, doll/house,* and *ball/can.*
- Tell the children that you are going to teach them a song about five little ducks that go out to play. Tell the children to listen for the rhyming words in the following song:

Five Little Ducks

Five little ducks went out one day
Over the hill and far away.
Mother Duck said, "Quack, quack, quack, quack,"
But only four little ducks came back.

Four little ducks went out one day
Over the hill and far away.
Mother Duck said, "Quack, quack, quack, quack,"
But only three little ducks came back.

Three little ducks went out one day
Over the hill and far away.
Mother Duck said, "Quack, quack, quack, quack,"
But only two little ducks came back.

Two little ducks went out one day
Over the hill and far away.
Mother Duck said, "Quack, quack, quack, quack,"
But only one little duck came back.

One little duck went out one day
Over the hill and far away.
Mother Duck said, "Quack, quack, quack, quack,"
But none of the five little ducks came back.

Sad Mother Duck went out one day
Over the hill and far away.
The sad mother duck said, "Quack, quack, quack."
And all of the five little ducks came back.

Note: "Five Little Ducks" is a traditional song. If you do not know the tune, there are many CDs available that feature this song such as *Animal Favorites*. It is also featured on many websites such as songsforteaching.com and kididdles.com.

- Emphasize the counting aspect of the song by holding up your hand and using your fingers to show how many ducks go out to play in each verse. Put down one finger each time the ducks return.
- Once the children know the song, have them act it out. Select five children. Give each child a number tag (1–5) and signal which ducks go out to play and which come back.

Simplify It

Sing the song using five ducks. Place one behind your back after each verse. Bring them all back after singing the last verse. Also consider singing about three ducks instead of five ducks.

Add a Challenge

Tape a set of number cards onto the floor in numerical order. Have the children count forward as they hop or walk the number path. Then, challenge them to walk and count backward.

Assessment

To assess each child's learning, consider the following:

1. Is the child able to learn the song?
2. Is the child able to recognize the sound of rhyming words?

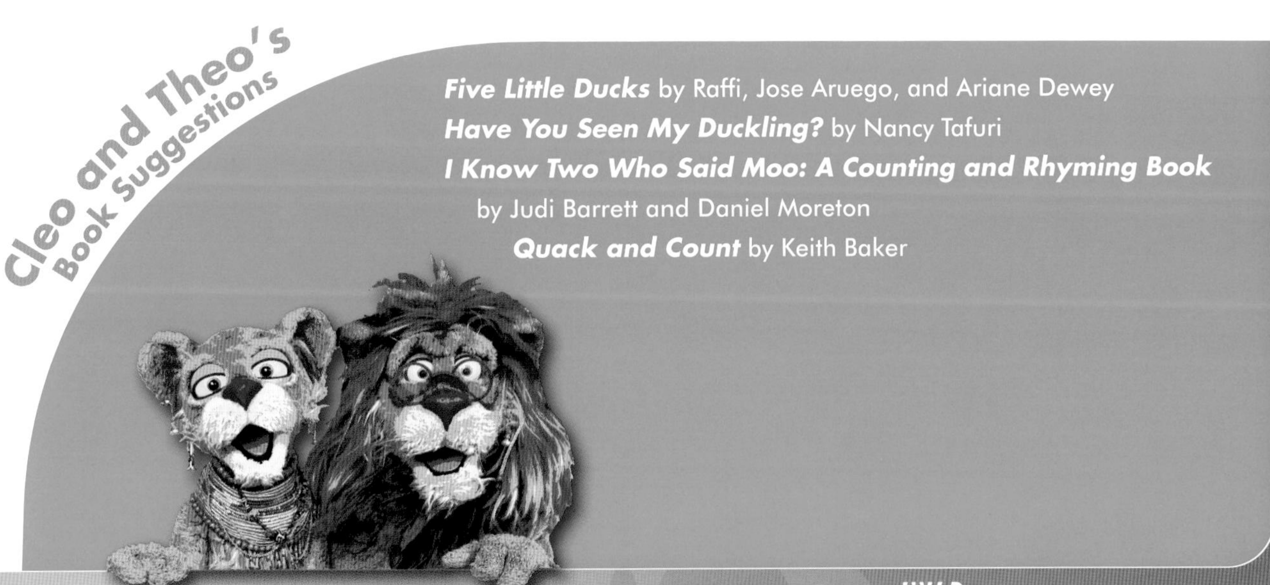

Cleo and Theo's Book Suggestions

Five Little Ducks by Raffi, Jose Aruego, and Ariane Dewey

Have You Seen My Duckling? by Nancy Tafuri

I Know Two Who Said Moo: A Counting and Rhyming Book by Judi Barrett and Daniel Moreton

Quack and Count by Keith Baker

Note to Families About the Topic of Helping

FAMILY LETTER

Date ____________________

Dear Families,

In our classroom, we are learning about the importance of helping, cooperation, and teamwork. We are reading a book about a little red hen who asks her friends to help her make bread. When they say no, she does it herself! We are also reading a modern version of the tale, *The Little Red Hen (Makes a Pizza)*, which gives the story a new twist. Ask your child to tell you about the story.

Here are some things you can do at home with your child:

- Bake bread, make pizza, or prepare some other food together. Ask your child to help you measure and mix the ingredients.
- Together, write or draw a thank-you card for a friend or family member.
- Write a shopping list together. Have your child check off each item as you put it in the cart. Thank your child for helping.
- Visit your neighborhood post office, fire station, health center, and/or library with your child. Talk about how mail carriers, firefighters, doctors, nurses, and librarians help us.

Thank you!

Things That Grow

CHAPTER 8

With this topic, the children in your classroom take a look at two fascinating animals—worms and butterflies. After listening to a nonfiction book about worms, the children help build a worm habitat, observe what worms look like and how they move, and learn how worms help plants grow.

Setting Up the Room

- Create and display a diagram of the four stages of the life cycle of a butterfly: 1) egg, 2) caterpillar, 3) chrysalis, and 4) butterfly.

- Give the children the opportunity to observe and study real worms. You can dig up worms, purchase worms from a bait shop, or order worms from a biological supply catalogue such as Carolina Biological Supply Company (www.carolina.com) or Connecticut Valley Biological (www.ctvalleybio.com). Set up a habitat to house the worms. Use a large glass container with a screen cover or a clear plastic or glass jar and lid filled with holes. Fill the container with soil, worms, and food for the worms (leaves and grass clippings). Keep the soil moist and cool. Cover the container with dark paper or drape it with a dark cloth. Keep a spray bottle filled with water next to the habitat so you can keep the soil damp.

- At the top of a large sheet of chart paper, write the question *Do worms have heads?* Then draw a vertical line down the middle of the paper to create two columns. Label the left column *YES* and the right column *NO*. Display the chart on an easel or a wall at the children's eye level and place markers nearby. As the children arrive and settle down in the morning, direct them and their parents or caregivers to the chart. Encourage parents and caregivers to read the question to their children. Have the children write their names in the *YES* or *NO* columns.

  Change the question each day. Here are some possibilities:
  - Can worms hear us?
  - Do caterpillars eat ice-cream cones?
  - Have you ever seen a butterfly?
  - Did you tell your family about our wonderful worms?

  Refer to the questions and the children's answers during the day. For example, you may want to conduct simple experiments to help answer the question of whether worms can hear or if they have heads.

Family Letter

Prepare and make photocopies of the Family Letter on page 192 that explains this topic. Give the letter to parents at pick-up time before you begin the topic.

Worms KWL Chart

Literacy Skill Focus

Active Listening
Concepts of Print
(Print Conveys Meaning)
Listening and Speaking
Observing and Describing
Vocabulary

Vocabulary

chart
earthworms
know
learn
long
skinny
tunnels
underground
want to know
wiggly
worms

Materials

chart paper
live worm, if possible
markers
paper towel

What Children Will Learn

1. What they know about worms
2. What they want to learn about worms

Related Themes

Animals
Nature

What to Do

- Have the children sit in a circle. Sing a greeting song such as, "Good Morning to You" on page 40, "Sing, Sing, Sing with Me" on page 108, or another greeting song.
- After singing this song, tell the children that they are going to be learning about worms. Ask, *Have you ever seen a worm? Where did you see it? What did it look like?* If possible, show the children a live worm on a damp paper towel. Explain that worms are long, skinny, wiggly animals. There are many types of worms. Earthworms live underground, or under the dirt or soil where we can't see them.
- Make a KWL chart on a large sheet of chart paper, as shown. Write what the children know about worms in the first column. Ask, *What do you want to know about worms?* Write children's questions in the second column of the Worms KWL chart.

Note: A KWL chart can be used for any topic. Make three columns on a sheet of chart paper. At the top of the first column write "What We Know About [the topic]," at the top of the second column write "What We Want to Know About [the topic]," and at the top of the third column write "What We Learned About [the topic]." Ask the children what they know about the topic. Record their answers in the first column. Ask the children what they want to know about the topic and record their responses in the second column. After reading books, doing activities, and exploring materials related to the topic, ask the children what they learned about the topic. Record their responses in the third column. An example of a KWL chart about hippos appears on page 63.

All About Worms KWL Chart		
What We **K**now About Worms	What We **W**ant to Know About Worms	What We **L**earned About Worms
Worms live in the dirt.	Do worms have feet?	
	How do worms eat?	

- Say, *One way to answer our questions is to read a book about worms.* Tell the children that tomorrow you are going to read a book called *Wonderful Worms.*

Simplify It

Read a book about worms and then create the chart.

Add a Challenge

Ask each child to move like a worm.

Assessment

To assess each child's learning, consider the following:

1. Is the child able to say what he knows about worms?
2. Is the child about to say what he wants to learn about worms?

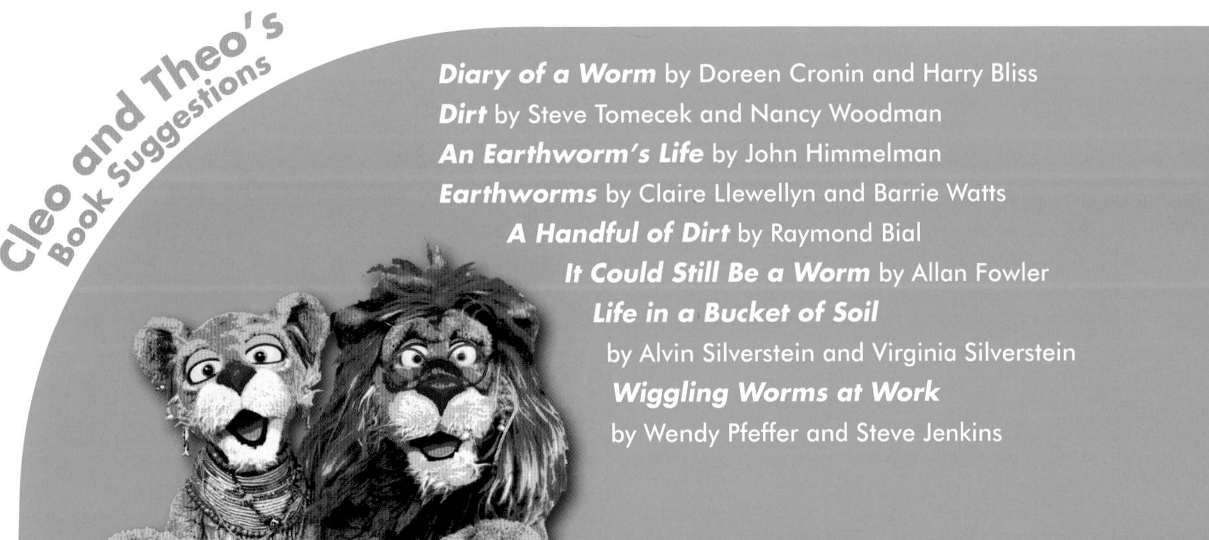

Cleo and Theo's Book Suggestions

Diary of a Worm by Doreen Cronin and Harry Bliss
Dirt by Steve Tomecek and Nancy Woodman
An Earthworm's Life by John Himmelman
Earthworms by Claire Llewellyn and Barrie Watts
A Handful of Dirt by Raymond Bial
It Could Still Be a Worm by Allan Fowler
Life in a Bucket of Soil by Alvin Silverstein and Virginia Silverstein
Wiggling Worms at Work by Wendy Pfeffer and Steve Jenkins

Reading *Wonderful Worms*

Literacy Skill Focus
Book Appreciation (Seeking Information from a Nonfiction Book)
Concepts of Print (Identifying Author and Illustrator)
Listening and Speaking
Story Comprehension
Vocabulary

Vocabulary

author
below
burrows
cover
damp
earthworms
illustrator
long
moist
move
nonfiction
passageways
plants
roots
skinny
soil
spread out
stretch
tail ends
title
tunnels
underground
wiggly
worms

Materials

Wonderful Worms by Linda Glaser and Loretta Krupinski

What Children Will Learn

1. About worms
2. That nonfiction books contain facts

Related Theme

Animals

What to Do

- Show the children the cover of *Wonderful Worms*. Ask a volunteer to point to the title of the book. Read aloud the title, pointing to each word. Then read aloud the names of the author and illustrator, and ask the children what each did to make the book.
- Ask the children what they see on the front cover. Tell the children that *Wonderful Worms* is a nonfiction book. It tells us true facts about earthworms and how they live. The boy on the cover tells us everything he knows about worms.
- Display the first page. Ask a volunteer to point to the worms. As you sweep your hand across the part of the picture that is below ground, say, *This part of the picture is underground, where worms live.* Ask, *What do you see underground in this picture?* Point to the burrows and ask, *What do you think these are?* Explain that they are *tunnels* that worms dig. They are also called *burrows* or *passageways*. Say, *Let's read the book and see what else we can find out about worms.*
- Read slowly and with expression. Ask the children to listen for answers to their questions about worms. Use the illustrations to reinforce the meaning of words such as *roots, passageways, burrows, soil, plants,* and *tail ends*. Use hand motions to demonstrate the meaning of the phrase *spread out*.

- Display the Worms KWL chart (see page 173) and review the children's questions about worms in the second column. Ask, *Can we answer any of these questions now?* Write the children's responses in the third column of the chart. Then ask, *Did you learn anything else about worms?* Prompt with specific questions such as:
  - *Where do worms like to live? Why?*
  - *What do worms eat?*
  - *How do worms dig tunnels?*

  Record the children's responses in the third column of the KWL chart.

Simplify It

Each time you read the book, focus on teaching the children two or three new words.

Add a Challenge

Ask, How do worms move? Yes, they stretch their bodies. When they stretch their bodies, they get long and skinny, just like a rubber band gets long when we stretch it. (Demonstrate by stretching a rubber band.) Then worms squeeze up their back ends and make their bodies short and fat. Have the children lie down on the floor and stretch and squeeze, stretch and squeeze, just like a worm on the move.

Assessment

To assess each child's learning, consider the following:

1. What did the child learn about worms?
2. Is the child able to understand that nonfiction books contain facts about a certain subject matter?

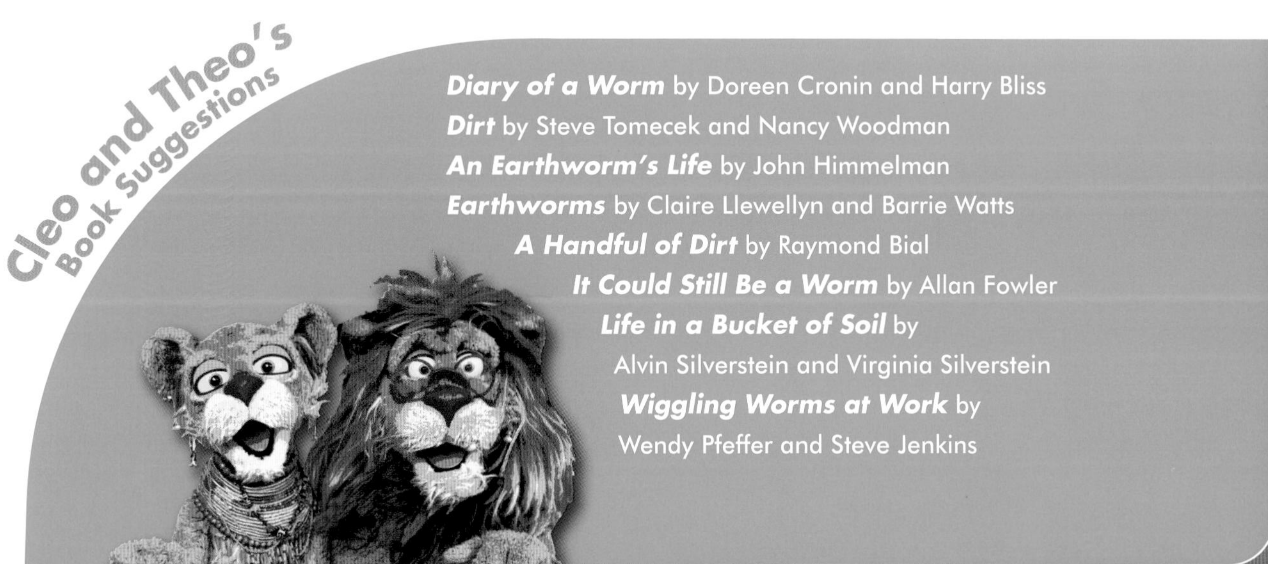

Cleo and Theo's Book Suggestions

Diary of a Worm by Doreen Cronin and Harry Bliss
Dirt by Steve Tomecek and Nancy Woodman
An Earthworm's Life by John Himmelman
Earthworms by Claire Llewellyn and Barrie Watts
A Handful of Dirt by Raymond Bial
It Could Still Be a Worm by Allan Fowler
Life in a Bucket of Soil by Alvin Silverstein and Virginia Silverstein
Wiggling Worms at Work by Wendy Pfeffer and Steve Jenkins

"The Worms Go Digging"

Literacy Skill Focus

Phonological Awareness (Rhythm and Repetition)

Vocabulary

Vocabulary

cover
deep
dig
far and wide
letter
side by side
squeeze
stretch
title
tunnels
under
wiggly
worms

Materials

Wonderful Worms by Linda Glaser and Loretta Krupinski

What Children Will Learn

1. To listen to and say a poem
2. About the letter "W"

Related Themes

Animals

Sounds

What to Do

- Encourage the children to stretch and squeeze their bodies like worms as you recite "The Worms Go Digging."

The Worms Go Digging
The worms go digging side by side,
Stretch, squeeze; stretch, squeeze.
The worms go digging side by side,
Stretch, squeeze; stretch, squeeze.
The worms go digging side by side,
Making tunnels far and wide.

- Invite the children to say the poem with you.
- Explain to the children that the word *worm* begins with the letter "W."
- Tell the children that the letter "W" makes the /w/ sound. Repeat the word *worms,* emphasizing the initial /w/ sound: *wwworms.*
- Hold up the book cover of *Wonderful Worms* and point to the words as you read aloud the title. Ask, *How many words does this title have? Yes, it has two words:* Wonderful Worms. *Let's look at the word* Wonderful. *What is the first letter in the word* Wonderful? (W) *Now, let's look at the second word,* Worms. *What is the first letter in the word* Worms? (W)

Simplify It

Teach the children the poem one line at a time. Ask the children to repeat the line after you say it.

Add a Challenge

Ask the children to look around the room at signs, charts, books, and other materials to find words that have the letter "W" in them.

Assessment

To assess each child's learning, consider the following:

1. Is the child able to say the poem with the class?
2. Is the child able to recognize the letter "W"?

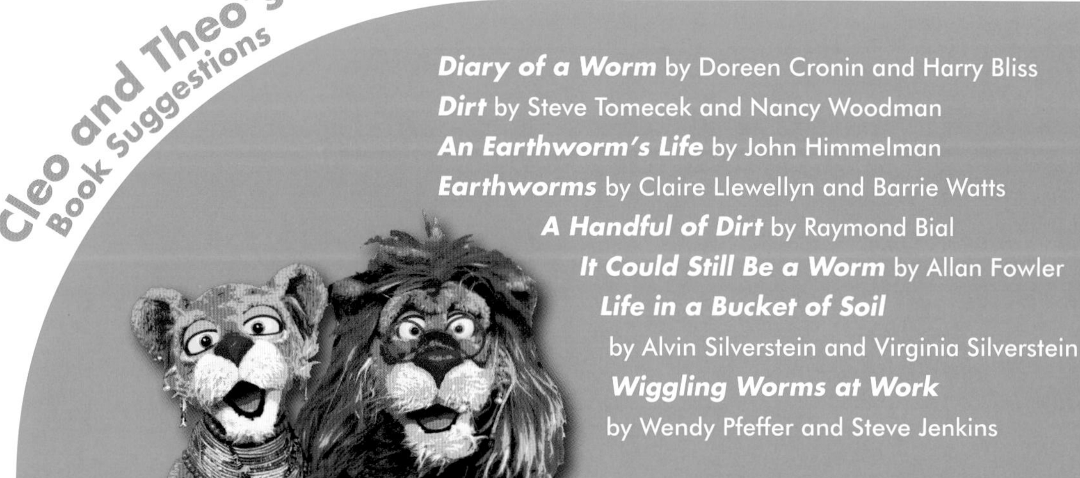

Cleo and Theo's Book Suggestions

Diary of a Worm by Doreen Cronin and Harry Bliss
Dirt by Steve Tomecek and Nancy Woodman
An Earthworm's Life by John Himmelman
Earthworms by Claire Llewellyn and Barrie Watts
A Handful of Dirt by Raymond Bial
It Could Still Be a Worm by Allan Fowler
Life in a Bucket of Soil by Alvin Silverstein and Virginia Silverstein
Wiggling Worms at Work by Wendy Pfeffer and Steve Jenkins

Friend or Foe?

Literacy Skill Focus
Book Appreciation (Seeking Information from Nonfiction Books)
Concepts of Print (Return Sweep)
Phonological Awareness (Rhythm, Rhyme, and Repetition)
Vocabulary

Vocabulary

burrows	predators
foes	quickly
hiding	safely
hole	squirm
moles	wiggle

Materials

chart paper
index card
markers
Wonderful Worms by Linda Glaser and Loretta Krupinski
Worms KWL chart (see page 173)

After reading the book, display the Worms KWL chart (see page 173). Read the third column. Ask, *Who can tell us something new about worms to add to our chart?* Read the children's questions in the second column. Select some of the questions and answers at the back of the book to read aloud. Add new knowledge to the Worms KWL chart.

What Children Will Learn

1. About worms
2. About predators

Related Themes

Friends
Sounds

Preparation

Write the words to "Wiggle, Wiggle" on chart paper.

What to Do

- Tell the children that some animals eat worms to help them grow just like we eat food to help us grow. Say, *As I read* Wonderful Worms, *I want you to look carefully at the illustrations of other animals.*
- As you read, point to the animals. Ask, *What is this animal? Do you think (birds) eat worms? Do (birds) live above ground or below ground?* (**Note**: Birds, frogs, snakes, moles, and lizards eat worms. Dogs, mice, chipmunks, snails, rabbits, and butterflies do not.)
- Before reciting the following poem, explain that the animals that eat other animals are sometimes called its *foes* or *predators*.
- Display the poem "Wiggle, Wiggle" written on chart paper. Point to each word as you read aloud the title. Say, *Let me see you wiggle like worms!* Tell the children that the poem is about how worms hide from their foes—the animals that eat them. Ask a volunteer to point to and name the picture of the worm's foe on the chart.
- Recite the poem on the next page. Move your finger under the words, exaggerating slightly the return sweep of your hand to the beginning of the next line.

Wiggle, Wiggle
Wiggle, wiggle, little worm
How I like to watch you squirm!
Down your hole you quickly go
Safely hiding from your foe.
Wiggle, wiggle, little worm
How I like to watch you squirm.
Down your hole you quickly run
Safely hiding from the sun.

- After reciting the poem, ask, *Why do worms hide from their foes the frogs? Why do worms hide from the sun?* (They like the dark. They like to keep their skin wet.)

Simplify It

Read the book one day and teach the children the song the next day.

Add a Challenge

Write the uppercase and lowercase "Ww" on an index card. Show the card to the children and ask them to identify the letter. Ask, *Who can find the uppercase letter "W" on our poem chart? Who can find the lowercase letter "w"?* Invite volunteers to come up to the poem chart to touch and name any other letters that they recognize.

Assessment

To assess each child's learning, consider the following:

1. What did the child learn about worms?
2. What did the child learn about predators?

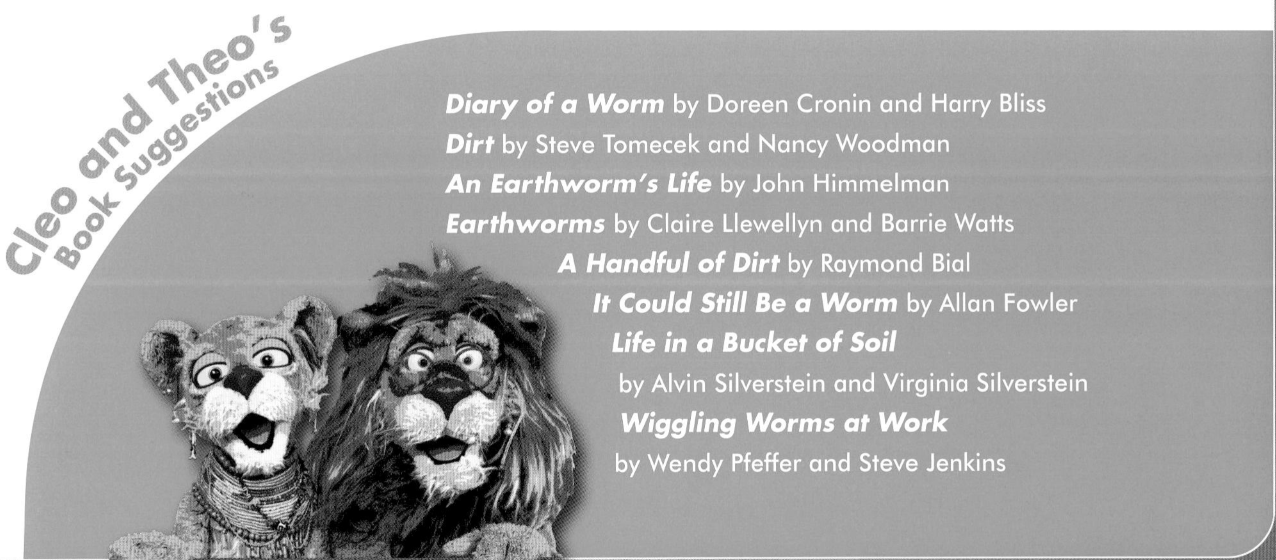

Cleo and Theo's Book Suggestions

Diary of a Worm by Doreen Cronin and Harry Bliss
Dirt by Steve Tomecek and Nancy Woodman
An Earthworm's Life by John Himmelman
Earthworms by Claire Llewellyn and Barrie Watts
A Handful of Dirt by Raymond Bial
It Could Still Be a Worm by Allan Fowler
Life in a Bucket of Soil by Alvin Silverstein and Virginia Silverstein
Wiggling Worms at Work by Wendy Pfeffer and Steve Jenkins

"I Have No Eyes"

Literacy Skill Focus
Compare and Contrast
Listening and Speaking
Story Comprehension
Vocabulary

Vocabulary

different	poem
ears	same
eat	see
eyes	smell
hear	squeeze
legs	stretch
nose	walk

Materials

Wonderful Worms by Linda Glaser and Loretta Krupinski (optional)

What Children Will Learn

1. About comparisons
2. About bodies

Related Themes

All About Me
Animals

What to Do

- Ask the children to remember the book *Wonderful Worms* and what they have learned about worms. Talk about how a worm's body is different from our bodies. Ask:
  - *Do worms have eyes?* (no)
  - *Do worms have ears?* (no)
  - *Do worms have a nose?* (no)
  - *Do worms have legs?* (no)
- Teach the children "I Have No Eyes" to help them remember what they have learned about a worm's body.

I Have No Eyes
I have no eyes to help me see. (*Touch eyes with fingers.*)
I have no nose to help me smell. (*Touch nose with finger.*)
I have no ears to help me hear. (*Touch ears with fingers.*)
I have no legs to help me walk. (*Touch legs with hands.*)
But I have a mouth to help me eat. (*Touch mouth with finger.*)
And I have muscles to help me move.
Stretch, squeeze; stretch, squeeze . . . BYE! (*Wave goodbye.*)

- You may also want to recite "Here Is My Body." Before reciting the poem, ask the children to take a deep breath and let it out. Explain that we breathe through our noses and mouths. Worms breathe through their skin!

Here Is My Body
Here is my body
So long and thin.
I eat with my mouth
And breathe through my skin.

Simplify It

Recite "I Have No Eyes" with the motions and ask the children to copy your motions.

Add a Challenge

Make the letter "W" on the floor or playground with chalk or tape. Mark the starting point at the top left. Have the children walk the letter "W," beginning at the starting point and following the line.

Assessment

To assess each child's learning, consider the following:
1. Is the child able to make comparisons between his body and worms' bodies?
2. What does the child know about his body and worms' bodies?

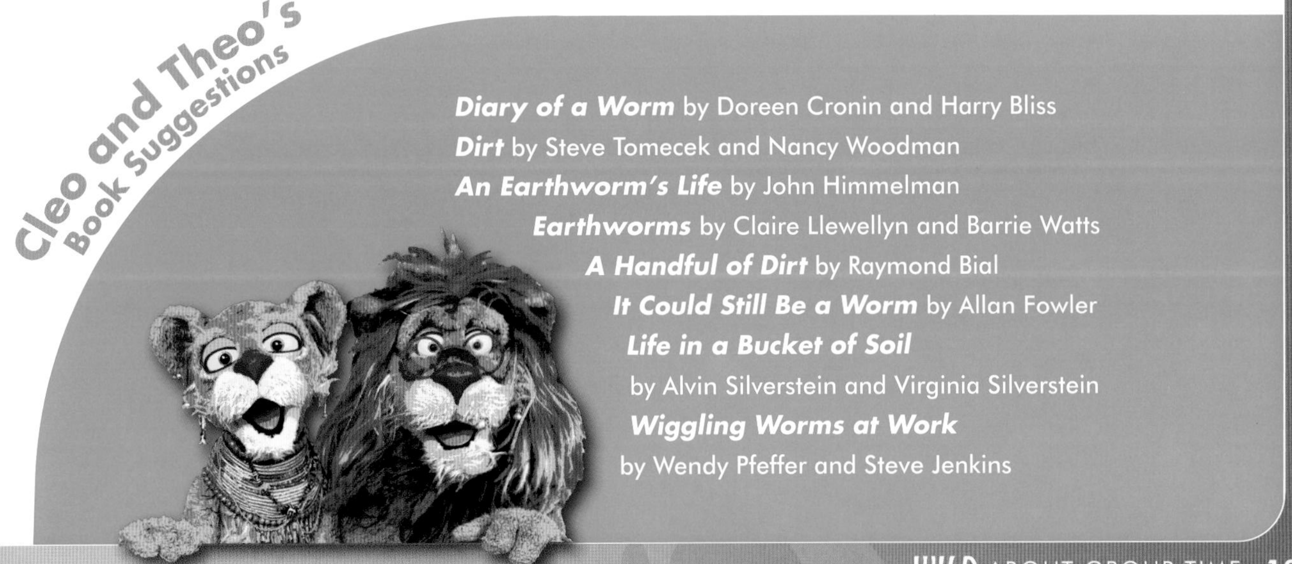

Cleo and Theo's Book Suggestions

Diary of a Worm by Doreen Cronin and Harry Bliss
Dirt by Steve Tomecek and Nancy Woodman
An Earthworm's Life by John Himmelman
Earthworms by Claire Llewellyn and Barrie Watts
A Handful of Dirt by Raymond Bial
It Could Still Be a Worm by Allan Fowler
Life in a Bucket of Soil by Alvin Silverstein and Virginia Silverstein
Wiggling Worms at Work by Wendy Pfeffer and Steve Jenkins

Reading The Very Hungry Caterpillar

Literacy Skill Focus

Compare and Contrast
Concepts of Print
Interpreting Illustrations
Listening and Speaking
Predicting
Recall and Retell
Sequencing (Days of the Week)

Vocabulary

author
butterfly
caterpillar
chrysalis
cocoon
cover
days of the week
egg
food
hungry
illustrator
insect
leaf
life cycle
moon
moths
nibble
title

Materials

a live caterpillar, a rubber caterpillar, or a picture of a caterpillar

The Very Hungry Caterpillar by Eric Carle

What Children Will Learn

1. About caterpillars
2. About the life cycle of a butterfly

Related Themes

Animals
Days of the Week

What to Do

- Show the children a live caterpillar, a rubber caterpillar, or a picture of a caterpillar. Ask, *Have you ever seen a caterpillar? Where did you see it? What did it look like?* Explain that caterpillars look like worms, but they are not worms. They are insects.
- Point to the words as you read aloud the title and the name of the author/illustrator. Ask the children to describe the caterpillar on the cover. Reread the title of the book. Ask, *What do you think our very hungry caterpillar eats?*
- Set a listening focus. Ask the children to notice what happens to the very hungry caterpillar. Read slowly and with expression.
- Show the children the book's unusual format and how it works. When the caterpillar eats through the apple, show the children how the page is cut shorter than the other pages. Point out the hole in the apple. Ask, *Why do you think there is a hole in the apple?* Turn the page and look at the back together. Ask, *What is coming out of the apple? It's the very hungry caterpillar. He ate a hole in the apple!* Have the children find and point to the caterpillar as he eats his way through the fruit and other foods.
- Encourage the children to join in on the repeating phrase in the book.
- After you read what the caterpillar ate each day, ask, *What do you think the caterpillar will eat tomorrow?*

- Point to the illustrations to clarify the meaning of the words *moon*, *egg*, *leaf*, *cocoon*, and the food words. When you read the word *nibbled*, make a nibbling motion and sound with your mouth.
- Talk about the book with the children. Ask questions such as:
  - *Where does the caterpillar come from at the very beginning of the book?* (He comes from a little egg.)
  - *What happens to the very hungry caterpillar after he eats all the food?* (He gets a stomachache. He gets big and fat.)
  - *What does the big, fat caterpillar do?* (He builds a house around himself.)
  - *What comes out of the caterpillar house?* (A beautiful butterfly!)

Simplify It

Read the book to the children once or twice and then ask them one question about the book.

Add a Challenge

Ask the children to draw pictures of the different stages in the life of a butterfly.

Assessment

To assess each child's learning, consider the following:

1. What did the child learn about caterpillars?
2. Is the child able to understand the life cycle of a butterfly?

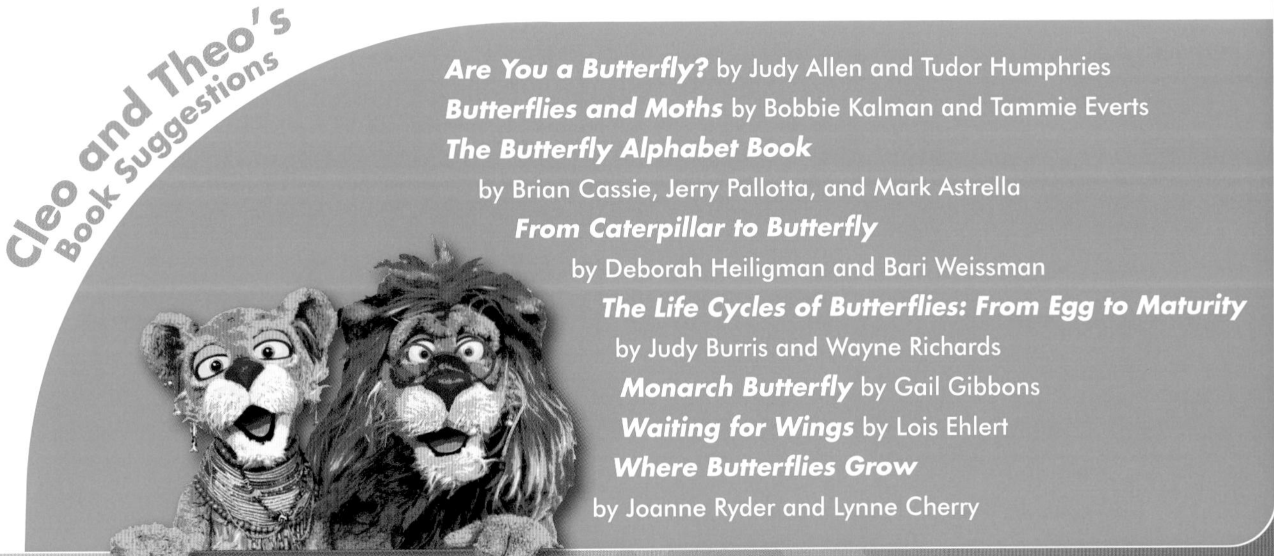

Are You a Butterfly? by Judy Allen and Tudor Humphries

Butterflies and Moths by Bobbie Kalman and Tammie Everts

The Butterfly Alphabet Book by Brian Cassie, Jerry Pallotta, and Mark Astrella

From Caterpillar to Butterfly by Deborah Heiligman and Bari Weissman

The Life Cycles of Butterflies: From Egg to Maturity by Judy Burris and Wayne Richards

Monarch Butterfly by Gail Gibbons

Waiting for Wings by Lois Ehlert

Where Butterflies Grow by Joanne Ryder and Lynne Cherry

Butterfly Life-Cycle Chart

Literacy Skill Focus
Active Listening
Concepts of Print
Recall and Retell
Sequencing
Vocabulary

Vocabulary

butterfly
caterpillar
chrysalis
cocoon
days of the week
egg
food
hungry
insect
leaf
life cycle
moon
moths
nibble

Materials

chart paper
classical music, optional
marker

What Children Will Learn

1. About the life cycle of a butterfly
2. To act out the life cycle of a butterfly

Related Theme

Insects

What to Do

- Create a butterfly life-cycle chart with the children. Draw the different stages in a circular format to help the children see a never-ending cycle.
- Ask, *How does a butterfly's life begin? Yes, it starts with an egg. I'll draw a little egg here and write the word* egg *above it.* Ask, *Who remembers the first letter in the word* egg?
- Ask, *What happens next? Yes, a caterpillar pops out of the egg. Pop!* Draw and label a picture of a caterpillar. Draw an arrow clockwise between the egg and the caterpillar.
- Ask, *After the caterpillar eats and grows, what does it do? Yes, it makes a chrysalis.* Draw and label a picture of a chrysalis. Draw an arrow clockwise between the caterpillar and the chrysalis.
- Ask, *What happens next? A butterfly comes out of the chrysalis.* Draw and label a picture of a butterfly. Draw an arrow clockwise between the chrysalis and the butterfly.
- *Point to each picture and review the stages. Tell the children that the butterfly will lay an egg. Draw an arrow between the butterfly and the egg. As you move your hand along the arrows, explain that a caterpillar will hatch from the egg, make a chrysalis, and grow into a butterfly. Say, This is the* life cycle *of a butterfly!*

- Invite the children to act out the life cycle of a butterfly. Ask, *How can you make your body look like a teeny egg? a caterpillar? a butterfly?* Slowly tell the life story of a butterfly (see below). Prompt the children to act out each transformation. You may want to play classical music as the butterflies fly from flower to flower.

Life Story of a Butterfly

Once upon a time there was a teeny, weeny egg resting on a leaf. Pop! Out crawls a little caterpillar. The caterpillar is very hungry. It eats and eats and grows bigger and bigger. Chomp. Chomp. Chomp. Nibble. Nibble. Nibble. The caterpillar spins a chrysalis. It stays very still. Slowly, its body starts to change. It pushes and pushes. Out comes a beautiful butterfly. The butterfly spreads its wings and flies. Higher and higher. The butterfly flies from flower to flower. It lands on a leaf and lays a little egg. And you know what happens next!

Simplify It

Ask the children to select a book about butterflies that they want you to read to them.

Add a Challenge

At rest time, invite the children to wrap themselves in a blanket and pretend they are turning into a butterfly inside their chrysalis. When naptime is over, have them wake up and flap their butterfly wings.

Assessment

To assess each child's learning, consider the following:

1. What did the child learn about the life cycle of a butterfly?
2. Is the child able to act out the life cycle of a butterfly?

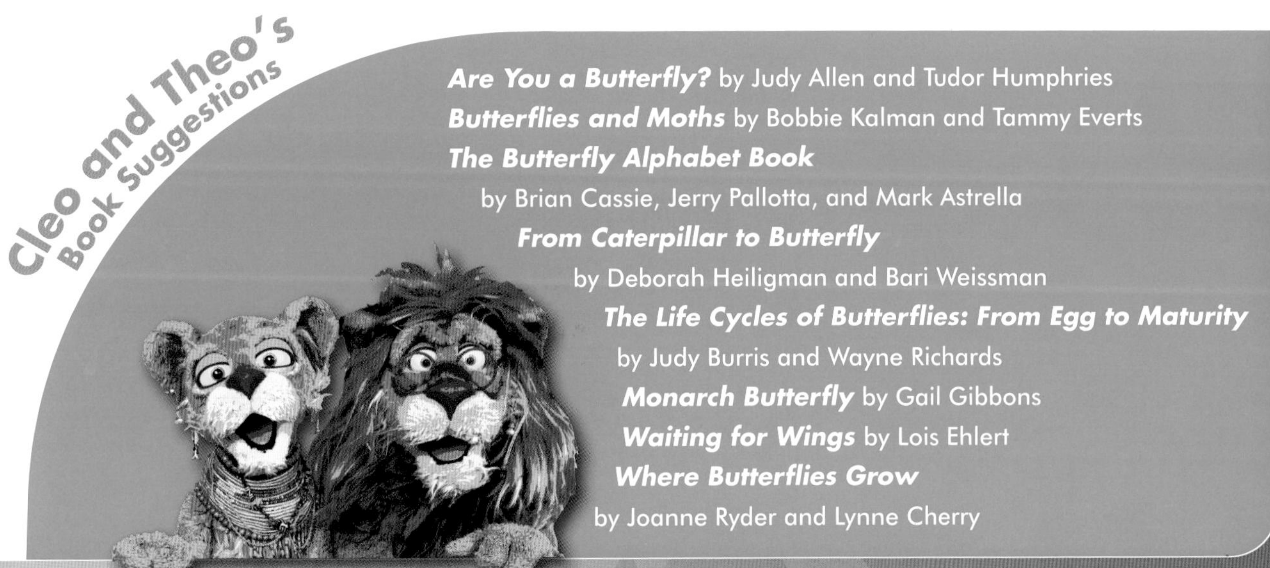

Cleo and Theo's Book Suggestions

Are You a Butterfly? by Judy Allen and Tudor Humphries
Butterflies and Moths by Bobbie Kalman and Tammy Everts
The Butterfly Alphabet Book by Brian Cassie, Jerry Pallotta, and Mark Astrella
From Caterpillar to Butterfly by Deborah Heiligman and Bari Weissman
The Life Cycles of Butterflies: From Egg to Maturity by Judy Burris and Wayne Richards
Monarch Butterfly by Gail Gibbons
Waiting for Wings by Lois Ehlert
Where Butterflies Grow by Joanne Ryder and Lynne Cherry

Days of the Week

Literacy Skill Focus

Concepts of Print (Functions of Print, Identifying Author and Illustrator)
Sequencing
Vocabulary

Vocabulary

author
calendar
caterpillar
cycle
day
days of the week
illustrator
today
tomorrow
week
yesterday

Materials

calendar
The Very Hungry Caterpillar by Eric Carle

What Children Will Learn

1. About the days of the week
2. About yesterday, today, and tomorrow

Related Themes

Days of the Week
Counting

What to Do

- Show the children *The Very Hungry Caterpillar* and point to the title and ask, *Who remembers the title of this book?* Point to the words as you read the name of the author/illustrator. Tell the children that Eric Carle has written and illustrated lots of books, many about animals. Ask, *Do you know any other books by Eric Carle?* If available, show the children some of Eric Carle's other books such as *The Mixed-up Chameleon*, *The Grouchy Ladybug*, *The Very Busy Spider*, and *The Very Quiet Cricket*. Read aloud the titles. Encourage the children to look at these books in the Library Center.
- Show the children a calendar. Say, *A week has seven days. Let's say the days of the week together.* Point to each day on the calendar as you recite the days of the week, starting with Sunday. After Saturday *say, Then it starts all over again with Sunday!* Do this a few times so the children recognize how the cycle of the week repeats itself.
- Point to the days on the calendar as the children answer the following questions. Ask:
  - *Who can tell me what day is today?* (Today is Thursday.)
  - *Who can tell me what day was yesterday, the day before today?* (Yesterday was Wednesday.)
  - *Who can tell me what day it will be tomorrow, the day after today?* (Tomorrow will be Friday.)

- Say, *I'm going to read* The Very Hungry Caterpillar *again. As I read, listen for the days of the week in the story.*

Simplify It

Show the children the current day on the calendar. Tell them the name of the day, the name of the month, and the number of the day. After doing this for a while, introduce the concept of today, and then yesterday and tomorrow.

Add a Challenge

Show the children photographs of caterpillars and worms, or have them look at real caterpillars and worms. Ask, *How are caterpillars and worms the same? How are they different?* Point out that worms and caterpillars look alike. They both have long bodies. But caterpillars have eyes and legs and worms do not. Caterpillars also have fuzzy hairs on their bodies. Caterpillars are insects that change and become butterflies. Worms don't do this. Worms stay worms. You may want to make a chart comparing the differences between caterpillars and worms.

Assessment

To assess each child's learning, consider the following:

1. Is the child able to learn the days of the week?
2. Is the child able to understand the meaning of *yesterday*, *today*, and *tomorrow*?

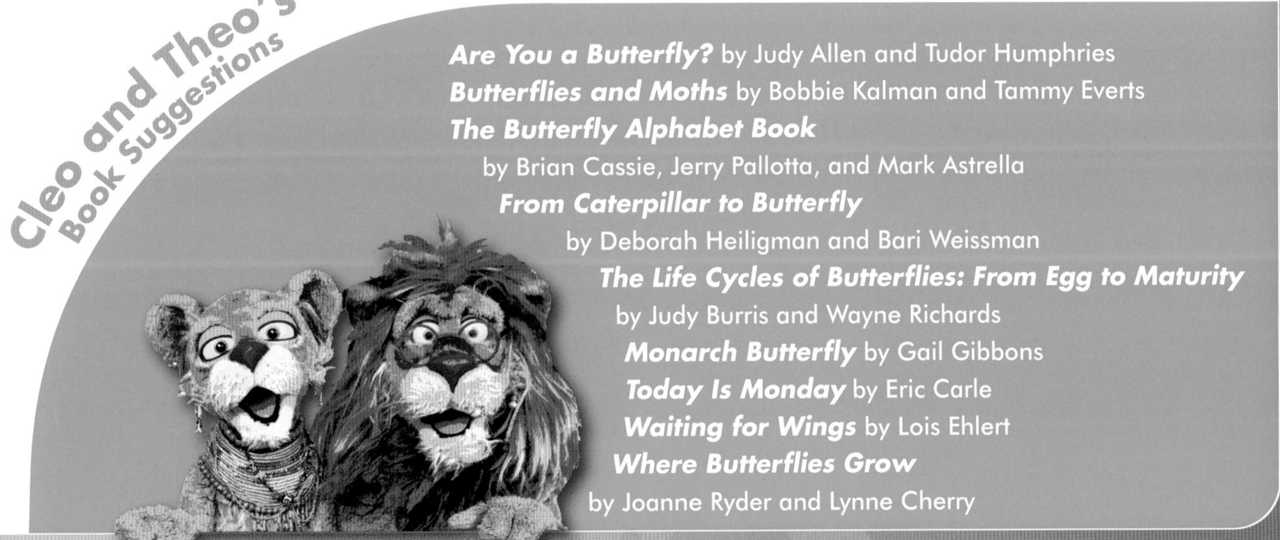

Cleo and Theo's Book Suggestions

Are You a Butterfly? by Judy Allen and Tudor Humphries
Butterflies and Moths by Bobbie Kalman and Tammy Everts
The Butterfly Alphabet Book by Brian Cassie, Jerry Pallotta, and Mark Astrella
From Caterpillar to Butterfly by Deborah Heiligman and Bari Weissman
The Life Cycles of Butterflies: From Egg to Maturity by Judy Burris and Wayne Richards
Monarch Butterfly by Gail Gibbons
Today Is Monday by Eric Carle
Waiting for Wings by Lois Ehlert
Where Butterflies Grow by Joanne Ryder and Lynne Cherry

Hopping Syllables

Literacy Skill Focus
Following Directions
Phonological Awareness
(Counting Syllables in Words;
Rhyme,
Rhythm, and Repetition)
Vocabulary

Vocabulary

beautiful
blanket
butterfly
caterpillar
corner
crept
earthworm
garden
gardeners
hop
roly-poly
slept
soil
spun
syllables
wakened

Materials

none needed

What Children Will Learn

1. About syllables
2. A poem about caterpillars

Related Themes

Counting
Sounds

What to Do

- Have the children stand in a circle. Say, *This is our garden. Caterpillars, butterflies, and earthworms live in our garden.*
- Ask a few children to come inside the garden. Say, *Each of you is an earthworm. Let's say the word together:* earthworm. *I'm going to say the word again and clap the word parts:* earth-worm.
- Say, *I'm going to say the word again. This time, I want the earthworms to hop the word parts. Ready:* earth–worm.
- Ask the children outside the circle, *How many times did the earthworms hop? Two times. There are two syllables in the word* earthworm.
- Repeat the process for the words *but-ter-fly* and *cat-er-pil-lar.*
- Make sure each child has a chance to stand inside the circle and hop.
- Teach the children the poem "Roly-Poly Caterpillar."

Roly-Poly Caterpillar
Roly-poly caterpillar
Into a corner crept, *(Walk fingers into bend of arm.)*
Spun a blanket around itself *(Make fist; spin finger from other hand around fist.)*
And for a long time slept. *(Rest head on hands with palms pressed together.)*
Roly-poly caterpillar
Wakened by and by, *(Stretch and yawn.)*
Roly-poly caterpillar
Is a beautiful butterfly! *(Flutter arms like wings.)*

- Recite the poem with the children and teach them the motions.
- "Hop" the syllables in *caterpillar* and *butterfly* as you recite the poem again.

Simplify It

Practice how to hop and then have the whole group of children hop each word together.

Add a Challenge

Ask one child to act out the poem as the group recites it.

Assessment

To assess each child's learning, consider the following:

1. Is the child able to understand that words have syllables?
2. Is the child able to learn the poem?

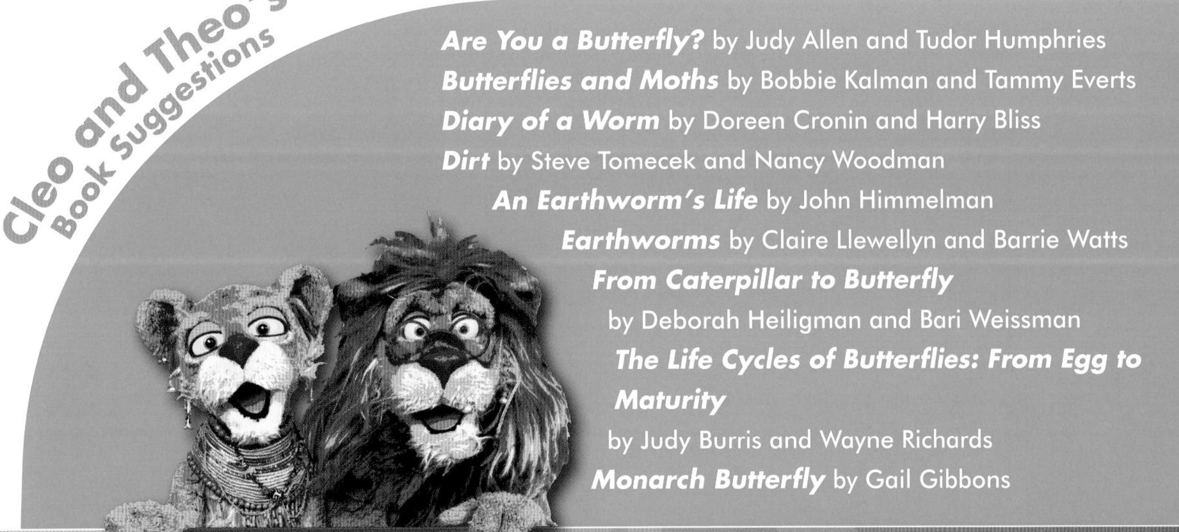

Cleo and Theo's Book Suggestions

Are You a Butterfly? by Judy Allen and Tudor Humphries

Butterflies and Moths by Bobbie Kalman and Tammy Everts

Diary of a Worm by Doreen Cronin and Harry Bliss

Dirt by Steve Tomecek and Nancy Woodman

An Earthworm's Life by John Himmelman

Earthworms by Claire Llewellyn and Barrie Watts

From Caterpillar to Butterfly by Deborah Heiligman and Bari Weissman

The Life Cycles of Butterflies: From Egg to Maturity by Judy Burris and Wayne Richards

Monarch Butterfly by Gail Gibbons

"Thank You, Worms"

Literacy Skill Focus
Phonological Awareness (Ending Sounds, Rhythm and Repetition)
Vocabulary (Plurals)

Vocabulary

count
dig
diggers
eat
end
grow
mix
more than
move
one
plant
plural
soil
sound
thank you
turn
two
word
worm

Materials

rubber or plastic worms
Wonderful Worms by Linda Glaser and Loretta Krupinski

What Children Will Learn

1. About worms
2. About plurals

Related Themes

Counting
Sounds

What to Do

- Review the Worms KWL chart (page 173). Add new knowledge to the third column. You may want to read more questions and answers from the back of *Wonderful Worms*.
- Remind the children that worms help plants grow. Then sing "Thank You, Worms."

Thank You, Worms
(Tune: "Frère Jacques")
Little diggers,
Little diggers,
Eat and move.
Eat and move.
Mix and turn the soil.
Mix and turn the soil.
Thank you, worms.
Thank you, worms.

- Sing the song again. This time tell the children to listen for the /s/ sound at the end of words.
- Ask the children to say the word *worm* with you. Ask, *What sound did you hear at the end of the word* worm? Say the word again, stretching the final /m/ sound: *wormmm.*
- Ask the children to say the word *worms* with you. Say the word again, emphasizing the final /s/ sound: *wormsss.* Ask, *What is the last sound that you hear in the word* worms? *The word* worms *ends in the /s/ sound.*

- Hold up a rubber or plastic worm. Ask, *How many worms do I have? I have one worm.* Then hold up two worms. Ask, *How many worms do I have now? I have two worms.*
- Explain that sometimes when we hear the /s/ sound at the end of a word, it means that there is more than one. Say, *One worm. Two worms.*
- Repeat the process with the words *digger(s), butterfly(ies)* and *caterpillar(s).*

Simplify It

Throughout the day, help the children count objects in the classroom. For example, count the blocks the children are using to build or count apple slices at snack time.

Add a Challenge

Have the children pretend they are worms at the Olympics. Set up a tunnel with a series of chairs or a table draped with a sheet. Give out Wonderful Worm medals for the longest stretch, the shortest squeeze, and the wiggliest wiggle. Make sure that every child receives a medal.

Assessment

To assess each child's learning, consider the following:

1. What did the child learn about worms?
2. Is the child able to understand that a plural means more than one?

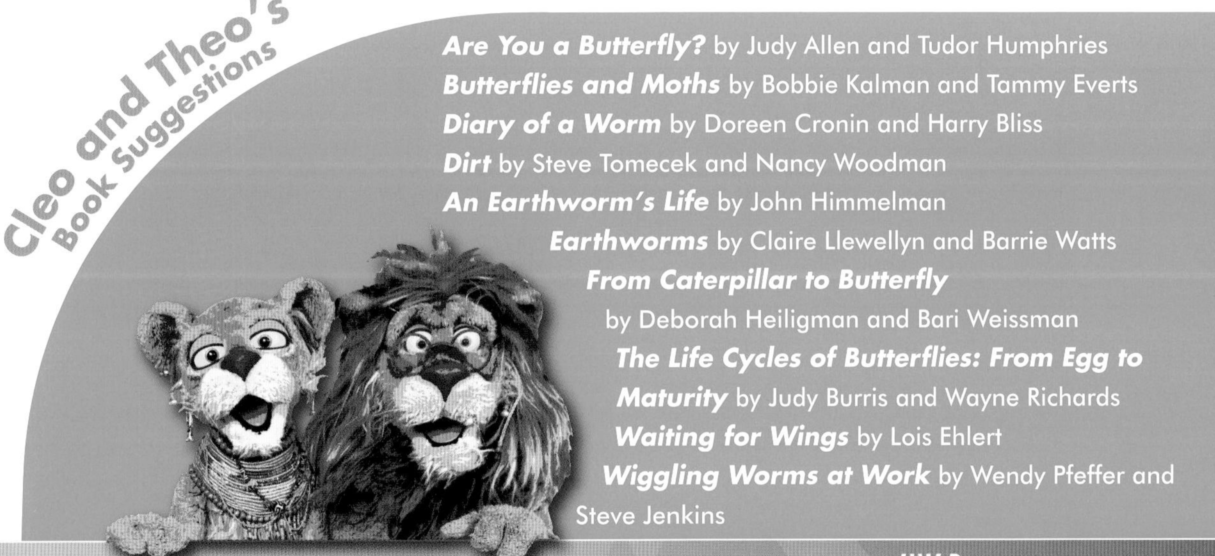

Cleo and Theo's Book Suggestions

Are You a Butterfly? by Judy Allen and Tudor Humphries
Butterflies and Moths by Bobbie Kalman and Tammy Everts
Diary of a Worm by Doreen Cronin and Harry Bliss
Dirt by Steve Tomecek and Nancy Woodman
An Earthworm's Life by John Himmelman
Earthworms by Claire Llewellyn and Barrie Watts
From Caterpillar to Butterfly by Deborah Heiligman and Bari Weissman
The Life Cycles of Butterflies: From Egg to Maturity by Judy Burris and Wayne Richards
Waiting for Wings by Lois Ehlert
Wiggling Worms at Work by Wendy Pfeffer and Steve Jenkins

Note to Families About the Topic of Things that Grow

FAMILY LETTER

Date ______________________

Dear Families,

In our classroom, we are learning about two fascinating animals: worms and caterpillars. We are reading a book called *Wonderful Worms* and making our own worm habitat with real worms! Ask your child to tell you why worms are wonderful. We are reading a book about a very hungry caterpillar that eats everything in sight. Ask your child to tell you how a caterpillar grows into a butterfly. We are also learning about the days of the week and the letter "W."

Here are some things that you can do at home with your child:

- Dig a hole in the soil. Can you find any worms? Watch what they do.
- Look for butterflies and caterpillars when you are outside. What colors are the butterfly's wings?
- Show your child a calendar and recite the days of the week together. Talk about what family members are doing each day of the week. Say, *On Saturday, we are going to Belinda's baseball game.*
- Search for the letter "W" on signs and labels. Say, *Look,* Wednesday *begins with the letter "W."*

Thank you!

Food

CHAPTER 9

With this topic, the children in your classroom learn about nutrition and eating healthy foods that help their bodies grow strong. An alphabet book teaches about the many varieties of fruits and vegetables. A funny story about some adventurous farm animals encourages the children to try new foods. The children also begin to learn where food comes from.

Setting Up the Room

- Cut out pictures from grocery-store flyers to create a Food wall display. You may want to sort the foods into categories—fruits, vegetables, meat and poultry, and so on. Label each picture. In addition to grocery-store flyers and magazines, you can find food pictures on the Internet.

- At the top of a large sheet of chart paper, write the question: *Do you like salsa?* Then draw a vertical line down the middle of the paper to create two columns. Label the left column *YES* and the right column *NO*. Display the chart on an easel or on a wall at the children's eye level and place markers nearby. As the children arrive and settle down in the morning, direct them and their parents or caregivers to the chart. Encourage parents and caregivers to read the question to their children. Have the children write their names in the *YES* or *NO* columns. Change the question each day. Here are some possibilities:
  - *Have you ever eaten nachos?*
  - *Do you like carrots?*
  - *Have you ever picked an apple from an apple tree?*

- Create a Tasting Center by displaying four to five different foods on a table. Label each food. You may want to include chips and salsa, guacamole, and an unfamiliar food that the children might like to try. Next to the table, display a chart at the children's eye level. Make four to five columns, labeled with the names of each of the foods. If possible, include a picture or symbol to help the children read the food labels. When the children try a food, have them write their name in the corresponding column. If they like the food, have them put a star sticker next to their name. Congratulate the children on trying new foods and being great food tasters! (**Note**: Be aware of food allergies.)

Family Letter

Prepare and make photocopies of the Family Letter on page 214 that explains this topic. Give the letter to parents at pick-up time before you begin the topic.

Wonderful Aromas

Literacy Skill Focus
Listening and Speaking
Phonological Awareness (Rhythm and Repetition)
Vocabulary

Vocabulary

aroma
chips
cilantro
dip
garden
garlic
hello
hola
lime
onion
recipe
salsa
scent
see
smell
spices
spicy
tomato
touch

Materials

garlic, lime, onion, cilantro, tomato (optional)

What Children Will Learn

1. To sing a song with the class
2. Words in another language (Spanish)

Related Themes

All About Me
Appreciating Diversity

What to Do

- Before singing "Hola Greeting Song," ask if anyone knows how to say hello in Spanish. Tell the children that in Spanish, people say *hola* (*hi*) or *buenos días* (*good day*). Ask the children to repeat the word *hola* with you (*pronounced OH-lah*).
- Tell the children that the song uses another word in Spanish—Olé. Explain that olé (OH-lay) is a Spanish word that people say when they like something, when something is done well, or when they feel happy.
- Have the children sit in a circle. Sing a verse of the "*Hola* Greeting Song," greeting by name the first three children to your left.

Hola Greeting Song
(Tune: "Goodnight Ladies")
Hola, *(child's name), (Children wave.)*
Hola, *(child's name), (Children wave.)*
Hola, *(child's name), (Children wave.)*
We're happy that you're here.
Olé!

- Invite the children to join you as you sing to the next group of three. Continue until everyone has been greeted. If the final group includes only one child, sing the verse using that child's name three times. If the final group includes two children, join the group and have the class sing *hola* to you as well.
  Note: Consider repeating this welcome song each day at group time.

- After you finish singing the song, ask the children, *Have you ever walked into the kitchen and smelled something wonderful? Could you tell what was cooking just by the smell?* Explain that *aroma* and *scent* are other words for *smell*. Use the new words in a sentence such as, *I can tell by the aroma coming from the kitchen that we are going to have chocolate chip cookies for dessert! Don't you love the smell, or scent, of cookies baking in the oven?*
- Tell the children that tomorrow you will read them a book called *Chicks and Salsa* about farm animals that are tired of eating the same old thing and decide to try some new foods. *Ask, Have you ever eaten chips and salsa? Do you like it?* If necessary, explain that *salsa* is a Spanish word that means "sauce." Say, *It's a cold and spicy dip made with tomatoes, onions, and spices. People often eat salsa with chips—chips and salsa!* If possible, display some of the ingredients (tomato, onion, garlic, cilantro, and lime) for the children to see, touch, and smell.

Simplify It

Sing the song to one child at a time.

Add a Challenge

Make salsa for snack.

Assessment

To assess each child's learning, consider the following:

1. Is the child able to sing the song with the class?
2. Is the child able to understand *hola*, the Spanish word for *hello*?

Cleo and Theo's Book Suggestions

Delicious Hullabaloo/Pachanga Deliciosa by Pat Mora and Francisco X. Mora

Farmer's Market by Carmen Parks and Edward Martinez

Gregory, the Terrible Eater by Mitchell Sharmat, Jose Aruego, and Ariane Dewey

I Will Never Not Ever Eat a Tomato by Lauren Child and Corina Fletcher

Lunch by Denise Fleming

To Market, To Market by Anne Miranda and Janet Stevens

"What Aroma Do I Smell?"

Literacy Skill Focus

Concepts of Print (Identifying Author and Illustrator, Locating Title)
Listening and Speaking
Phonological Awareness (Rhythm and Repetition)
Vocabulary

Vocabulary

aroma
author
bull
chicken
chips
cilantro
dip
duck
garden
garlic
guacamole
hola
horse
illustrator
lime
mice
nachos
onion
pig
publisher
recipe
rooster
salsa
scent
solution
spices
spicy
tamales
tomato

Materials

Chicks and Salsa by Aaron Reynolds and Paulette Bogan

What Children Will Learn

1. To sing a song
2. That food has different smells

Related Theme

Appreciating Diversity

What to Do

- Say, *In the book* Chicks and Salsa, *there are lots of wonderful smells when the animals and the farmer's wife cook salsa, guacamole, nachos, and tamales.* Remind the children that two other words that mean the same thing as *smell* are *aroma* and *scent*.
- Teach the children the song "What Aroma Do I Smell?" When you sing the last line, point to a picture of a food on the Food wall display (see page 193) and sing the name of that food. For the second verse, have a volunteer point to a food on the Food wall display that she likes and sing the name of that food in the last line.

What Aroma Do I Smell?
(Tune: "London Bridge Is Falling Down")
What aroma do I smell?
Do I smell, do I smell?
What aroma do I smell?
I smell __________!

- After singing the song, ask a volunteer to point to the book title. As you point to the words, ask, *Who can tell me the title of this book?* Chicks and Salsa*!* Ask, *Do you see any other words on the cover?* Let the children point them out, then ask, *What do you think those words tell us?* (the names of the author, illustrator, and publisher) Read aloud the names and ask the children to tell you what an author and illustrator do.

Food

- Before reading, flip through the pictures of the book and ask the children to name the farm animals (rooster, chickens, ducks, pigs, bull, horses, mice, and so on). Then set a listening focus: Say, *The animals in the story have a problem. They are tired of eating the same food all the time. As I read the book, I want you to think about how the animals solve this problem. What is their solution?* Explain that a *solution* is the way you answer, or solve, a problem.
- Read slowly and with expression. To help clarify the meaning of the some of the words in the story, point to the illustrations of the different foods: tomatoes, onions, chips, salsa, guacamole, avocados, chiles, nachos, and grapes. After reading, ask, *How do the animals solve their problem? What solution do they come up with?*

Simplify It

In addition to pointing to pictures of food on the Food wall display, show the children the actual food that is pictured.

Add a Challenge

Turn the song into a guessing game. Place a small amount of different spices in non-see-through containers and punch holes into the top. You may want to use some of the spices from the story, such as garlic and cilantro. Sing "What Aroma Do I Smell?" as you pass the container to the children and have them guess what's inside.

Assessment

To assess each child's learning, consider the following:

1. Is the child able to sing the song with the class?
2. What did the child learn about food having different smells?

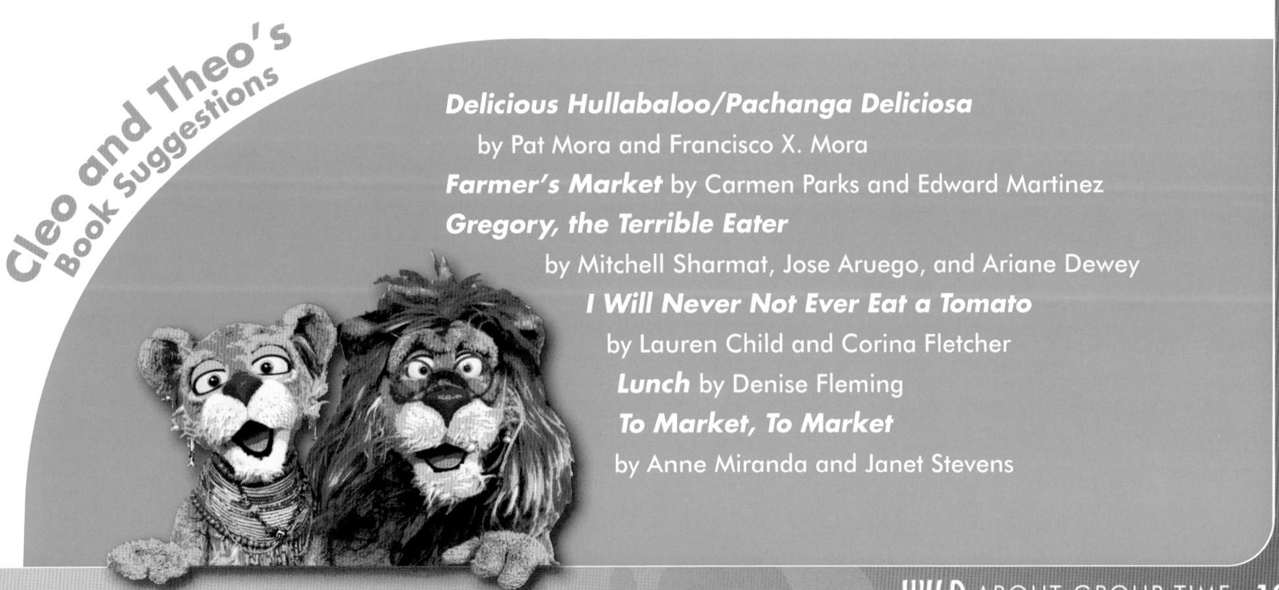

Cleo and Theo's Book Suggestions

Delicious Hullabaloo/Pachanga Deliciosa by Pat Mora and Francisco X. Mora

Farmer's Market by Carmen Parks and Edward Martinez

Gregory, the Terrible Eater by Mitchell Sharmat, Jose Aruego, and Ariane Dewey

I Will Never Not Ever Eat a Tomato by Lauren Child and Corina Fletcher

Lunch by Denise Fleming

To Market, To Market by Anne Miranda and Janet Stevens

Olé and Ooh, La, La

Literacy Skill Focus
Listening and Speaking
Recall and Retell
Vocabulary

Vocabulary

avocado
beans
beret
brim
collided
crêpes
crept
garlic
gathered
guacamole
leader
nachos
olé
plodded
salsa
sombrero
spices
tamales
taste
tortilla chips
uprooted

Materials

Chicks and Salsa by Aaron Reynolds and Paulette Bogan
chips and salsa, guacamole, and/or nachos (optional)

What Children Will Learn

1. About new foods
2. About languages

Related Themes

Animals
Appreciating Diversity

What to Do

- Hold up *Chicks and Salsa* and ask, *Who can tell me the name of this book? What was it about? Did the animals like the new foods they tried?* Ask the children if they have ever eaten the foods the animals and farmer make (salsa, guacamole, nachos, tamales, and crêpes). Explain briefly what each food is. (You may want to bring in some chips and salsa, guacamole, or nachos for a snack.)
- Ask, *Have you ever tried a new food—something you never ate before? What did it taste like? Did you like it? Do you want to eat it again?*
- *What new foods do the animals eat?* (The chickens eat chips and salsa, the ducks eat guacamole, and the pigs eat nachos.) If possible, show the children an avocado. Explain that *guacamole* is a Spanish word for a dip that is made from mashed avocado, garlic, and spices. Say, *You eat guacamole with chips. Nachos are tortilla chips with beans and melted cheese on top.*
- Tell the children that *Chicks and Salsa* has some words in Spanish and in French. Ask, *What word do the rooster, ducks, and pigs say when they finish eating?* Say, *Olé is a Spanish word that people say when they like something, when something is done well, or when they feel happy. Let me hear you say it—Olé!*
- Show the children the book cover and ask them to describe the hat the rooster is wearing. Tell them that the hat is called a sombrero. Explain that a *sombrero* is a Spanish word for a hat with a big, wide brim.

Food

- Show the last illustration and point to the hat the rooster is wearing. Say, *When the rooster is eating crêpes, a French kind of pancake, he wears a French hat called a beret. He says "Ooh, la, la!" French people say "Ooh, la, la" when they are very happy about something. Let's say it together—Ooh, la, la!*
- Ask, *Do you think this story is a real story or a make-believe story? Why?*

  Note: *Chicks and Salsa* is full of wonderful new vocabulary words. When you read the book, point to the illustrations to explain the meaning of unfamiliar words and phrases, such as *perched on a fence post.* Act out the action words such as *crept, uprooted, gathered, plodded,* and *collided.* Rephrase challenging sentences and insert phrases to clarify meaning.

Simplify It

Focus on teaching the children one or two new words each time you read the story.

Add a Challenge

Make chips and salsa, guacamole, or nachos for snack.

Assessment

To assess each child's learning, consider the following:

1. What new foods did the child learn about?
2. Is the child able to understand the words in Spanish and French?

Cleo and Theo's Book Suggestions

Cool Foods for Fun Fiestas: Easy Recipes for Kids to Cook by Lisa Wagner

Delicious Hullabaloo/Pachanga Deliciosa by Pat Mora and Francisco X. Mora

Farmer's Market by Carmen Parks and Edward Martinez

El Gusto del Mercado Mexicano/A Taste of the Mexican Market by Nancy Maria Grande Tabor

The International Cookbook for Kids by Matthew Locricchio

Market Day: A Story Told with Folk Art by Lois Ehlert

To Market, To Market by Anne Miranda and Janet Stevens

"The Chicks Make the Salsa"

Literacy Skill Focus
Early Writing
Phonological Awareness (Rhyme, Rhythm, and Repetition)
Recall and Retell
Sequencing
Story Comprehension
Vocabulary

Vocabulary

avocado
beans
beret
brim
cheese
chicks
chips
crêpes
ducks
farmer
garlic
guacamole
jig
leader
mouse
nachos
olé
pig
rooster
salsa
sombrero
spices
tamales
taste
tortilla chips
wife

Materials

Chicks and Salsa by Aaron Reynolds and Paulette Bogan

What Children Will Learn

1. To sing and act out a song with the class
2. About recipes

Related Themes

Appreciating Diversity
Cooking

What to Do

- Tell the children you are going to teach them a song about *Chicks and Salsa.* Before singing the song, ask, *What food do the chickens make?* (salsa) *Who brings the chips?* (the mouse) *What food do the ducks make?* (guacamole) *Who brings the avocados?* (the mouse) *What food do the pigs make?* (nachos) *Who brings the cheese?* (the mouse)
- Sing "The Chicks Make the Salsa." As you sing, you may want to show the illustrations from the book to help the children remember the animals and the foods they make.
- Sing the song again and invite the children to join in and act it out the same way they would act out "The Farmer in the Dell."

The Chicks Make the Salsa
(Tune: "Farmer in the Dell")
The chicks make the salsa,
The mouse brings the chips.
Hi ho the derry-o
The rooster says, "Olé!"

The ducks make guacamole,
The mouse brings the avocado.
Hi ho the derry-o
The rooster says, "Olé!"

The pigs make the nachos,
The mouse brings the cheese.
Hi ho the derry-o
The rooster says, "Olé!"

The wife makes tamales,
The farmer does a jig.
Hi ho the derry-o
The wife says, "Olé!"

The rooster makes crêpes,
The mouse reads the book.
Hi ho the derry-o
The rooster says, "Ooh la la!"

- After singing the song, show the children the recipes at the back of *Chicks and Salsa* and read the funny names. Choose one of the recipes to read aloud.

Food

Simplify It

Read the book again before singing the song with the children.

Add a Challenge

Together, choose something simple that most children like to eat and might know how to make, such as a simple fruit salad or a peanut butter and jelly sandwich. Bring in the required ingredients and cooking tools. Write a recipe together. Write the title, ingredients, and the steps. Ask prompting questions, *What ingredients do we need? What do we do first? What do we do next?* Think aloud as you write, emphasizing that you begin at the top of the paper and write from left to right. Together, read the completed recipe as you point to the words. Then invite the children to help you make it!

Assessment

To assess each child's learning, consider the following:

1. Is the child able to sing and act out the song with the class?
2. Is the child able to understand how recipes are used?

Cleo and Theo's Book Suggestions

Cool Foods for Fun Fiestas: Easy Recipes for Kids to Cook by Lisa Wagner

Delicious Hullabaloo/Pachanga Deliciosa by Pat Mora and Francisco X. Mora

Eight Animals Bake a Cake by Susan Middleton Elya and Lee Chapman

Farmer's Market by Carmen Parks and Edward Martinez

Good Enough to Eat: A Kid's Guide to Food and Nutrition by Lizzy Rockwell

El Gusto del Mercado Mexicano/A Taste of the Mexican Market by Nancy Maria Grande Tabor

Kids' First Cookbook by The American Cancer Society

Market Day: A Story Told with Folk Art by Lois Ehlert

Reading *Eating the Alphabet*

Literacy Skill Focus

Concepts of Print
Interpreting Illustrations
Letter Recognition
Listening and Speaking
Parts of a Book
Story Comprehension
Vocabulary

Vocabulary

author	hair
banana	illustrator
blueberries	mouth
cherry	nose
cover	seeds
different	sweet
fruits	teeth
green beans	vegetables

Materials

Eating the Alphabet: Fruits & Vegetables from A to Z by Lois Ehlert

real or plastic apple, banana, carrot, lemon, potato, and other fruits and vegetables

What Children Will Learn

1. About fruits and vegetables
2. About the alphabet

Related Theme

The Alphabet

What to Do

- Hold up a piece of fruit and ask, *What is this?* Hold up another piece of fruit and repeat the question. Point out that both are different kinds of fruit. Say, *Most fruits have seeds inside. Most fruits are sweet to eat. There are many different kinds of fruit. Which fruits do you like to eat?* Repeat the process with vegetables. Say, *Most vegetables are not sweet. There are many different kinds of vegetables.* Ask, *What vegetables do you like to eat?*
- Show the children the cover of *Eating the Alphabet*. Point to the words as you read aloud the complete title and the name of the author/illustrator. Explain that this is an alphabet book about fruits and vegetables.
- Ask the children to name the different fruits and vegetables they see on the cover.
- Look at the title page together. Ask, *What do you notice about the illustration?* Say, *Yes, Lois Ehlert, the author and illustrator, made a face out of different fruits and vegetables.* Ask, *Which fruit did she use to make the mouth?* (a banana) *Which fruit did she use for the teeth?* (blueberries) *Which fruit did she use for the nose?* (a cherry) *Look, she made the hair out of green beans!*
- Point to the featured letter on each page and its name. Use the following routine for the "Aa" page and adapt for the other letter pages.
- Say, *This is the letter "Aa" page. All the fruits and vegetables on this*

page begin with the letter "A." Point to the apples and say, *Look, here is a picture of an apple. The word* apple *is right next to it! The word* apple *is written two times! Here it is written with uppercase letters and here it is written again with lowercase letters. The word* apple *begins with the letter "A."* Point to the avocados and say, *Look, here's an avocado, the fruit that the ducks use to make guacamole!*

- Point to and read the names of each fruit and vegetable on the pages. Ask, *Have you eaten any of the fruits and vegetables on the letter "Aa" page? Which ones?*

Teacher Tip: In the glossary at the back of *Eating the Alphabet*, you will find a pronunciation guide as well as interesting facts about each fruit and vegetable. You may want to share some of these facts with the children.

Simplify It

Look at each letter page. Say the name of each fruit and vegetable that the children point to.

Add a Challenge

Ask the children to name another fruit or vegetable for each letter.

Assessment

To assess each child's learning, consider the following:

1. What did the child learn about fruits and vegetables?
2. What did the child learn about the alphabet?

Cleo and Theo's Book Suggestions

Delicious Hullabaloo/Pachanga Deliciosa by Pat Mora and Francisco X. Mora

Farmer's Market by Carmen Parks and Edward Martinez

Good Enough to Eat: A Kid's Guide to Food and Nutrition by Lizzy Rockwell

El Gusto del Mercado Mexicano/A Taste of the Mexican Market by Nancy Maria Grande Tabor

Market Day: A Story Told with Folk Art by Lois Ehlert

To Market, To Market by Anne Miranda and Janet Stevens

"Apples and Bananas"

Literacy Skill Focus

Active Listening
Listening and Speaking
Phonological Awareness (Rhyming, Rhythm and Repetition, Sound Substitution)
Vocabulary

Vocabulary

apples	lime
bananas	me
bean	pea
bear	pear
big	queen
born	rare
corn	rhyme
dig	sea
dime	slime
eat	taste
favorite	tear
fig	time
fruits	torn
green	tree
horn	vegetables
like	wig

Material

Eating the Alphabet: Fruits & Vegetables from A to Z: by Lois Ehlert

Note: "Apples and Bananas" is a traditional song. If you do not know the tune, there are many CDs available that feature this song such as *Apples & Bananas* and *Raffi's Box of Sunshine*. It is also featured on many websites such as songsforteaching.com and kididdles.com.

What Children Will Learn

1. A song about fruits and vegetables
2. About rhyming

Related Themes

Colors
Sounds

What to Do

- Ask the children to name some of their favorite fruits and vegetables. Ask, *Did you see any fruits or vegetables in* Eating the Alphabet *that you would like to taste? Which ones?*
- Tell the children you are going to teach them a silly song about two fruits: apples and bananas. The song is silly because you play with the sounds of the words and sing them differently each time. Say, *First you sing apples, then you sing ay-ples, then ee-ples, then i-ples, then oh-ples, and then oo-ples. Banana goes from bananas, to bay-nay-nays, to bee-nee-nees, to by-ny-nys, to bo-no-nos, and to boo-noo-noos. The word* eat *also changes. I'll sing a line. Then you repeat it with me.*

Apples and Bananas
I like to eat, eat, eat apples and bananas.
I like to eat, eat, eat apples and bananas.

I like to ate, ate, ate ay-ples and bay-nay-nays.
I like to ate, ate, ate ay-ples and bay-nay-nays.

I like to eet, eet, eet ee-ples and bee-nee-nees.
I like to eet, eet, eet ee-ples and bee-nee-nees.

I like to ite, ite, ite i-ples and by-ny-nys.
I like to ite, ite, ite i-ples and by-ny-nys.

I like to ote, ote, ote oh-ples and bo-no-nos.
I like to ote, ote, ote oh-ples and bo-no-nos.

I like to oot, oot, oot oo-ples and boo-noo-noos.
I like to oot, oot, oot oo-ples and boo-noo-noos.

Food

Teacher Tip: Each of the long vowel sounds are substituted for the beginning sound in the words *apples* and *eat* and for the three short /a/ sounds in the word *bananas*.

- After singing the song, tell the children that they are going to play a rhyming game about fruits and vegetables. Say, *I am going to say a fruit or vegetable and you are going to think of a word that rhymes with it.*
- Point to a picture of a bean on the Food wall display (see page 193) or in the book *Eating the Alphabet* and say the word. Ask, *Can you think of a word that rhymes with* bean? *Yes,* green. Green *rhymes with* bean. *What else rhymes with* bean? Queen *rhymes with* bean. *Some words have lots of words that rhyme with them. Let's try it!*

Simplify It

Say two words that rhyme and one that does not rhyme (*bean, green, lime*) and ask the children which word does not rhyme.

Add a Challenge

Repeat the process with the words pear (bear, tear, rare); corn (horn, torn, born); fig (big, dig, wig); lime (dime, slime, time); and pea (me, tree, sea).

Assessment

To assess each child's learning, consider the following:

1. Is the child able to sing the song with the group?
2. Is the child able to identify words that rhyme?

Delicious Hullabaloo/Pachanga Deliciosa by Pat Mora and Francisco X. Mora

Eight Animals Bake a Cake by Susan Middleton Elya and Lee Chapman

Farmer's Market by Carmen Parks and Edward Martinez

Good Enough to Eat: A Kid's Guide to Food and Nutrition by Lizzy Rockwell

El Gusto del Mercado Mexicano/A Taste of the Mexican Market by Nancy Maria Grande Tabor

Market Day: A Story Told with Folk Art by Lois Ehlert

To Market, To Market by Anne Miranda and Janet Stevens

Fruits and Vegetables

Literacy Skill Focus
Concepts of Print (Directionality, Print Carries Meaning)
Phonological Awareness (Beginning Sounds)
Vocabulary

Vocabulary

banana
carrot
chart
column
fruit
guess
lemon
names
pictures
potato
sound
vegetable

Materials

bag
chart paper
index cards
markers
pictures of fruits and vegetables from magazines
real or plastic banana, carrot, lemon, potato, or other fruits and vegetables
tape

What Children Will Learn

1. To use clues to identify fruits and vegetables
2. To make a chart

Related Themes

Colors
Sounds

Preparation

Place real or plastic fruits and vegetables in a bag. Use chart paper to make a chart called Our Favorite Fruits and Vegetables. Attach the name and/or pictures of six to eight fruits and vegetables in a column on the left side of the chart. Use index cards to make a name card for each child in the class.

What to Do

- Play a guessing game that helps the children identify fruits and vegetables while recognizing beginning sounds.
- In a bag, place a real or plastic banana, carrot, lemon, and potato. Reach into the bag. Say, *I have in my hand a fruit that begins with the /b/ sound. It is yellow. You peel it. Monkeys love to eat it.* Ask, *What is it?*
- Pull the banana out of the bag to confirm the children's guess. Say, *Yes, it's a banana.* Banana *begins with the /b/ sound.* Ask, *Who likes to eat bananas?*
- Reach into the bag again. Say, *I have in my hand a vegetable that begins with the /k/ sound. It is orange. It's long. It is crunchy when you eat it.* Ask, *What is it?* Pull the carrot out of the bag and say, *Yes, it's a* carrot. Carrot *begins with the /k/ sound.* Ask, *Who likes to eat carrots?*
- Repeat the process with the lemon and potato.

- Tell the children that you are going to chart their favorite fruits and vegetables. Display Our Favorite Fruits and Vegetables chart on the wall at the children's eye level. Ask the children to identify the names of the fruits and vegetables as you attach or display the pictures. Invite each child to choose a fruit or vegetable that he likes best.
- Have the children take turns attaching their name card next to their favorite fruit or vegetable, forming a row from left to right. Talk about the completed graph. Ask, *How many people chose (apples) as their favorite fruit or vegetable? Let's count. Which fruit or vegetable has the (longest, shortest) line of names after it?*

Simplify It

Show the children the fruit or vegetable and ask them to say the beginning sound of that word.

Add a Challenge

Create a chart that is organized by color. Ask, *Which color has the most fruits or vegetables?*

Assessment

To assess each child's learning, consider the following:

1. Is the child able to use the clues to recognize fruits and vegetables?
2. Is the child able to understand how to use and read the chart?

Cleo and Theo's Book Suggestions

Delicious Hullabaloo/Pachanga Deliciosa by Pat Mora and Francisco X. Mora
Eight Animals Bake a Cake by Susan Middleton Elya and Lee Chapman
Farmer's Market by Carmen Parks and Edward Martinez
Good Enough to Eat: A Kid's Guide to Food and Nutrition by Lizzy Rockwell
El Gusto del Mercado Mexicano/A Taste of the Mexican Market by Nancy Maria Grande Tabor
Market Day: A Story Told with Folk Art by Lois Ehlert
To Market, To Market by Anne Miranda and Janet Stevens

A Is for ________

Literacy Skill Focus
Alphabet Awareness
Concepts of Print
Letter Recognition
Listening and Speaking (Describing)
Vocabulary

Vocabulary

alphabet
banana
blue
cooked
cover
first
fruit
green
last
letter
orange
raw
red
sentence
smell
taste
title
vegetable
yellow

Materials

Eating the Alphabet: Fruits & Vegetables from A to Z by Lois Ehlert

What Children Will Learn

1. The letters of the alphabet
2. To identify the colors of fruits and vegetables

Related Theme

Colors

What to Do

- Before reading *Eating the Alphabet*, review colors with the children.
- Display the front cover of the book. Ask the children to show you where the title is. Read aloud the title and ask if the children can recognize and name any of the letters.
- After you read the poem on the first page, point to the letters printed in red. Ask, *Do you recognize these letters? Yes, the first red letter is the letter A, the first letter in the alphabet. The second red letter is the letter Z, the last letter in the alphabet.*
- As you turn the pages, ask each child to name a fruit or vegetable and its color. Encourage the children to use complete sentences: *There is a yellow banana. I see a red strawberry.*
- Linger over each page to allow the children to talk about the fruits and vegetables they like to eat. Talk about their colors, tastes, and smells and the different ways to eat them. Ask, *Do you like to eat carrots raw or cooked? Do you like applesauce or apple pie?*

Simplify It

Look at each page and ask the children to point to the fruit or vegetable that you describe. For example, open to a page with a yellow banana on it. After you say, *I see a yellow banana on this page*, ask one child to point to the banana on the page.

Add a Challenge

Say the sound of a letter and then ask the children to name a fruit or vegetable that begins with that sound.

Assessment

To assess each child's learning, consider the following:

1. Is the child able to identify the letters of the alphabet?
2. Is the child able to identify the colors of fruits and vegetables?

Cleo and Theo's Book Suggestions

The ABCs of Fruits and Vegetables and Beyond by Steve Charney, David Goldbeck, and Marie Burgaleta Larson

Alphabet Soup by Kate Banks

Good Enough to Eat: A Kid's Guide to Food and Nutrition by Lizzy Rockwell

Growing Colors by Bruce McMillan

Growing Vegetable Soup by Lois Ehlert

El Gusto del Mercado Mexicano/A Taste of the Mexican Market by Nancy Maria Grande Tabor

Market Day: A Story Told with Folk Art by Lois Ehlert

The Vegetable Alphabet Book by Jerry Pallotta, Bob Thomson, and Edgar Stewart

We Love Fruit! by Fay Robinson

Words Have Parts

Literacy Skill Focus
Phonological Awareness (Clapping and Counting Syllables in Words; Rhythm, Rhyme, and Repetition)

Vocabulary

apple
banana
bean
blueberry
clap
corn
fast
four
fruit
how many
lemon
listening
name
one
part
potato
rhythm
slow
syllable
three
two
vegetable
watermelon
word

Materials

basket
real, toy, or pictures of fruits and vegetables

What Children Will Learn

1. That words have parts (syllables)
2. To sing a song about word parts (syllables)

Related Themes

All About Me
Counting

Preparation

Place the real, toy, or pictures of fruits and vegetables into a basket.

What to Do

- Have the children sit in a circle. Sing "Clapping All Our Names."

Clapping All Our Names
(Tune: "Twinkle, Twinkle, Little Star")
We can play a listening game,
Let's all clap and say our name.
Clapping, clapping, fast and slow,
Ready, set, now here we go.
Everybody clap with me,
Clap the name parts carefully.

- Say, *Now let's clap our names together. Listen carefully and clap when I do.* First say your name slowly in its natural rhythm, then say your name and clap for each part (syllable) as you say it.

Ms.	Pe	ter	son
clap	clap	clap	clap

- Together, practice clapping each child's name. Sing the song again, then go around the circle and clap each child's name once more.

- Say, *Now we are going to clap the syllables of the names of fruits and vegetables we have been learning about.*
- Hold up an apple from the basket and ask, *What is this?* Then repeat the word, breaking it down into its parts, or syllables, (*ap-ple*). Say *ap-ple* again, clapping the word parts, or syllables, as you say them. Say, *I'm going to say and clap the word* apple *again. Listen very carefully and tell me how many times I clap.* Ap-ple. *How many times did I clap? Yes, I clapped two times.* Ap-ple *has two parts.* Have the children repeat the word *apple* and clap the word parts with you.
- Repeat the process with other familiar fruits and vegetables. Begin with ones that have one or two syllables (*bean*, *corn*, *le-mon*) and then move on to three- and four-syllable words (*ba-na-na*, *po-ta-to*, *blue-ber-ry*, *wa-ter-me-lon*).

Simplify It

Have the child say her name while you clap the syllables.

Add a Challenge

Food

Make large number cards for the numbers 1, 2, and 3. Place one dot on the number 1 card, two dots on the number 2 card, and so on. Put the number cards in front of you in numerical order. Point to the numbers and identify them. Say, *We clapped two times for apple so I am going to place the apple under the number two.* Repeat the process with other fruits and vegetables. Be sure to have several words for each number. Once you have sorted all the fruits and vegetables by word parts, look at the display and say, *Let's clap all the food with one word part, two word parts, three word parts (and so on).*

Assessment

To assess each child's learning, consider the following:

1. Is the child able to understand that words have parts (syllables)?
2. Is the child able to sing the song about word parts (syllables)?

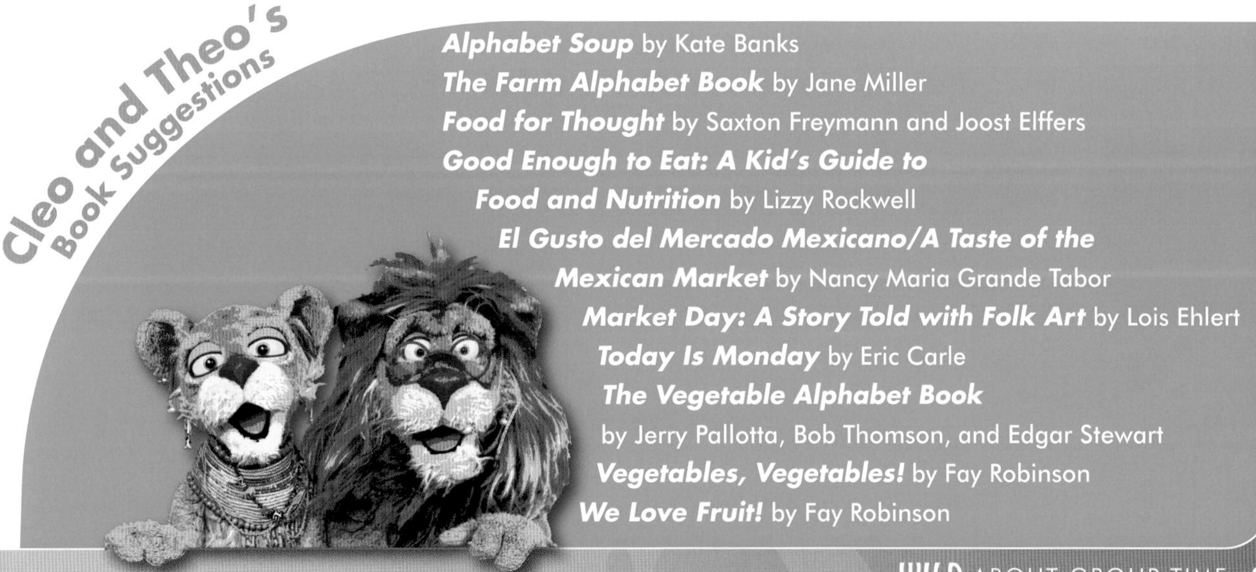

Alphabet Soup by Kate Banks
The Farm Alphabet Book by Jane Miller
Food for Thought by Saxton Freymann and Joost Elffers
Good Enough to Eat: A Kid's Guide to Food and Nutrition by Lizzy Rockwell
El Gusto del Mercado Mexicano/A Taste of the Mexican Market by Nancy Maria Grande Tabor
Market Day: A Story Told with Folk Art by Lois Ehlert
Today Is Monday by Eric Carle
The Vegetable Alphabet Book by Jerry Pallotta, Bob Thomson, and Edgar Stewart
Vegetables, Vegetables! by Fay Robinson
We Love Fruit! by Fay Robinson

"Eat Every Color"

Literacy Skill Focus

Concepts of Print
Listening and Speaking
Vocabulary

Vocabulary

apple
banana
blueberry
bodies
broccoli
color
fruit
healthy
orange
plum
strong
taste
vegetable

Materials

chart paper
markers
real, toy, or pictures of an apple, banana, orange, plum, broccoli, and blueberry

What Children Will Learn

1. About colors
2. About healthy eating

Related Theme

Colors

What to Do

- Ask the children, *Have you ever heard a grownup say, "An apple a day keeps the doctor away"? What do you think it means?* Say, *Apples and other fruits and vegetables help our bodies grow healthy and strong. When you are healthy, you feel good and don't get sick.* Explain that some foods taste good but are not very healthy for us, such as candy and cake. Ask, *What are some foods that help our bodies grow strong?*
- Say, *Remember all the colors of the fruits and vegetables we saw in* Eating the Alphabet? *Fruits and vegetables come in all colors of the rainbow.*
- While the children watch or help, draw a rainbow with wide stripes of solid colors. Include the colors red, orange, yellow, green, blue, and purple. Red should be on the outer ring. Give a child a real or toy apple or a picture of a red apple. Ask, *What color is this apple? Can you find the color red on the rainbow?* Repeat with a banana, an orange, a plum, broccoli, and blueberries.

- Tell the children that eating different-colored fruits and vegetables is very healthy for their bodies and their minds. Then recite the poem "Eat Every Color."

Eat Every Color
Eat every color
Of the rainbow,
And into a healthy
Child you'll grow.

Simplify It

Identify the color of the fruit or vegetable and then ask the children where it belongs on the rainbow.

Add a Challenge

Ask the children to say other fruits and vegetables, identify their colors, and say where on the rainbow each belongs. Suggest that the children find pictures of fruits and vegetables in magazines and tape them to the rainbow.

Assessment

To assess each child's learning, consider the following:

1. Is the child able to recognize the colors of the fruits and vegetables?
2. Is the child able to understand that eating a variety of fruits and vegetables is good for you?

Cleo and Theo's Book Suggestions

The ABCs of Fruits and Vegetables and Beyond by Steve Charney, David Goldbeck, and Marie Burgaleta Larson
Food for Thought by Saxton Freymann and Joost Elffers
Good Enough to Eat: A Kid's Guide to Food and Nutrition by Lizzy Rockwell
El Gusto del Mercado Mexicano/A Taste of the Mexican Market by Nancy Maria Grande Tabor
Market Day: A Story Told with Folk Art by Lois Ehlert
The Vegetable Alphabet Book by Jerry Pallotta, Bob Thomson, and Edgar Stewart
Vegetables, Vegetables! by Fay Robinson

Note to Families About the Topic of Food

FAMILY LETTER

Date ____________________

Dear Families,

In our classroom, we are learning about food. We are reading a book called *Chicks and Salsa* about farm animals that are tired of eating the same old thing and decide to cook up some new recipes, including salsa, guacamole, and nachos! Ask your child to tell you about the story. We are also reading an alphabet book about fruits and vegetables and learning how they help our bodies grow healthy and strong.

Here are some things that you can do at home with your child:

- Talk to your child about healthy foods that help our minds and bodies grow.
- Encourage your child to try a new fruit or vegetable.
- Find a new recipe that you want to try and ask your child to help you make the recipe.
- Visit the produce section at the grocery store. Together, look at and talk about the different fruits and vegetables. Find one for each color of the rainbow: red, orange, yellow, green, blue, and purple.

Thank you!

CHAPTER 10

Silly Stories

Silly songs, stories, and poems offer wonderful opportunities for the children in your classroom to play with the sounds in words. With this topic, the children will enjoy a silly rhyming story about Mrs. McNosh and her wacky wash. In *Chicka Chicka Boom Boom*, the rambunctious letters of the alphabet lead the children on a rhyming trip up and down a coconut tree. The children listen to and recognize the beginning and ending sounds in words as they come up with their own silly rhymes and nonsense words.

Setting Up the Room

- Hang a clothesline in a corner of the room. Supply clothespins and an assortment of clothes. Also provide rhyming objects or rhyming picture cards (for example, *cat/hat, pen/hen*) for the children to hang up on the clothesline.

- Display alphabet charts at the children's eye level in different parts of the classroom.

- Create a book-browsing box with silly stories, such as *Silly Sally* by Audrey Wood and *Bark, George* by Jules Feiffer. Add new alphabet books, such as *The Alphabet Tree* by Leo Lionni and *What Pete Ate from A to Z* by Moira Kalman, to the classroom ABC book-browsing box.

Family Letter

Prepare and make photocopies of the Family Letter on page 236 that explains this topic. Give the letter to parents at pick-up time before you begin the topic.

I Feel Silly

Literacy Skill Focus
Listening and Speaking
Name Recognition
Phonological Awareness (Rhythm, Rhyme, and Repetition)
Vocabulary

Vocabulary

bend
clap
everyone
fun
hands
silly
songs
stories
toes
welcome

Materials

index cards
markers

What Children Will Learn

1. To sing a song with their class
2. To recognize their names in print

Related Themes

All About Me
Feelings

Preparation

Use index card and markers to create a name card for each child.

What to Do

- Sit in a circle with the children.
- Sing "Welcome, Welcome."

Welcome, Welcome
(Tune: "Twinkle, Twinkle, Little Star")
Welcome, welcome, everyone. (or name of a child).
Now you're here,
We'll have some fun.
We'll clap our hands, and touch our nose;
Then we'll bend and touch our toes.
Welcome, welcome, everyone. (or name of a child).
Now you're here,
We'll have some fun.

- Hold up each child's name card as you sing his or her name.
- When you sing the fourth and fifth lines, have the children clap their hands and touch their toes.
- Sing more funny songs that can be accompanied by clapping, such as "Miss Mary Mack" and "A Sailor Went to Sea, Sea, Sea," and "Flea Fly Flow."

- Ask the children, *How do you feel today?* After getting a few responses, say, *This morning, I feel a little silly. I feel silly because I'm thinking of silly songs and silly stories. It makes me smile and laugh just to think about them.* Ask, *Does anyone else feel a little silly?* Engage the children in a discussion about things that are silly.

Simplify It

Say each child's name when you hold up each card.

Add a Challenge

Ask the children to make up additional actions to the song.

Assessment

To assess each child's learning, consider the following:

1. Is the child able to sing the song with the other children?
2. Is the child able to recognize the names of the children in the class?

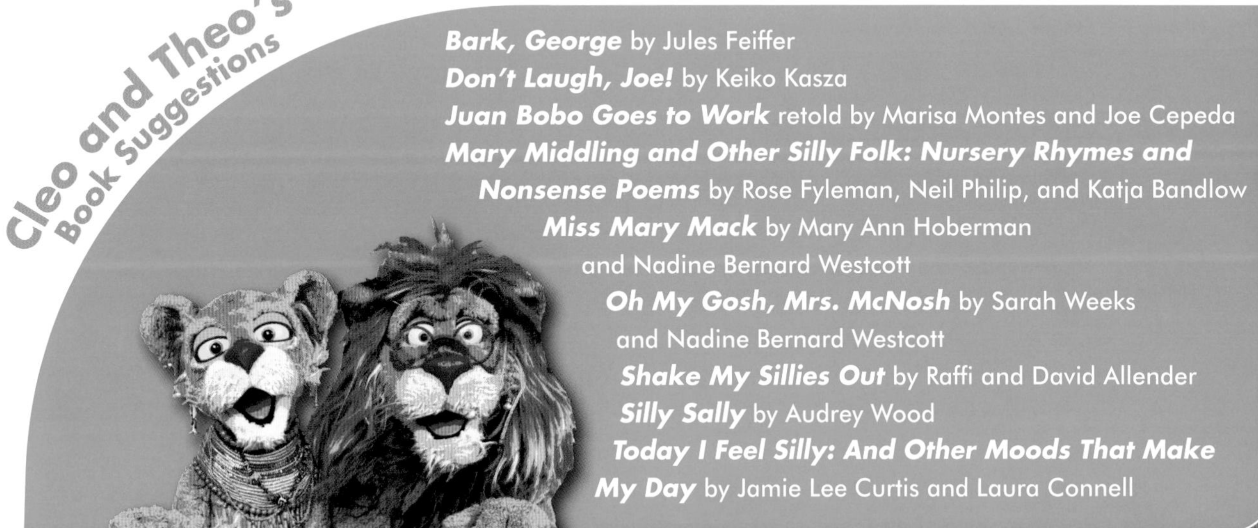

Cleo and Theo's Book Suggestions

Bark, George by Jules Feiffer
Don't Laugh, Joe! by Keiko Kasza
Juan Bobo Goes to Work retold by Marisa Montes and Joe Cepeda
Mary Middling and Other Silly Folk: Nursery Rhymes and Nonsense Poems by Rose Fyleman, Neil Philip, and Katja Bandlow
Miss Mary Mack by Mary Ann Hoberman and Nadine Bernard Westcott
Oh My Gosh, Mrs. McNosh by Sarah Weeks and Nadine Bernard Westcott
Shake My Sillies Out by Raffi and David Allender
Silly Sally by Audrey Wood
Today I Feel Silly: And Other Moods That Make My Day by Jamie Lee Curtis and Laura Connell

Reading Mrs. McNosh Hangs Up Her Wash

Literacy Skill Focus
Compare and Contrast
Concepts of Print
Listening and Speaking
Phonological Awareness (Rhyming)
Story Comprehension
Vocabulary

Vocabulary

author	newspaper
barrel	phone
clip	removable teeth
clothesline	shirts
clothespin	silly
dog	socks
dresses	title
dry	turkey
gown	wash
illustrator	wet
laundry	wrings
news	

Materials

Mrs. McNosh Hangs Up Her Wash by Sarah Weeks and Nadine Bernard Westcott

What Children Will Learn

1. About a silly story
2. New vocabulary words

Related Themes

Families
Humor

What to Do

- Talk about different ways families wash and dry their clothing. Tell the children that in the story you are going to read, *Mrs. McNosh Hangs Up Her Wash*, a woman called Mrs. McNosh washes her clothes in a barrel and then hangs the wet clothes on a clothesline to dry in the fresh air.
- Show the children the classroom clothesline (see Setting Up the Room, page 215) and explain that a clothesline is a long piece of rope that people hang outside to dry wet clothes on. Explain that a clothespin is a wooden or plastic clip that helps keep clothes on a clothesline. Demonstrate how to use a clothespin.
- Read the book slowly and with expression, emphasizing the rhythm of the words. Use the illustrations to explain the meaning of unfamiliar words such as *barrel, news, gown,* and *removable teeth.*
- Talk with the children about why the story is so funny and silly.
  - Say, *Mrs. McNosh washes shirts, dresses, and socks. Does your family wash shirts, dresses, and socks? Mrs. McNosh washes a phone, a dog, and a turkey. Does your family wash the phone? the dog? a turkey?* (No, that would be silly!)
  - Ask, *Do you remember what Mrs. McNosh does to the newspaper before she hangs it up on the clothesline?* (She wrings out the water.) *That means she twists the newspaper to squeeze the water out. Pretend that you have a wet shirt in your hands. Show me how you wring the water out of the shirt before hanging it up to dry.*

Silly Stories

Simplify It

Give the children clip-type clothespins and suggest that the children practice opening and closing the clothespins.

Add a Challenge

Make a Venn diagram by drawing two overlapping circles. Write the heading *Mrs. McNosh's Wash* on top of the left circle. Write the heading *Our Wash* on top of the right circle. Say, *Let's list in the middle of this chart the things that our families wash and the things Mrs. McNosh washes.* Together, go through the book and look at the illustrations of the things that Mrs. McNosh hangs up on her clothesline. Ask questions such as, *What is this? Does your family wash shirts, too? Yes. Let's draw a shirt here, in the middle.* Continue the process. Write and/or draw the silly items that only Mrs. McNosh washes in the left circle. Ask, *Are there things that your family washes that Mrs. McNosh didn't wash?* Draw any additional items in the *Our Wash* circle. Review the diagram with the children.

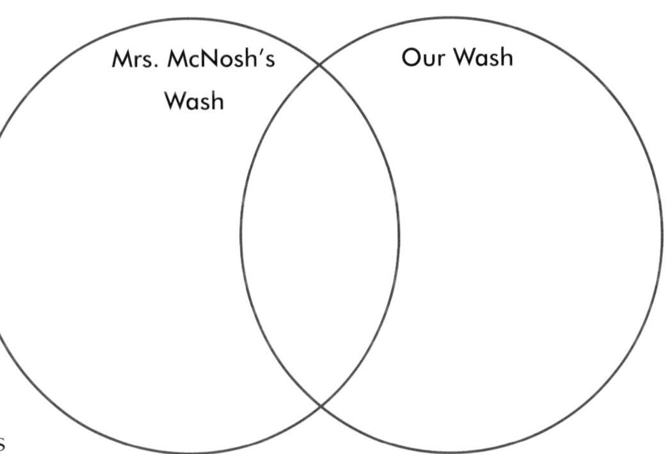

Assessment

To assess each child's learning, consider the following:

1. Is the child able to understand why the story is silly?
2. Is the child able to learn new vocabulary words?

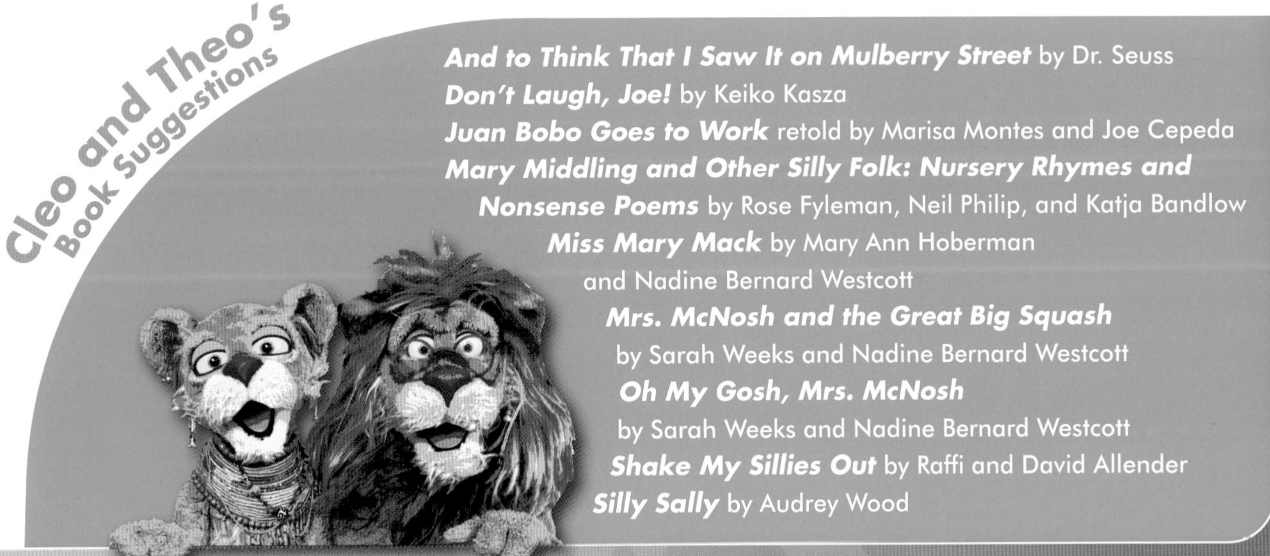

Cleo and Theo's Book Suggestions

And to Think That I Saw It on Mulberry Street by Dr. Seuss
Don't Laugh, Joe! by Keiko Kasza
Juan Bobo Goes to Work retold by Marisa Montes and Joe Cepeda
Mary Middling and Other Silly Folk: Nursery Rhymes and Nonsense Poems by Rose Fyleman, Neil Philip, and Katja Bandlow
Miss Mary Mack by Mary Ann Hoberman and Nadine Bernard Westcott
Mrs. McNosh and the Great Big Squash by Sarah Weeks and Nadine Bernard Westcott
Oh My Gosh, Mrs. McNosh by Sarah Weeks and Nadine Bernard Westcott
Shake My Sillies Out by Raffi and David Allender
Silly Sally by Audrey Wood

"Silly, Silly Mrs. McNosh"

Literacy Skill Focus
Concepts of Print
Phonological Awareness (Rhyming)
Vocabulary

Vocabulary

blocks
cat
clothesline
clothespin
dry
hat
laundry
news
rain
rhyme
shine
shirts
shoes
silly
skirts
socks
wash

Materials

hat
markers
sentence chart
sentence strips
small stuffed-animal cat (or picture of a cat)
two objects that don't rhyme with the word *cat*

What Children Will Learn

1. To say a silly poem
2. About rhyming

Related Theme
Sounds

Preparation

Write each line of the poem "Silly, Silly Mrs. McNosh" on sentence strips. Display in a sentence chart. Leave a space between the seventh and eighth line to insert additional sets of rhyming words.

What to Do

- Tell the children you are going to recite a poem called "Silly, Silly Mrs. McNosh."

Silly, Silly Mrs. McNosh
Silly, silly Mrs. McNosh,
Now it's time to do your wash.
Hang your laundry on a line,
Hang it up, rain or shine.
Shirts and skirts,
Shoes and news,
Socks and blocks,
Silly, silly Mrs. McNosh,
Now it's time to do your wash.

- Read the poem through several times, pointing to each word every time you read it. Then invite the children to recite the poem with you.
- Use the "Silly, Silly Mrs. McNosh" poem chart to help the children hear, recognize, and identify rhyming words.

- Point to the words *shirts* and *skirts* on the poem chart as you say them aloud. Have the children repeat the words with you. Ask, *What do you notice about the way these two words sound?* Emphasize that the words rhyme—they both sound the same at the end.
- Repeat the process with the rhyming pairs *shoes/news* and *socks/blocks*.
- Explain that Mrs. McNosh washes and hangs up objects that rhyme. Say, *Let's think of two more silly things that Mrs. McNosh can wash and hang up to dry on her clothesline.* Show the children a small stuffed-animal cat (or picture of a cat). Say, *Here's a cat for Mrs. McNosh to wash.* Show the children a hat and two other objects that don't rhyme with the word *cat*. Ask, *What else can Mrs. McNosh wash that rhymes with the word* cat? Have the children select the hat. Say, *Yes,* hat *rhymes with* cat!
- Write the words *a cat and a hat* on a sentence strip. Draw or attach a simple picture next to each word. Insert the sentence strip after the seventh line. Then point to each word as you read the entire poem. Invite the children to recite the poem with you.

Simplify It

Clap to the rhythm of the poem. Once the children understand the rhyming nature of the poem, talk about adding additional rhyming words.

Add a Challenge

Ask the children to say more words that rhyme with *cat*, *shoes*, or *blocks*.

Assessment

To assess each child's learning, consider the following:

1. Is the child able to learn the poem?
2. Is the child able to recognize the rhyming words in the poem?

Cleo and Theo's Book Suggestions

How Do Dinosaurs Say Good Night? by Jane Yolen and Mark Teague

Mary Middling and Other Silly Folk: Nursery Rhymes and Nonsense Poems by Rose Fyleman, Neil Philip, and Katja Bandlow

Miss Mary Mack by Mary Ann Hoberman and Nadine Bernard Westcott

Mrs. McNosh and the Great Big Squash by Sarah Weeks and Nadine Bernard Westcott

Silly Sally by Audrey Wood

Today I Feel Silly: And Other Moods That Make My Day by Jamie Lee Curtis and Laura Cornell

Rhyming Clothesline

Literacy Skill Focus
Active Listening
Phonological Awareness (Rhyming)
Vocabulary

Vocabulary

bats
clothesline
clothespins
end
news
next
objects
pairs
phone
rhyming
same
skirts
sound
teeth
title
wash
words

Materials

Mrs. McNosh Hangs Up Her Wash by Sarah Weeks and Nadine Bernard Westcott
rhyming picture cards

What Children Will Learn

1. About active listening
2. About rhyming

Related Theme
Sounds

What to Do

- Hold up the book *Mrs. McNosh Hangs Up Her Wash.* Ask, *Who can tell me the title of the book?* Say, Mrs. McNosh Hangs Up Her Wash *is fun to read because it has lots and lots of rhyming words.* Remind the children that when words rhyme, they sound the same at the end. Say, McNosh. Wash. *The words rhyme.* McNosh. Wash. *They sound the same at the end.*
- Say, *When I read the story this time, I want you to use your rhyming skills to figure out what comes next in the story. When I pause, I want you to fill in the missing rhyming word.*
- Pause before the last word on each page and invite the children to supply the rhyming word. Whenever possible, point to the illustrations to help the children identify the rhyming word (*skirts, news, phone, bats, teeth*). Congratulate the children on their rhyming skills.
- Tell the children they are going to make their own rhyming clothesline!
- Gather children around the classroom clothesline (see Setting Up the Room, page 215). Show the children the rhyming picture cards. As you point to each object, ask the children to say what it is.

- Ask the children to raise their hand if they can name two objects from the cards that rhyme. Have a volunteer pick up two picture cards and say the names of the objects. Ask the children, *Do they rhyme?* If they do, ask the child to hang up the rhyming card pair on the clothesline. If they don't rhyme, hold up one of the picture cards and ask the child to choose another card that rhymes with it.
- Continue the process until all the picture cards are hanging in rhyming pairs. Point to each set of rhyming picture cards and say the names of the objects together.
- Continue to add to the rhyming clothesline throughout this topic.

Simplify It

Show the children three picture cards–two that rhyme and one that does not. Ask the children to pick out the two that rhyme.

Add a Challenge

Read "Silly, Silly Mrs. McNosh" (see page 220) with the children. Use the rhyming picture-card pairs on the rhyming clothesline to add new lines to the poem.

Assessment

To assess each child's learning, consider the following:

1. Is the child able to hear when a rhyming word needs to be inserted into the text?
2. Is the child able to identify words that rhyme?

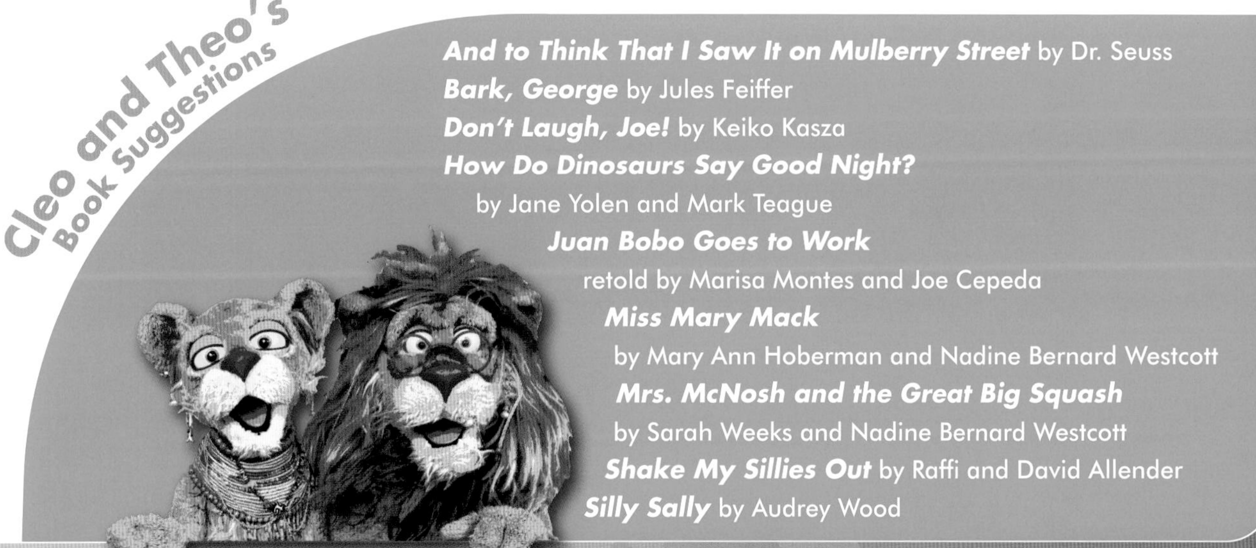

Cleo and Theo's Book Suggestions

And to Think That I Saw It on Mulberry Street by Dr. Seuss
Bark, George by Jules Feiffer
Don't Laugh, Joe! by Keiko Kasza
How Do Dinosaurs Say Good Night? by Jane Yolen and Mark Teague
Juan Bobo Goes to Work retold by Marisa Montes and Joe Cepeda
Miss Mary Mack by Mary Ann Hoberman and Nadine Bernard Westcott
Mrs. McNosh and the Great Big Squash by Sarah Weeks and Nadine Bernard Westcott
Shake My Sillies Out by Raffi and David Allender
Silly Sally by Audrey Wood

Silly Wash Class Book

Literacy Skill Focus
Concepts of Print
Name Recognition
Vocabulary

Vocabulary

basket
book
dry
hang
laundry
letters
name
sentence
silly
wash
write

Materials

crayons, markers, pencils
laundry basket filled with a variety of silly objects to wash
paper

What Children Will Learn

1. Beginning writing skills
2. Beginning reading skills

Related Theme

Imagination

What to Do

- Tell the children that you are going to write a class book about doing a silly wash, just like Mrs. McNosh.
- Begin with an introductory sentence such as, *On Monday morning, Ms. (or Mr.) _________ does the wash.* Write the sentence on a piece of paper as the children watch you.
- Display a laundry basket filled with a variety of objects. Tell the children to imagine that the class is going to do its own silly wash, just like Mrs. McNosh.
- Model by choosing a silly object, such as a clock, from the laundry basket. On another piece of paper, draw a simple picture of a clock. Under the picture write, "Ms. (or Mr.) ______________is washing the clock."
- Point to each word as you read aloud the sentence.
- Invite each child to pick a silly object from the laundry basket to wash. Have each child draw a picture of the object on a piece of paper. Below the picture, write: (name of child) washes the (name of object). As you write, have the child say the letters in his name.
- Point to each word as you read the sentence aloud. Then have the child read the sentence with you as you point to each word.

Teacher Tip: Make a cover and bind the pages together to make a class book. Read the completed book to the children and then put it in the Library Center for the children to read and enjoy.

Simplify It

Say the letters in the child's name and the child can repeat the letters after you say them.

Add a Challenge

Cut out a T-shirt shape from construction paper for each child. Encourage the children to decorate their paper T-shirts using crayons and markers. Invite the children to hang their T-shirts on a clothesline, just like Mrs. McNosh!

Assessment

To assess each child's learning, consider the following:

1. Is the child able to accomplish beginning writing skills?
2. Is the child able to accomplish beginning reading skills?

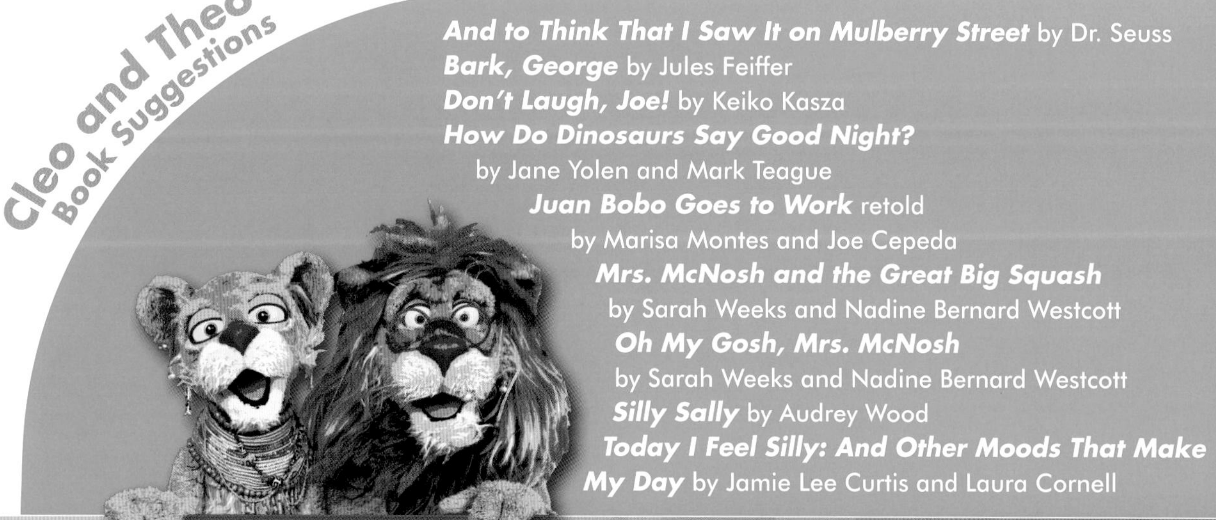

Cleo and Theo's Book Suggestions

And to Think That I Saw It on Mulberry Street by Dr. Seuss
Bark, George by Jules Feiffer
Don't Laugh, Joe! by Keiko Kasza
How Do Dinosaurs Say Good Night? by Jane Yolen and Mark Teague
Juan Bobo Goes to Work retold by Marisa Montes and Joe Cepeda
Mrs. McNosh and the Great Big Squash by Sarah Weeks and Nadine Bernard Westcott
Oh My Gosh, Mrs. McNosh by Sarah Weeks and Nadine Bernard Westcott
Silly Sally by Audrey Wood
Today I Feel Silly: And Other Moods That Make My Day by Jamie Lee Curtis and Laura Cornell

Reading Chicka Chicka Boom Boom

Literacy Skill Focus
Alphabet Awareness
Letter Recognition
Listening and Speaking
Parts of a Book
Phonological Awareness (Rhythm, Rhyme, and Repetition)

Vocabulary

author
coconuts
cover
down
enough
fruits
fun
green
grow
illustrator
leaves
letter
milk
nonsense
silly
title
top
up
whole
words

Materials

chart paper
Chicka Chicka Boom Boom by Bill Martin Jr., John Archambault, and Lois Ehlert
markers

What Children Will Learn

1. About the alphabet
2. About the concepts of *up* and *down*

Related Themes

Opposites
Sounds

What to Do

- Ask the children if they remember the name of the silly story you read to them. Ask, *What silly things did Mrs. McNosh do?*
- Tell the children that today you are going to read another silly story called *Chicka Chicka Boom Boom.* Ask the children to repeat the title with you. Say, *Those are silly words. They don't mean anything, but they are fun to say. Listen to these other silly words you will hear in the story.*
- Ask, *What are other silly words that are fun to say? How about, "Pip pop biddle bop. Flim flam wee!"* Encourage the children to make up other silly nonsense words. Write the words on chart paper. Then lead the children in a silly word chant.
- Show the cover of the book. Point to the words as you read aloud the title, the authors, and the illustrator. Then point to the tree and explain that it is a coconut tree. *These circles are the coconuts that grow under the big green leaves near the top of the tree.* Coconuts *are large fruits that grow on special trees. Coconuts have a very hard shell. If you break open the shell, you can drink the sweet coconut milk inside!*
- Open to the end pages and exclaim, *Look, here are the letters of the alphabet!* Chicka Chicka Boom Boom *is an alphabet book.* Invite the children to recite the alphabet or sing the ABC song as you point to each letter. Then ask, *What do you think a coconut tree is doing in an alphabet book? Let's read the book and find out.*

- *Chicka Chicka Boom Boom* has a lively musical rhythm. As you read, have fun with the beat and rhythm of the words. Read the text straight through without pause. Invite the children to join in when you read the repeating lines. Point to each letter as you read its name.
- After you finish reading the book, talk about it with the children. Ask questions such as:
  - *Why do you think the letters of the alphabet run up the coconut tree?*
  - *What happens when all the letters get to the top of the tree? (They fall down!) Why do you think they fall down?*
  - *How many letters are there in the whole alphabet? Let's count them. (Count together as you point to each letter on the alphabet chart.) There are 26 letters in the alphabet. That's a lot of letters. Was there enough room for all 26 letters on top of the coconut tree?*

Simplify It

Focus on one or two letters each time you read the book.

Add a Challenge

Pause before each of the repeating phrases in the book and wait for the children to say the words.

Assessment

To assess each child's learning, consider the following:

1. Is the child able to learn some or all of the letters of the alphabet?
2. Is the child able to understand the concepts of *up* and *down*?

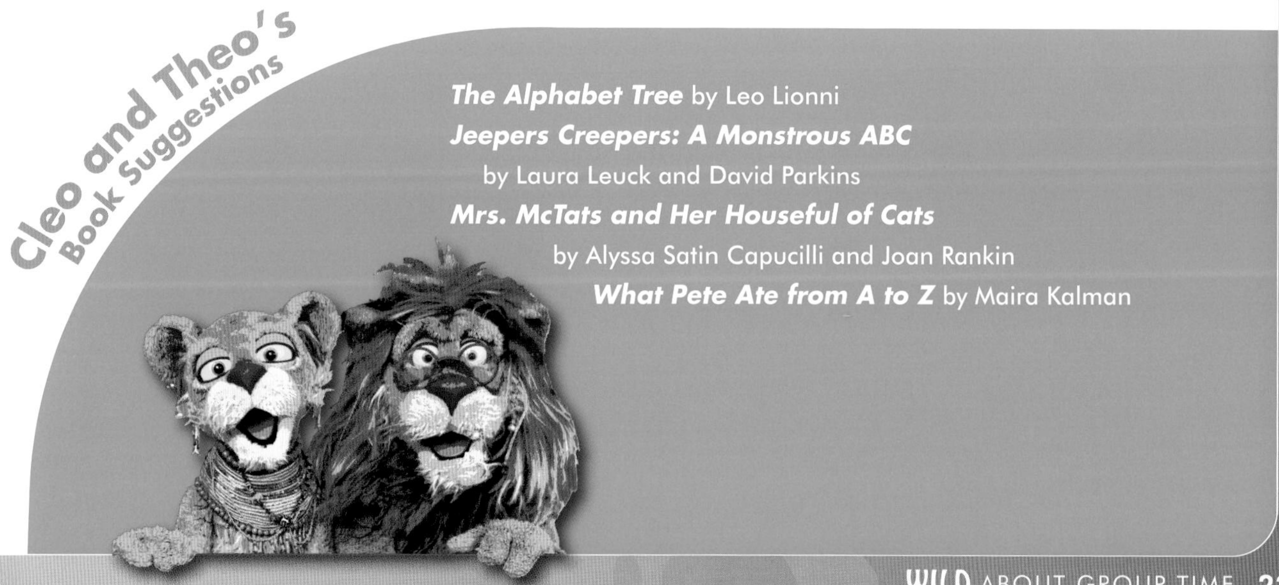

Cleo and Theo's Book Suggestions

The Alphabet Tree by Leo Lionni

Jeepers Creepers: A Monstrous ABC by Laura Leuck and David Parkins

Mrs. McTats and Her Houseful of Cats by Alyssa Satin Capucilli and Joan Rankin

What Pete Ate from A to Z by Maira Kalman

The Sillies

Literacy Skill Focus

Concepts of Print
Dictating Sentences
Listening and Speaking
Phonological Awareness (Alliteration; Beginning Sounds; Rhythm, Rhyme, and Repetition)

Vocabulary

around, down, face, object, sentence, silly, sound, story, up

Materials

chart paper
markers
objects that begin with one of the following sounds: /k/, /h/, /l/, or /p/

What Children Will Learn

1. About rhyming
2. To create a silly sentence

Related Themes

Friends
Sounds

What to Do

- Ask the children, *How do you feel today? Does anyone feel silly? Can you make a silly face?* Recite the following chant and ask the children to do the motions:

  Look up.
  Look down.
  Turn around.
  Make a silly face,
  But don't make a sound!

- Tell the children that you are going to write a silly story.
- Display a variety of objects that begin with one of the following sounds: /k/, /h/, /l/, or /p/.
- Ask the children to select three or more objects. Then ask them to think of one or two sentences about the selected objects. For example, "The pink pig ate pizza with popcorn on top!"
- Repeat the sentence as you write it on a piece of chart paper. Arrange the selected objects in front of you in the order in which they appear in the silly sentence.
- As you write, point to or pick up the corresponding object. Point to each word as you read the sentence aloud.
- Congratulate the children on their silly story. Then point to the objects in front of you. Say, *I notice something fun about the way these words sound. They all begin with the same sound. Say the words with me*—pink, pig, pizza, popcorn. *What sound do you hear?* (the /p/ sound)

Simplify It

Instead of "Look Up" use the following simple rhyme.

Chicka chicka boom boom!
Will there be enough room?
Here comes (name of child)
Up the coconut tree!

Add a Challenge

Ask the children to make silly faces on paper plates. If possible, take photographs of the children making silly faces. Create a Silly Faces wall display with the paper-plate faces and photographs.

Assessment

To assess each child's learning, consider the following:

1. Is the child able to recognize rhyming words?
2. Is the child able to create a silly sentence?

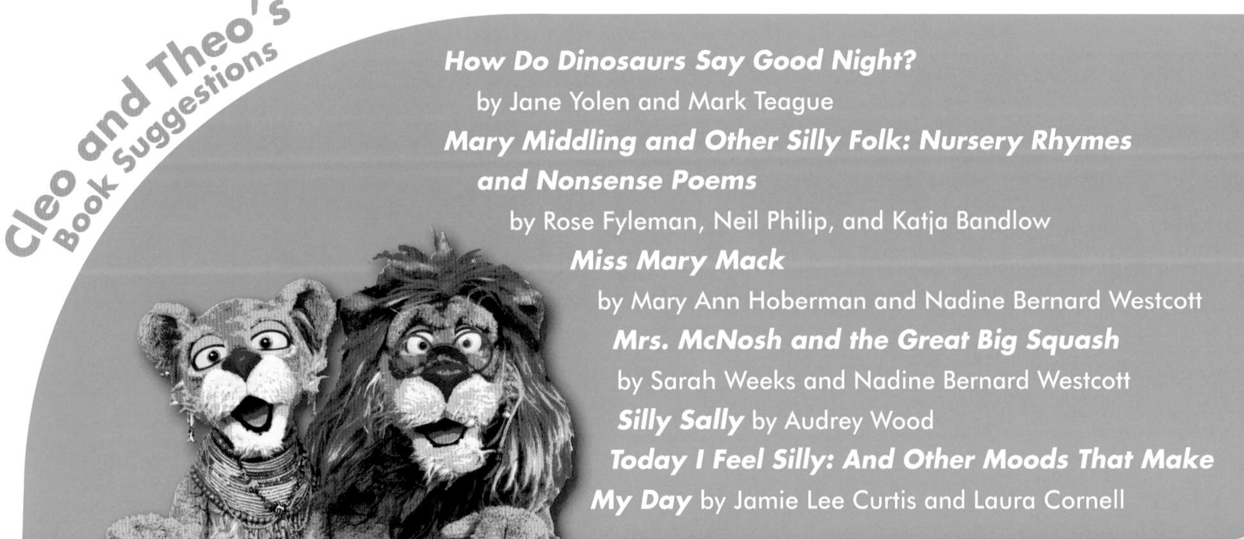

Cleo and Theo's Book Suggestions

How Do Dinosaurs Say Good Night? by Jane Yolen and Mark Teague

Mary Middling and Other Silly Folk: Nursery Rhymes and Nonsense Poems by Rose Fyleman, Neil Philip, and Katja Bandlow

Miss Mary Mack by Mary Ann Hoberman and Nadine Bernard Westcott

Mrs. McNosh and the Great Big Squash by Sarah Weeks and Nadine Bernard Westcott

Silly Sally by Audrey Wood

Today I Feel Silly: And Other Moods That Make My Day by Jamie Lee Curtis and Laura Cornell

Up and Down Letters

Literacy Skill Focus

Active Listening
Alphabet Awareness
Listening and Speaking
Phonological Awareness (Rhyming)
Story Comprehension
Vocabulary

Vocabulary

alphabet
coconut
down
knotted
letter
looped
lowercase
rhyming
tangled
tree
twisted
up
uppercase

Materials

Chicka Chicka Boom Boom by Bill Martin Jr., John Archambault, and Lois Ehlert
string or ribbon

What Children Will Learn

1. About lowercase and uppercase letters
2. About rhyming

Related Themes

Shapes
Sounds

What to Do

- Hold up the book and ask the children if they can tell you the title. Remind the children that *Chicka Chicka Boom Boom* is an alphabet book about letters racing up a coconut tree. Say, *This book is fun to read because it has lots of rhyming words, just like* Mrs. McNosh Hangs Up Her Wash. *When I read the story this time, I want you to help me say some of the rhyming words.* At the end of a rhyming sequence, pause long enough for the children to provide the rhyming word.
- Invite the children to join in when you read the repeating lines. Pause each time before you read the word *tree* so the children can supply the word. On subsequent readings, invite the children to supply different rhyming words.
- After you read the book, look at the pictures with the children to help them understand what happened to the letters when they fell from the tree and to explain the meaning of unfamiliar vocabulary words.
- Look at the page that shows all the letters falling into a pile. Say, *Look at the letters in the pile. Are they lowercase (little) letters or uppercase (big) letters?* (They are lowercase letters.) *Now let's look at the next page where the mamas, papas, aunts, and uncles come running to help the lowercase letters that fell from the tree. Look, the mamas and the papas are uppercase letters! Here's the uppercase letter "R" helping the lowercase letter "r." Here's the uppercase letter "J" helping the lowercase letter "j"!*

- As you say the words, describe the way the letters are *tangled, looped, twisted*, or *knotted* together. Use a string or ribbon and demonstrate the words *tangled, twisted, looped,* and *knotted*.

Simplify It

Read the story without pausing for the children to say the rhyming words. Read it a second time, this time pausing to wait for the children to say the rhyming words.

Add a Challenge

Pause before reading each letter, point to the letter in the illustration, and ask children to name the letter.

Assessment

To assess each child's learning, consider the following:

1. Is the child able to understand the difference between lowercase and uppercase letters?
2. Is the child able to say the missing rhyming words?

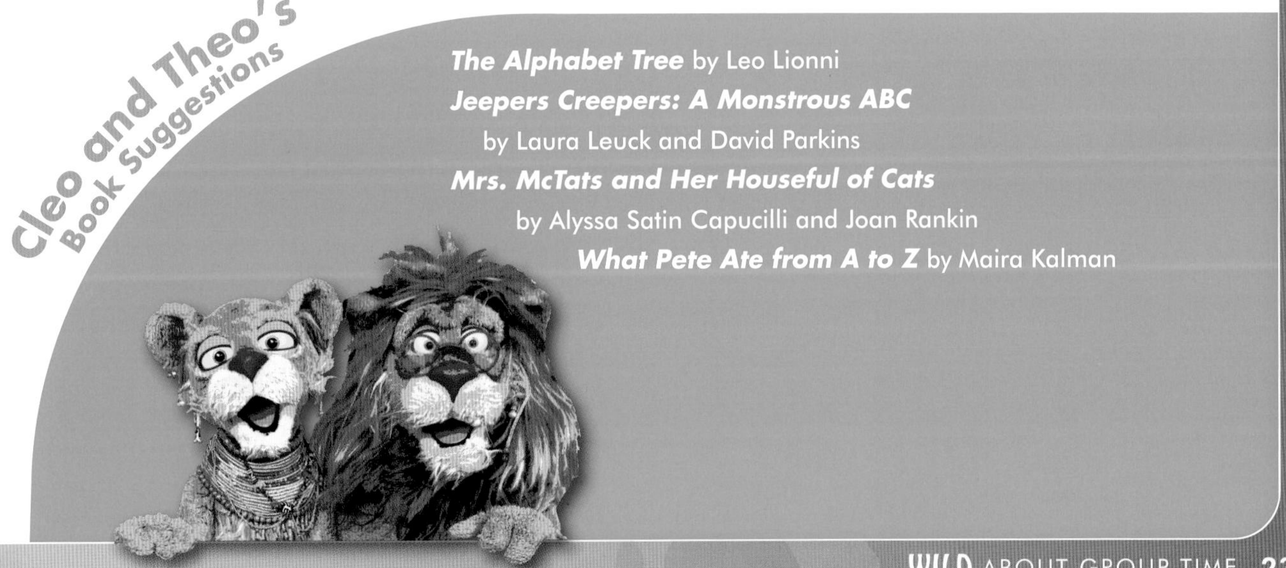

The Alphabet Tree by Leo Lionni

Jeepers Creepers: A Monstrous ABC by Laura Leuck and David Parkins

Mrs. McTats and Her Houseful of Cats by Alyssa Satin Capucilli and Joan Rankin

What Pete Ate from A to Z by Maira Kalman

Once, Twice, Three Times

Literacy Skill Focus
Concepts of Print (Directionality)
Letter Recognition
Phonological Awareness (Distinguishing Sounds; Rhythm, Rhyme, and Repetition)
Word Recognition

Vocabulary

coconut
down
fun
listen
nonsense
once
poem
race
repetition
silly
three
tree
twice
up
word

Materials

chart paper
markers

What Children Will Learn

1. About the concepts of *up* and *down*
2. That reading is done from left to right and top to bottom

Related Themes

Counting
Sounds

Preparation

Write the poem "Up, Up, Up" on chart paper.

What to Do

- Talk with the children about the repetition of silly words in *Chicka Chicka Boom Boom*. Say, *In the book, sometimes we hear the same word twice, one right after the other.* Chicka Chicka. *That's the same word twice. What's another word that's said twice?* (Boom Boom) *Both words are silly, nonsense words. Saying them twice adds to the fun. I am going to say some words. Listen carefully. Tell me if I'm saying the same word two times.*
    - chicka, chicka
    - cat, ball
    - boom, boom
    - skit, scat
    - kit, cat
    - dear, dear
    - up, up
- Tell the children you are going to recite a poem about *Chicka Chicka Boom Boom* that uses a word three times.
- Display the chart with the poem "Up, Up, Up" written on it. Point to the first word *Up* in the title. Ask, *Does anyone know what this word says?* Say, *Yes, it's the word* up. Point to the second and third words in the title and say, *Here it is again—and again. The title of the poem is "Up, Up, Up."*
- Ask, *Where do I start to read the poem? Yes, I start to read here—on the top of the page on the left side. I read this way—across the page.*

- Point to the words as you read aloud the poem.

Up, Up, Up

Up, up, up
The coconut tree,
Raced 26 letters
As silly as can be.
Down, down, down
The coconut tree,
Fell 26 letters.
What a sight to see!
Chicka chicka BOOM! BOOM!

- Invite the children to recite it with you.
- Open the book to an illustration of a coconut tree. As you read the first four lines, move your finger up the trunk of a coconut tree. As you read the last four lines, move your hands down the trunk of the tree.

Simplify It

To help the children understand the concepts of *up* and *down*, give each child a plastic letter. Ask the children to raise the letters up over their heads when you say the first four lines of the poem, and then drop the letters down to the floor when you say the last four lines of the poem.

Add a Challenge

Have the children help you make a list of some of the silly songs they know. Some possibilities include "Down by the Bay," "Shake My Sillies Out," and so on. Invite the children to choose their favorite silly song to sing.

Assessment

To assess each child's learning, consider the following:

1. Is the child able to understand the concepts of *up* and *down*?
2. Is the child able to understand that you read from left to right and top to bottom?

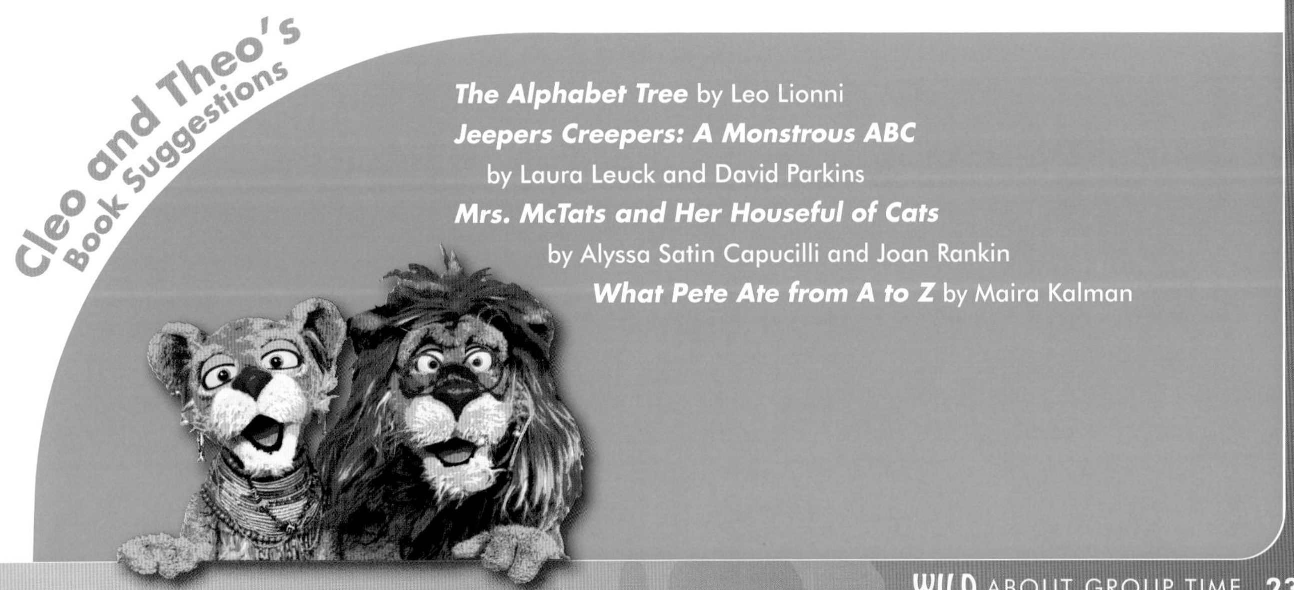

The Alphabet Tree by Leo Lionni
Jeepers Creepers: A Monstrous ABC by Laura Leuck and David Parkins
Mrs. McTats and Her Houseful of Cats by Alyssa Satin Capucilli and Joan Rankin
What Pete Ate from A to Z by Maira Kalman

The Same or Different?

Literacy Skill Focus
Active Listening
Compare and Contrast
Making Connections
Story Comprehension
Vocabulary

Vocabulary

barrel
clothes
compare
contrast
cover
different
dirty
Laundromat
laundry
same
silly
story
title
wash
washing machine
wet

Materials

Knuffle Bunny: A Cautionary Tale by Mo Willems

Mrs. McNosh Hangs Up Her Wash by Sarah Weeks and Nadine Bernard Westcott (optional)

What Children Will Learn

1. To enjoy two silly stories
2. To compare and contrast two stories

Related Theme

Families

What to Do

- Hold up the book *Knuffle Bunny* and ask the children if they know the title of the book. Talk with the children about how Trixie and her dad washed their laundry in a washing machine. Remind the children that the word *laundry* means dirty clothes, or clothes that need to be washed. Then ask, *What do you think Trixie and her dad did with the wet clothes after they took them out of the washing machine?*
- Ask, *What silly thing does Trixie's dad put in the wash?* Read the book for enjoyment.
- After reading the book, help the children compare and contrast *Knuffle Bunny* and *Mrs. McNosh Hangs Up Her Wash.*
  Note: If necessary, reread *Mrs. McNosh Hangs Up Her Wash.*
- Ask, *In what ways are the two books the same?* (They are both about doing the wash. Both books are funny.) *In what ways are they different?* (Trixie and her dad wash their clothes in the washing machine at the Laundromat. Mrs. McNosh washes her clothes outside in a barrel.)

Simplify It

Read one book at a time. Ask the children what is silly about the book.

Add a Challenge

Make a Venn diagram by drawing two overlapping circles. Write the heading *Mrs. McNosh Hangs Up Her Wash* on top of the left circle. Write the heading *Knuffle Bunny* on top of the right circle. Go through the two books and look for things that are the same. Write these in the overlapping space of the circles. Go through the books a second time and look for things that are only true for *Mrs. McNosh Hangs Up Her Wash.* Write these in the left circle. Go through the books for the last time and look for things that are only true for *Knuffle Bunny.* Write these in the right circle.

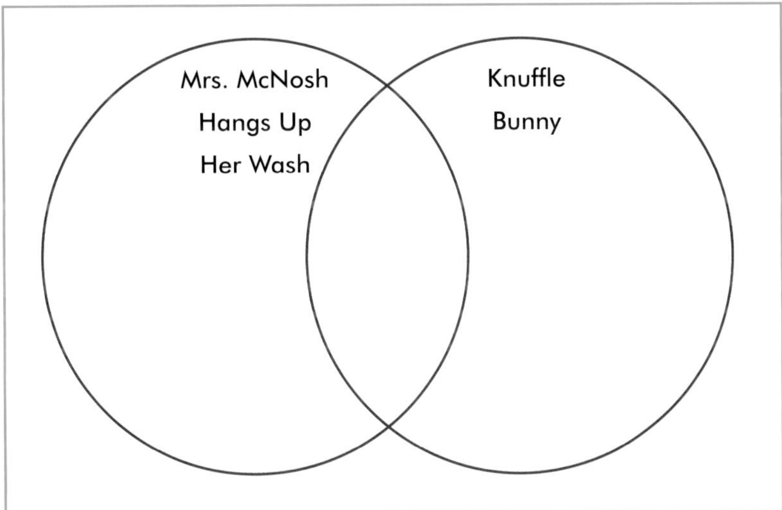

Assessment

To assess each child's learning, consider the following:

1. Is the child able to enjoy the humor in both stories?
2. Is the child able to compare and contrast the two stories?

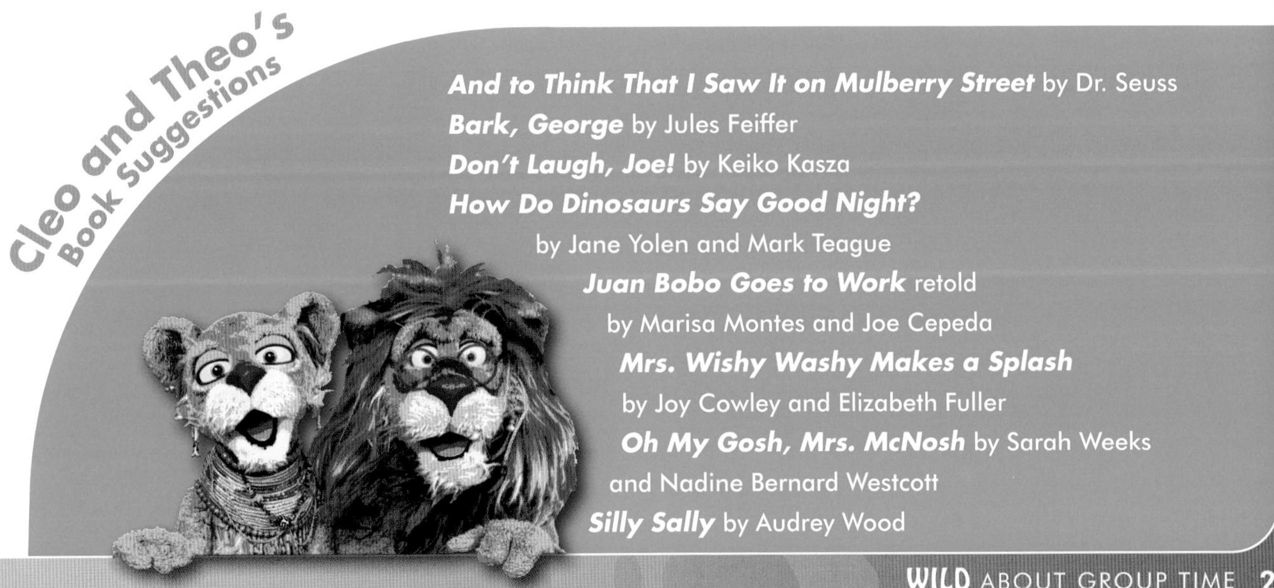

Cleo and Theo's Book Suggestions

And to Think That I Saw It on Mulberry Street by Dr. Seuss
Bark, George by Jules Feiffer
Don't Laugh, Joe! by Keiko Kasza
How Do Dinosaurs Say Good Night? by Jane Yolen and Mark Teague
Juan Bobo Goes to Work retold by Marisa Montes and Joe Cepeda
Mrs. Wishy Washy Makes a Splash by Joy Cowley and Elizabeth Fuller
Oh My Gosh, Mrs. McNosh by Sarah Weeks and Nadine Bernard Westcott
Silly Sally by Audrey Wood

Note to Families About the Topic of Silly Stories

FAMILY LETTER

Date ______________________

Dear Families,

In our classroom, we are playing with the sounds in words by enjoying reading silly books, singing silly songs, and writing silly stories. We are reading a book called *Mrs. McNosh Hangs Up Her Wash* about a woman who washes the news and her shoes, two bats and a hat, and other silly things. We are also reading an alphabet book—*Chicka Chicka Boom Boom*—about silly letters that climb a coconut tree.

Here are some activities that you can do at home with your child:

- Do silly things together: Read a silly book. Sing a silly song. Play silly games. Tell silly jokes. Make silly faces together. Have fun!
- Make up silly songs as you do the wash together or as your child washes in the tub. *Soapy Simone in the tub. Rub, rub, rub; rub-a-dub-dub!*
- Read an alphabet book together. Look for the first letter in your child's name.
- Try this healthy snack. Spread cream cheese in the middle of a celery stalk with a leafy top. Give your child cereal letters to put on the cream cheese. Help your child write his name with the letters.

Thank you!

Appendix

Theo

Cleo

Leona

Lionel

Feelings Chart

 happy	 sad
 angry	 scared
 silly	 worried

Index of Children's Books

W

Y

Z

Index

T

U

V

W

Z